THE ARMY'S NAVY

THE ARMY'S NAVY

British Military Vessels and their History since Henry VIII

David Habesch

CHATHAM PUBLISHING
LONDON

Copyright © David Habesch 2001

First published in Great Britain in 2001 by Chatham Publishing,
61 Frith Street, London W1D 3JL

Chatham Publishing is an imprint of Gerald Duckworth & Co Ltd

British Library Cataloguing in Publication Data
A catalogue record for this book is available from the
British Library

ISBN 1 86176 157 0

Designed and typeset by Trevor Ridley

Printed and bound in Great Britain by the Cromwell Press, Trowbridge, Wilts

Contents

List of Illustrations		6
Preface		8
Introduction and Acknowledgements		9

1	From Henry VIII to the Great War	13
2	The Great War and After: 1914-39	23
3	The Second World War (I): 1939-43	41
4	The Second World War (II): 1944-45	60
5	The Inland Water Transport RE: 1939-45	89
6	RASC to RCT: 1945-65	107
7	RCT to RLC: 1965-93	152
8	The Royal Logistic Corps: 1993 to the Present	189

Appendices

I	Board of Ordnance Fleet taken from Estimates of 1839/40	197
II	War Department Fleet List 1911	198
III	War Department Vessels 1898-1914	200
IV	Vessels Constructed 1920-39	204
V	Responsibilities Regarding Waterborne Craft: War Office Directive, June 1944	205
VI	Control of Water Transport Services, Post-War Policy	209
VII	Particulars of RASC Craft 1939-45	213
VIII	Military Crew Complements of RASC Vessels	217
IX	Organisation of IWT, Persia and Iraq, 31 December 1942	218
X	Organisation Chart of the RASC Fleet as at 1 September 1945	219
XI	Marine Craft - RASC Vessels	221
XII	Brief Record of the Names of the LCT Mk VIIIs operated by RASC/RCT Crews	228
XIII	RASC Fleet List 1964	229
XIV	HMAV *Ardennes* - Commissioning Order 1977	231
XV	Army Fleet Review, 30 September 1988	232

Bibliography	235
Abbreviations	236
Index	238

List of Illustrations

Illustrations for Chapters 1 and 2   *Between pp32-41*

Spritty sailing barge. (Painting by Major Bill Wynn-Werninck)
WDV *Wyndham*. (Author's collection)
Steam target tower *Gordon*. (Reg Cooley collection)
Gun barge *Gog*.
Miners of the Submarine Mining Service. (RE Library, Chatham)
Divers of the SMS. (RE Library, Chatham)
Ensign of the Royal Engineers. (Author's collection)
Inland Water Transport barge, 1917. (Museum of Army Transport, Beverley)
Train ferries of the IWT. (RE Library, Chatham)
Paddle-steamer *S.47*. (Museum of Army Transport, Beverley)
Motor Boat Patrol, Macedonia 1916. (Museum of Army Transport, Beverley)
Improvised motor boat 1919. (Museum of Army Transport, Beverley)
WDV *Sir Hastings Anderson*. (Author's collection)
The coaster *Malplaquet*. (Author's collection)

Illustrations for Chapters 3, 4 and 5   *Between pp72-81*

Mediterranean *caique*. (Museum of Army Transport, Beverley)
Soldier-sailors learning boat pulling.
RASC motor boat security patrol, 1941.
Review of RASC Motor Boat Co.
A launch of No.2 Motor Boat Co.
Target tower off Portsmouth. (By permission of the Trustees of the
Imperial War Museum: H15034)
'Queen Gull' target boat. (Author's collection)
Military Oil Barge.
'Battle' class target tower.
61ft Motor Fishing Vessel. (Museum of Army Transport, Beverley)
90ft MFV fire boat.
Training recruits in East Africa.
Ramped Cargo Lighters in Burma.
WDV *Oma*, 12 May 1945. (John De La Haye collection)
A DUKW. (HMSO/Crown Copyright)
A TID tug.
IWT launch *Karmala*, 1942. (RE Library, Chatham)

Illustrations for Chapter 6   *Between pp112-121*

Taking the salute at Army's Navy review 1945. (Bill Wynn-Werninck collection)
Ambulance launch *Benson*. (Museum of Army Transport, Beverley)
Ammunition disposal craft.
Ammunition disposal.
Soldiers of the RASC Fleet.
Civilian seaman of the RASC Fleet. (Museum of Army Transport, Beverley)
LST *Evan Gibb*. (Author's collection)
Captain Alan Marr. (Author's collection)
'Derby Winner' class launch *Isinglass*.
RASCV *Mull*. (Author's collection)
LST *Audemer*, St Kilda.
RASCV *Arakan*. (HMSO/Crown Copyright)
HMAV *Audemer*. (Author's collection)

Illustrations for Chapters 7 and 8   *Between pp168-177*

Army hovercraft 1966. (HMSO/Crown Copyright)
Launch of LCL *Arakan* 1977.
HMAV *Aachen*. (HMSO/Crown Copyright)
Audemer rescuing *Sine Boye*, 1976. (Painting by Major Bill Wynn-Werninck)
RCTV *Alfred Herring VC*. (Painting by Major Bill Wynn-Werninck)
Range safety craft, 1980s. (HMSO/Crown Copyright)
Ramped powered lighters, Belize. (Author's collection)
HMAV *St George*.
Mexeflote with flying boat.
The Falkands War:
          RCL loading on P&O ship. (HMSO/Crown Copyright)
          RCL *Arromanches* at Port Stanley, 1982.
          Argentine POWs aboard *Arromanches*.
Arakan landing U-boat conning tower.
Officer being 'piped over the side' of HMAV *Ardennes*.
(HMSO/Crown Copyright)
Ardennes at Royal Review 1990. (Painting by Major Bill Wynn-Werninck)
Ex-RASC RPL in Belize 1994. (Author's collection)

Preface

Her Majesty's Army Vessel *St George*, proudly flying the Blue Ensign with Crossed Swords and Lion and Crown superimposed, made her way to a designated anchorage at Spithead, with senior officers of the Royal Corps of Transport and Royal Navy aboard. Although the weather was perfect, with calm seas, bright sunshine and a slight breeze, nonetheless a deep depression lay over the anchorage as the occasion, an Army Fleet Review, was a melancholy one, marking as it did the demise of the Army's civilian-manned fleet after over 400 years' continuous operation. The date was 30 September 1988 and this ceremony was to commemorate the forthcoming transfer of a large number of the Army's ships, including the *St George* herself, to the Director of Marine Services (Naval).

At noon the Reviewing Officer, Major General C.E.G. Carrington CBE, Director General of Transport and Movements, standing on the flag deck of *St George*, took the salute as various craft from 18 Maritime Squadron RCT sailed past in formation led by RCTV *Yarmouth Navigator*, a training vessel providing facilities for the teaching of seamanship, navigation and engineering to the seagoing soldiers of the Maritime Regiment, Royal Corps of Transport. The other vessels participating were mainly range safety craft, which were deployed around the coasts of Britain to patrol military firing ranges from the English Channel to the Hebrides and usually manned by the civilian seamen of the Army Fleet. In contrast *St George*, an ammunition ship, was manned by military personnel.

Those present at the ceremony, especially the civilian officers and ratings, must have been keenly aware of the poignancy and nostalgia surrounding the Review as the ships faultlessly performed their various evolutions before returning to HM Gunwharf, their base at Portsmouth alongside HMS *Vernon*. Probably nobody was feeling a greater sense of loss than Lieutenant Colonel G.J. Yeoman MBE RCT, Commanding Officer 20 Maritime Regiment, who, with the transfer of HMAV *St George* to the Navy, had seen his complement of large ships reduced by a third. The late Frank Bourne, then Master Superintendent of 18 Maritime Squadron RCT, must also have had similar feelings of loss, as he looked back on his career in the Army's Navy from the time when he joined as a Boy Seaman in the mid-1940s.

However, despite the loss of the civilian-manned ships and their crews, this was by no means the end of the British Army's fleet of ships as the following pages will show.

Introduction and Acknowledgments

'The Army's Navy? What on earth is that?' This was the most frequent response received by the author from a wide variety of institutions and individuals while he was researching material for this book. It soon became apparent that there was almost total ignorance about a navy that had been in nearly continuous existence from the early sixteenth century right up to the present day. Even museums specialising in military history, including those dedicated to elements of the British Army with close links to the Army's Navy, usually only had sparse information on the story of this unique service.

Although the author had served as an officer in the civilian-manned RASC Fleet for only a short period of time in 1947, he soon realised that this organisation was quite unlike either the Royal or Merchant Navy. Many years later, in February 1988, he wrote a short article on this fascinating subject for the *Nautical Magazine*, but hardly had this been published when the RCT Fleet suffered a grievous blow, sadly the first of many, with the transfer of the entire civilian-manned fleet and its personnel to the Director of Marine Services (Naval). Also transferred was the flagship of the military-manned vessels, HMAV *St George*. This savage pruning of the Royal Corps of Transport Fleet prompted the author to write an updated and expanded history of the Army's Navy, which appeared as a two-part article in *Ships Monthly* in February and March 1991.

Having received many flattering comments on his work, the author then started to write a book on the history of the Army's Navy. Whereas the previous articles had mainly concentrated on the ships and men of the RASC/RCT Fleets, the book would also cover other fleets of the British Army, for example the Submarine Mining Service and the Inland Water Transport, both administered by the Royal Engineers. The task has now been completed and although it has occupied much of the author's spare time, it has taken several years. Much of this time has been spent in researching the subject, including considerable travel visiting museums, individuals with experience of service in Army craft and, of course, 17 Port and Maritime Regiment, Royal Logistic Corps, at Marchwood Military Port.

Several factors affected the completion of the book, including changes in the name of the service, such as from Royal Corps of Transport to Royal

Logistic Corps, swingeing cuts in craft and personnel by the powers that be, and also, and by no means least, much new information surfacing at intervals from ex-Army mariners relating their experiences with the Army's Navy. A significant proportion of the above information required the re-editing of certain sections of the original draft, culminating in the complete re-writing of the last two chapters following the Defence Review of 1998. It is now hoped that the final result will fulfil a need for a definitive history of a unique navy that has existed for nearly half a millennium.

Of course the work could never have come to fruition without the unstinting help of many people, several of whom had tales to tell of their experiences with the Army's Navy in war and peace. A great deal of help was given to the author by the following persons from the outset, and which continues to the present day. Major (Ret'd) David Nicholas MBE, late RASC/RCT and Major (Ret'd) B.V. Wynn-Werninck MNI, late RASC, must head the list, with both these gentlemen possessing encyclopaedic knowledge of the Army's Navy, particularly during the post-Second World War period. During the author's stay in the Officers' Mess at McMullen Barracks, Marchwood, David Nicholas not only spent a great amount of his valuable time in helping to select suitable photographs from his vast archives but also arranged interviews with other retired officers. In addition, David's hospitality in the Mess was kindness itself, even loaning linen and soap to the author who had not realised that these items were not supplied to guests! The author has no hesitation in stating categorically that if it had not been for David's assistance throughout the several years of writing this book, it would never have been completed. Bill Wynn-Werninck was always ready to offer his help in providing details of such occasions as the biggest Fleet Review ever of Army ships, which took place in the Solent a short while after VJ Day, and additionally recounting many of his experiences during and after the Second World War. He is also a well-known marine artist specialising in paintings of Army ships and personnel and he readily gave his permission to use any suitable prints from his paintings as illustrations in the book.

The author is also indebted to Lieutenant-Colonel J.M. Bowles MBE, Commanding Officer, 17 Port and Maritime Regiment, Royal Logistic Corps, who from the outset kindly agreed to the Regiment being the sponsor of the book.

Lieutenant-Colonel (Ret'd) Reg Cooley, late RASC/RCT, is the author of *The Unknown Fleet*, the only full and detailed history of the ships and men of the Army's civilian-manned fleet in war and peace from the reign of Henry VIII to the final stand-down in 1988. Reg was always more than willing to help the author with any information, and also supplied several unique photographs from his collection.

Information regarding the Royal Engineers Fleets, *ie* the Submarine Mining Service, the Inland Water Transport and the Port elements, was forthcoming from Captain (Ret'd) R.T. Arnold, late Royal Engineers, Librarian RE Library and his assistant, Mrs Maggie Magnuson. They were also most helpful in the supply of suitable photographs, whilst when the author's car developed a serious fault during the visit to Brompton Barracks at Chatham, they went to endless trouble to rectify the problem and thus enable the author and his wife to continue their travels.

Chief Officer Terry Holtham, Royal Fleet Auxiliary Service, together with his brother Tony, have, over many years, assembled an enviable collection of data covering British armed forces small craft, with the aim of eventually publishing a book on this subject. Both brothers have been of great help to the author with their wide-ranging knowledge of the smaller vessels in the Army's Navy whenever they were approached for information.

Other persons are acknowledged to have been most helpful in supplying details of their service in or with Army vessels. Jack Toft, author of *The Making of a Service Corps Seaman*, provided the story of his service in the WD/RASC Fleet during the Second World War, from private to staff sergeant. His experiences during the D-Day landings were particularly interesting. Ex-Corporal Peter Robinson RASC gave a wealth of reminiscences of his time with what is acknowledged to have been the smallest unit of the British Army during the Korean War. This was the LST Control Unit consisting of only two men, Peter himself and the late Major Vincent RASC. John de la Haye provided a detailed account of his Army craft leading the Liberation Fleet into Guernsey after VE Day. This vessel was WDV *Oma* and was the smallest vessel to take part in the operation. John was not only in the smallest craft but was believed to have been the youngest member of the Task Force, being just fifteen and on his first voyage as a Boy in the War Department Fleet. Despite being in poor health, Mr A.S. Blight CEng, MIMechE, retired Superintending Engineer and Constructor of Shipping, was kind enough to furnish details of the RASC Fleet Landing Ships (Tank), these vessels being the largest craft ever to fly the Blue Ensign with Crossed Swords. Major (Ret'd) Tony Pheby MNI, late RASC/RCT, gave fascinating accounts of two voyages made by his command, the LCT *Abbeville*, behind the Iron Curtain during the Cold War, the reasons being to deliver replacement power station equipment made in Britain to Helsinki, no commercial ships being available. Two retired officers based at Marchwood provided valuable information and notes on the Inland Water Transport Service and other maritime elements of the Royal Engineers. These gentlemen were Major (Ret'd) Ross Mason and Captain (Ret'd) Mike Richardson, both late of the Royal Engineers.

The author is indebted to the Museum of Army Transport, Beverley, especially for its kind permission for the loan of photographs and in particular to Major (Ret'd) J.A. 'Tubby' Robbins, late Royal Engineers, for imparting his knowledge of the IWT in both World Wars, including the use of train ferries in the Great War. The then archivist of the museum, Geoffrey Blewett, also kindly granted the author access to archives to select suitable photographs. Others rendering help were Ian Carter, Photograph Archive, Imperial War Museum, and Frank O'Connell of the Royal Logistic Corps Museum. The author also wishes to thank Mrs Joyce Smale for her kind permission to allow photographs from her late husband John Smale's wonderful collection depicting ships of the civilian-manned War Department/RASC Fleet from the turn of the century to after the Second World War. Thanks also to her son Robert for his assistance in this. It was very important that HM Stationery Office should grant permission to use Crown Copyright photographs and material in this book and Ian Quarterman, on behalf of the Controller HMSO, was most helpful in his guidance and advice in arranging this.

William Hawkins provided the author with his memories of his service in the RASC Fleet as a Boy Seaman after the Second World War. The author received these with appreciation, especially as William followed this with a letter to the editor of *Ships Monthly* extolling in glowing terms the articles in the magazine by the author on the Army's Navy!

The Secretary, the Institution of the Royal Army Service Corps and the Royal Corps of Transport, Lieutenant-Colonel R.F Grevatte-Ball, rendered a great service by granting the author a most generous authorisation to make reference in his book from any Corps publication. He also supplied many little-known facts of Corps maritime history and offered his most welcome assistance in spreading valuable publicity throughout his numerous connections in the field of the Army's Navy.

Finally the author is more than grateful for the sound advice and encouragement freely given by Captain Andrew Douglas, editor of *Sea Breezes*, especially on every aspect of the ways and means of publishing such a book. Should the author have inadvertently omitted any person of organisation in his acknowledgements, he offers his sincere apologies.

Chapter 1

From Henry VIII to the
Great War

Until 1597, vessels engaged in carrying military stores and cargoes were administered by the Office of Ordnance based at the Tower of London, which also served as the Royal Arsenal. In this period, there being no standing army, its principal duties involved supplying guns, ammunition, stores and equipment to the rapidly-expanding King's navy. In 1518 the first of the Royal 'gunwharves' had been built at Woolwich to facilitate the fitting of guns to the King's ships. HM Gunwharf at Portsmouth, built in 1662, served continuously as a base for the Army's ships for over 300 years, until the demise of the civilian-manned fleet in 1988. The ships employed in this service would have been hired or requisitioned by the Office from commercial owners. However, following a Royal Commission which found that in the 180 years of the Office of Ordnance's existence corrupt and fraudulent practices had become rife, it was replaced by a new body entitled the Board of Ordnance in 1597. The Board, headed by its Great Master, continued as an Office of the Crown until it was taken over by Parliament under the Commonwealth. The restoration of the monarchy in 1660 saw the Board restored to its original form, which continued until 1683 when it became a Civil Department of State.

The Board was now headed by the Master-General of the Ordnance, a post reserved for a soldier of great distinction and which carried with it, until 1828, a seat in the Cabinet. His Deputy was likewise a senior officer, and directly subordinate to them were four Principal Officers, with Inferior Officers and Under Ministers under them. Among this latter group was an official entitled the Purveyor, who was directly charged by the Board to 'provide such ships, vessels, lighters and boats as the Board might require at favourable contract rates'.

Ordnance storehouses had been established at the Royal Dockyards at Portsmouth, Sheerness, Chatham and Devonport, at Deptford and of course at Woolwich, which was destined to become the principal Royal Arsenal and the main supplier of the sinews of war to the armed forces throughout the British Empire. By 1796 there were fifty-four storehouses, rising to ninety-eight throughout the Empire by 1828.

The Birth of the Army's Navy

Finding dependence on chartered vessels unsuited for its requirements, the Board of Ordnance began to purchase its own small boats. The earliest surviving record of the Board's activities as a shipowner is a reconditioning order for £5 dated 1751 for the Woolwich Office boat, built in 1746 but having had no repairs since then. So from these humble beginnings, which probably gave rise to the popular saying among the older members of the Army's Navy when the author was serving as Second Officer of RASCV *Maxwell Brander* in 1947, to the effect that 'they had been serving in Army ships since the Fleet was a rowing boat', grew a unique fleet employed in the carriage of military stores. But even in these early days the activities of this fleet were not exclusively restricted to the transport of supplies. The Board's smaller craft also provided a safe and secure means of transport for officials and valuables in an age when the poor state of the roads and the prevalence of highwaymen made overland travel dangerous and time-consuming. Thus began the tradition of the Army Fleet performing duties outside the range of their routine tasks.

In 1777, the post of Superintendent of Shipping, reporting directly to the Board, came into being, charged with the duties of operator, purveyor and repairer of the Board's vessels. In wartime, he would also have been responsible for ensuring that any hired vessels came up to the stringent requirements of the Charter Agreements, as the owner of any hired vessel lost in action could claim the full value of the ship as compensation. Perhaps the best-known holder of this post was Captain Thomas Dickinson, who retired from the Board at the age of 72 in 1826 after forty-five years service, an early example of long service in the Army's Navy. During Captain Dickinson's term of office the Fleet began to expand, consisting of a variety of craft, the majority concentrated at Woolwich, and employed by various departments for a wide range of activities. One such was the operation of the Military Ferry between Woolwich and the north bank of the Thames, records showing that in 1803 the Superintendent of Shipping was required to provide two extra barges and a large boat for this service. Other departments of the Royal Arsenal, such as the Storekeeper, the Royal Laboratory and the Engineer's Department also operated vessels for their own requirements. For example, by 1812 the Engineer's Department was operating a diverse selection of water craft employed in clearing Thames sandbanks and in construction work at the Arsenal. These included barges used as horse ferries, with the pulling craft to tow them, sailing boats for the transport of stores and personnel, and ballast lighters with attendant skiffs. Captain Dickinson was succeeded by another retired naval officer, Captain James Steward, who served until 1831, followed by Captain Joseph Soady. In 1852 Captain Soady was followed by a civilian, Samuel B. Cook, whose term of office would be cut short by the dissolution of the Board of Ordnance in 1855. As time went on, the Board of Ordnance had acquired larger vessels used to convey stores to the various depots around the British Isles, and to supply ordnance stores to ships riding at anchor, and the Estimates of 1839-40 show that twelve such vessels were now on the strength (see Appendix I for details).

The War Department Fleet

The Crimean War of 1854-5 saw a further increase in the Army's Fleet, larger vessels now numbering twenty, but due to general mismanagement during that campaign, the Board of Ordnance was dissolved in 1855. Its fleet, however, survived under a new name, the War Department Fleet. As far as can be ascertained, the Fleet's ships continued to fly the Ordnance flag of a Red Ensign defaced with three cannons surmounted by three cannon balls until 1864, when the Admiralty ruled that in future ships belonging to government offices should fly a blue ensign bearing the insignia of the appropriate department. The Fleet's ensign therefore changed to blue, but retained the same insignia, until it in turn was replaced in 1890 when the Admiralty authorised a new 'blue ensign of Her Majesty's Fleet with the Badge of such other Military Services, on the Fly thereof, namely two crossed swords' and this has been the ensign flown, with some minor changes, by the ships of the Army's Navy ever since.

Apart from its change of name, and that it now consisted of a wide range of craft, relatively little is know of the activities of the Fleet in the next few years, but it is presumed that it was administered directly from the War Office, with local management in the hands of the Storekeeper's Department. Its main base continued to be at Woolwich Arsenal, where extensive improvements including dredging and the construction of a new pier allowed up to four large ships to be loaded alongside by crane, thus reducing the need for barges for loading and unloading. Records show that by 1862 the War Department owned and administered thirty-three vessels based not only at Woolwich but also at Portsmouth, Chatham and Devonport.

In 1847, the War Office had purchased land at Shoeburyness for use as a proof-testing range for heavy guns. As ordnance had grown more powerful and longer-ranged, the inhabitants of Woolwich and Plumstead had suffered from the effects of 'friendly fire' of guns being tested in the vicinity of Woolwich Arsenal itself, and they were doubtless greatly relieved by the move to Shoeburyness. But this move meant that heavy ordnance now had to be shipped to and from the new range for testing. Specially-built railway wagons came into service for the carriage of heavy gun barrels, but since there was no railway within 5 miles of Shoeburyness, and furthermore the sheer legs at the range could only lift 50 tons (some gun barrels could weigh up to 100 tons), another solution was required.

Water transport was the obvious answer, and large barges with rail tracks in the cargo space were constructed, able to carry a heavy gun on its proof carriage, which was loaded by running it into the barge through the bows. The barge was then towed to Shoeburyness by tug, and the gun, still on its carriage, was pulled off the barge by a powerful static engine, and then run on rails to its test-firing position. The first of these custom-built barges was named *Magog*, and she was joined in 1886 by a larger vessel, the 400-ton *Gog*. The original *Magog* was replaced by a 260-ton barge of the same name in 1900. The barges were towed by the steam tugs *Katharine* and *Katharine II*. All four of these vessels fully maintained the Fleet's tradition of long service, *Gog* serving from 1886 to 1948, the second Magog from 1900 to 1948, *Katharine* from 1882 to 1930 and her successor *Katharine II* from 1930 to 1959 (see Appendix II).

'Their Lordships felt it their bounden duty to discourage to the utmost of their ability the use of steam vessels, as they considered that the introduction of steam was calculated to strike a fatal blow at the naval supremacy of the Empire.' This was the view expressed by the First Lord of the Admiralty, Lord Melville, in 1828, and although technical and logistic developments in the following decades rendered such concerns unfounded, it was many years before the Royal Navy became an exclusively steam navy. The transition was equally slow in Army vessels. It appears that the first steamship in the War Department Fleet was the *Balaclava* in 1857, which was joined two years later by the *Lord Panmure*. The latter ship remained in service until about 1900, surviving a serious collision in 1869, but *Balaclava* was lost in 1865. No further steam vessels joined the Fleet until 1874 when the steam launches *Falcon*, a paddle steamer later converted to screw propulsion, and *Grand Duchess* came into service. Three years later more steam vessels were acquired, and from then on the trend was to replace sail vessels with steam. However, a group of sailing vessels was maintained for the carriage of gunpowder and other explosives, for safety reasons. Sailing barges were also operated by the Royal Gunpowder Factory at Waltham Abbey, and although these barges were never part of the War Department Fleet, personnel from the Fleet were sometimes seconded to this service. The Waltham Abbey powder-carrying fleet never employed powered vessels, and it is interesting to note that as late as 1931 an order was placed for two new sailing barges, one of which, *Lady of the Lea*, was reportedly the last wooden sailing barge built on the Thames. With the closure of the Waltham Abbey factory in 1945, the surviving vessels were sold off.

In 1869 the Army Service Corps came into being as part of the Supply and Transport sub-department of the Control Department of the Army, itself founded the same year. When the Control Department was abolished in 1875 owing to various shortcomings, the status of the ASC remained the same under the new Commissariat and Transport Department. In 1880, this Department was split into two sections, the Commissariat and Transport Staff and the Commissariat and Transport Corps, under the latter of which the ASC was organised until the two commissariats were united by Royal warrant in 1888, becoming the Army Service Corps with full responsibility for supply and transport, which of course included the War Department Fleet.

In 1895 the War Department Fleet consisted of fifteen steamers (including three new building), sixteen steam launches, twelve sailing vessels and 178 boats, while numerous dumb barges were employed on various duties. These vessels were stationed throughout the United Kingdom and also at Singapore, Hong Kong, Bermuda, Gibraltar, Barbados, Mauritius, Nova Scotia, Ceylon, Jamaica, Malta and Sierra Leone. Prime examples of ships having long lives in the Army's Navy were the coasters *Marquess of Hartington* (1886-1957) and *Sir Evelyn Wood* (1896-1957). Surviving both World Wars, and carrying out all tasks given to them, including several long ocean voyages, they were very popular with the officers and men of the Fleet, and it was a sad day when both finally paid off at Cairnryan in 1957.

This tradition was also reflected in the long service careers of the

17

officers and ratings of the Fleet. Many joined as boys and frequently served for as long as forty years, some for over fifty years, apparently disregarding any normal retiring age. There are also many instances of succeeding generations of the same family serving in the Fleet. Although the Fleet continued to be manned by civilian crews as it had been since its inception, records show that in the 1890s military personnel began to be employed afloat, although no specific details of their duties are given. It would appear, however, that such personnel were attached only temporarily to ships' crews for specifically military tasks. For example, Royal Artillery gunners from the coastal batteries may have been embarked aboard target-towing vessels to report the fall of shot or even help the permanent crew with the streaming and recovery of targets. Nonetheless, the manning of these ship continued to be by the officers and men of the War Department Fleet, whose status was firmly civilian, albeit holding the position of civil servants and thus subject to Government Employees' Regulations and Conditions as well as being bound by the Ship's Articles of Agreement. In fact the Fleet Regulations of 1859 appear very rigorous to modern eyes, bristling with stern injunctions to the Master to ensure that the vessel and crew under his command adhered strictly to the rules and regulations laid down by the War Office. Particular emphasis was laid on the safety rules to be observed when loading, carrying or discharging powder or ammunition, but many of the regulations appear self-evident, for example that when at sea the officer of the watch is to keep his watch on the bridge, and likewise that the engineer on duty should not leave the engine room unless relieved by another engineer. The only mention of any specific punishment is that any person found in possession of Lucifer matches aboard any War Department vessel will be immediately dismissed. Considering, however, that drunkenness was a widespread social problem at this time, it is very surprising that this is not mentioned at all in the regulations, and neither is what punishment should befall any crew member found guilty of stealing cargo or stores.

By 1890, despite the civilian status of the crews, strict dress regulations were in force, with Masters, Mates, Boatswains, Seamen and Boys being required to wear uniform. Officers' uniforms were based on the Royal Navy uniforms of the day, consisting of a peaked cap with a badge comprising a Royal Crown above the letters WD surrounded by a gold laurel wreath, and a blue reefer jacket with gilt buttons and appropriate symbols of rank on the sleeve in gold braid. Other items of the officers' uniform were a matching waistcoat and blue cloth trousers. Boatswains were similarly attired, with their rank indicated by three gilt buttons on the sleeve of the jacket. Seaman and Boys wore blue pea jackets and a blue jersey with trousers of inferior cloth to those worn by officers, but the men could choose whether the cloth was blue serge, boats' crews (as worn in the Royal Navy) or blue tweed. Caps were of naval round hat pattern, made of blue cloth with a black silk band inscribed 'War Department' in gold. Another form of headgear was a blue worsted cap, to be worn at sea. Both Officers and Ratings had to provide and maintain all these items of clothing at their own expense, the officers using a tailoring firm at Portsea, while the Seamen and Boys obtained theirs, on repayment, from the Services' clothing centre at Pimlico in London. As the cost of this uniform was rather high, various well-meaning people, including Members of Parliament, occasionally queried why the men had to pay for their own uniforms. This always received the reply that as the Fleet personnel received good rates of pay they could well afford the outlay. Whether the crews of War Department Fleet ships agreed with this is another matter. Engine room personnel were exempt from these uniform regulations, receiving instead two canvas suits of working clothes annually free of charge from the Services' clothing centre, given the dirty environment they worked in as distinct from the deck crew. There may also have been something of the snobbishness once evidenced towards engineering personnel in the Royal Navy in the early days of steam, when deck officers did not recognise engineers as being officers and insisted on them wearing civilian clothes, albeit frock coats and top hats!

With the development of steam-propelled, armoured warships the role of coastal artillery in the defence of ports and other strategic locations had changed considerably. Increases in the speed of warships, there being fast torpedo boats capable of 21kts by 1877, also required new forms of training, and the use of moving targets for practice shoots became increasingly common. Initially target towing was undertaken by a miscellaneous collection of vessels from a variety of sources, including Royal Navy torpedo boats and steam tugs, hired commercial vessels, and a few of the Army's ships, including War Department steam launches. However, it soon became apparent that it would be more logical for one organisation to control this activity, so gradually the Army took over the task of towing targets for coastal artillery, with vessels being provided by the War Department Fleet and the Submarine Mining Service, and this service was to continue until the abolition of coastal artillery in 1956-7. In 1895 the first steam ships specifically built for target towing were commissioned, *Sir Redvers Buller* and *Osprey*. Two years later *Osprey* was fitted with a special winch that allowed her targets to move across the field of fire at greatly increased speed. This innovation was enthusiastically received and became standard equipment on future target-towing vessels. As well as their designed role, both of these vessels were also used in routine shipping of military cargoes.

With the advent of moving targets it became clear that there was now an increased risk to civilian shipping from shells fired by coastal batteries, and in 1892 a committee was set up to investigate how range safety could be improved. The committee's report was presented to Parliament the following year, and among its recommendations was that provision should be made for towing away vessels that trespassed into firing areas. It was suggested that steam tugs should be allocated to the commanders of coastal batteries for this purpose. Although these recommendations do not seem to have been made law, by-laws were enacted under the Military Lands Act to prevent vessels entering target areas and allowing for those that did so to be towed away. It followed therefore that military vessels should undertake such duties and a new role of ensuring range safety was added to the duties of the War Department Fleet which was to continue in peace and war for many years to come. This role survived the abolition of coastal artillery in the 1950s as War Department vessels continued their range safety duties in the missile firing ranges off the Hebrides.

The Submarine Mining Service, 1871-1904

Another area in which the Army was involved in maritime activities in the nineteenth century was that of the defence of harbours and rivers by means of mines and torpedoes. The success of floating mines (called 'torpedoes' at this time) during the American Civil War lead to a joint naval and military committee being set up to look into the feasibility of this type of harbour defence. Somewhat surprisingly, given the influence wielded by the Admiralty and its traditional belief that 'anything that floats belongs to us', the recommendation was that the Army, specifically the Royal Engineers, should be responsible for these defences. It may have been the case that the committee was swayed by the Royal Engineers always having been 'Sappers and Miners', and it was a fact that at this time they were the acknowledged experts in the application of electricity to military science, and moored mines were electrically detonated. Also, the Navy may have considered itself an offensive-orientated, seagoing force, and craft for the support of static defences were outside their remit.

Be that as it may, the Submarine Mining Service (SMS) of the Royal Engineers was established in 1871. Although initially equipped with craft unsuitable for its tasks, by 1875 a purpose-built vessel had been commissioned, the first of the *Miner* class. In 1885 vessels of the *Gordon* class entered service. These were larger vessels equipped for laying cable and displaced between 100 and 125 tons. By 1891 even larger vessels, such as the 144-ton *General Skinner* and the 177-ton *Napier of Magdala*, had joined the SMS. These ships were all equipped to lay and recover floating mines, the *Miner* class being equipped with a steam winch and bow derrick. The larger vessels had bow and mast derricks as well as a large steam-powered lifting device. They also had the advantage of having twin screws. Like the War Department Fleet, the vessels of the SMS were civilian-manned, a typical crew consisting of a coxswain, two or three deckhands, two engineers, two stokers and a cook. Royal Engineers personnel would also be embarked as needed for purely military duties. Photographs of SMS vessels often show quite large RE parties on board carrying out various functions including signalling by 'flag wagging'.

By 1898 the SMS fleet had grown to sixty-eight vessels distributed throughout the British Empire, including some quite sophisticated ships (see Appendix III for details of SMS vessels between 1898-1904). However, in the early years of the twentieth century the Royal Navy's policy changed, and it sought to take control of the defence of harbours by mines and torpedoes, prompted in part by the recognition of the increased role in naval warfare played by the submarine. The Admiralty coveted the shore installations of the SMS for the support of these under-water craft, and suggested that it should take over all aspects of under-water warfare. Despite a hard-fought rearguard action by the War Office, the Committee for Imperial Defence decided in favour of the Navy, and in April 1904 the SMS, which now had a total military and civilian personnel of 5800, was disbanded, twenty-one of its vessels going to the Royal Navy and twenty-seven to the War Department. The largest of the SMS ships, the *Haslar*, came to the WD Fleet and in the best traditions of that Service soldiered on until 1951.

This account of the SMS has only briefly covered the history of an interesting, though short-lived, aspect of the British Army's maritime activities. But this was not to be the end of the Royal Engineers' water-borne activities, as will be seen in later chapters. A detailed history of the SMS can be found in *The History of Submarine Mining in the British Army* by Lieutenant-Colonel W. Baker-Brown RE.

The WD Fleet before the Great War

In the early years of the twentieth century the War Department Fleet continued to expand, the transfer of ships from the defunct SMS in 1904 being a particular boost. In 1908 a committee was set up under the chairmanship of Major General C.E. Heath CVO to enquire into whether the Army really needed to have its own fleet or whether its needs could be more economically met by hiring commercial vessels. The committee decided to retain the Army's Navy, but of perhaps greater interest is that contained within its report was a complete listing of Army ships, apparently the first detailed fleet list ever produced. The vessels of the Fleet, ranging from steamers to small craft, were divided into those stationed at home and those abroad, and showed a total of some 200 craft. However, many of these would have been little more than rowing boats or, on overseas stations, local craft. One interesting fact which emerges from this list is the existence of an oil-fuelled motor launch, unnamed but belonging to 76 MT Company ASC. Stationed at Shoeburyness for firing observation and range safety duties, it was manned by a corporal and a private, making it apparently the only military-crewed vessel in the Army's Navy (although of course RE personnel had long been shipped aboard civilian-crewed vessels for specifically military duties). The launch appears in the 1911 list of War Department vessels (see Appendix II). Also, the list records that at both Gibraltar and Malta, the Governor's launch was provided and manned by the War Department Fleet, and as we shall see, this practice was to continue for many years to come. However, as shown in Appendix III, an extract from the *Naval Pocket Book* listing War Department vessels 1898-1919, a great deal of change and expansion took place in the years under review.

Apart from this threat of an early form of privatisation in 1908, these were fairly tranquil years for the Fleet, but the assassination of the Archduke Franz Ferdinand of Austria and his wife by Serbian nationalists in the then little-known city of Sarajevo on 20 June 1914 brought all that to an end. Europe moved inexorably towards all-out war as Austria declared war on Serbia on 28 July, followed by Russian mobilisation in support of Serbia and a German declaration of war on Russia and France. The German invasion of Belgium as part of the Schlieffen Plan to knock Russia's ally France out of the war quickly brought Great Britain into the war on 4 August, and the stage was set for the then greatest conflict in history, resulting in the loss of millions of lives and the re-drawing of the map of Europe.

Chapter 2

The Great War and After: 1914-39

With the outbreak of the Great War there was of course a massive increase in all aspects of military operations, so it is surprising that there appears to have been no new building of vessels for the War Department Fleet between 1914 and 1918, in fact no new ships being commissioned until 1926. In 1914 Fleet strength stood at fifty-six steam or motor vessels, nine sailing craft (including 'hoys', these being sloop-rigged working boats of Continental design), numerous barges and lighters (mostly unnamed), and mention is also made of three 'tongkangs'. The reason for the lack of expansion of the Fleet is thought to have been the refusal by the Superintending Engineer and Constructor of Shipping of the day of a request to construct and maintain a new fleet of vessels for use on inland waterways, as he could not undertake any further commitments. As well as being responsible for the construction and maintenance of all War Department Fleet vessels, he was also charged with the management of the Woolwich Arsenal Gasworks, he was responsible for the supply of all Army fire-fighting equipment and also served as Superintending Engineer to HM Customs. The operation of inland water transport was therefore passed to the Royal Engineers, forming yet another branch of the Army's Navy.

Transportation Branch (Inland Water Transport) RE, 1914-24

Inland water transport was needed on the Western Front to supplement the French and Belgian railway networks by exploiting those countries' extensive canal systems. As such craft might find themselves operating close to, or even in, the front line, it was thought necessary that they should be manned by military, rather than civilian personnel, and therefore the RE was given the task.

The IWT initially came under the control of the Director of Railway Transport, RE, who appointed a Deputy Director to administer the new fleet. The first incumbent was Commander G.E. Holland who had served in the Royal Indian Marine and later as Marine Superintendent of the London and North Western Railway. But as the IWT expanded, it became clear it was not just an adjunct of railway transport, and rapidly evolved into an independent organisation. From the commencement of hostilities the IWT was active on the Continent, operating large numbers of craft on the canals and rivers, mostly large barges, both motorised and dumb, ferrying troops and supplies from the Channel ports and railheads to as close to the front line as possible. There were also several large hospital barges, evacuating the wounded back to base hospitals.

In 1916 it was decided to introduce a cross-Channel service of IWT vessels, and a military port and depot was established at Richborough, which by 1918 had become a major seaport capable of handling 30,000 tons of cargo per week, with over 200 barges crossing the Channel to French ports. Four large train ferries were also acquired to transport railway wagons from Southampton and Richborough across the Channel, mostly to Dieppe. The first three, *TF 1-3*, were new construction while *TF 4* was a requisitioned Canadian ship of extraordinary design with an enormous superstructure of steel girders. There is some argument as to whether these vessels, which in line with normal wartime merchant ship practice were armed with guns for defence against U-boats, were military or civilian-manned. It is recorded that there was a Marine Detachment RE at Richborough for employment aboard barges and train ferries, while photographs of these ferries show both soldiers and merchant seamen serving as deckhands. It is likely, however, that the new-construction ships were military-manned while the requisitioned Canadian ferry kept her merchant seaman crew.

Apart from this activity on the Western Front, and a presence in the East African campaign, the greatest concentration of IWT craft was to be found in the Middle East, following the entry of Turkey into the war as an ally of Germany. The scarcity of roads and railways in the Mesopotamian theatre meant that water transport on the great rivers Tigris and Euphrates was the only practical means of moving large bodies of men and supplies during the campaign to capture Baghdad. Large numbers of shallow-draught vessels were pressed into service, including paddle steamers, motor boats, barges and native craft. Although the majority of craft employed were obtained locally, several paddle steamers were built in Britain and shipped out in sections to the Middle East to be assembled in India or at the port of Basra. This kind of operation, using rivers to move troops through desert regions, was not new, the Sudan campaign of 1896-8 being a prime example, when large numbers of river vessels, including all of Thomas Cook's Nile steamers, were used to ferry an Anglo-Egyptian army up the Nile. By November 1918, the IWT Fleet in Mesopotamia numbered 1634 craft, of which 446 were steamers, 774 barges and 414 motor boats. Although all administered by the IWT, most of these would have been chartered or requisitioned vessels.

Although the growth of the IWT during the war had been meteoric, it was not to join the War Department Fleet in its tradition of longevity, being disbanded in 1924. But the RE-administered fleet was to be revived in the Second World War.

The War Department Fleet in the Great War

Despite the lack of new tonnage in this period, the War Department Fleet was kept busy as in peacetime, ferrying cargoes to military bases in the British Isles and to Egypt, Malta, Gibraltar and other Mediterranean ports. Target-towing duties also continued, but the war brought further commitments for the Fleet.

During the Gallipoli landings in 1915 the Fleet provided a water cooling ship and a cold store vessel, and during the Macedonian campaign of 1916 an Army Service Corps motor boat company operated patrol launches on Lakes Langazo and Beshik. These military-crewed companies were a wartime innovation and were disbanded in 1918. Closer to home, the Irish Rebellion of 1916 resulted in an increased presence by the British Army in Ireland, leading to further responsibilities for the Fleet in supplying the various garrisons in the south of that country. Three vessels, each with two crews, were also based at Queenstown in Ireland supporting the various coastal batteries in the area. Overseas commitments in areas not classed as war zones continued as in peacetime, vessels being manned by locally-recruited crews commanded by civilian Fleet officers from the UK.

The Fleet's most important role, however, remained the cross-Channel service in support of the Army in France and Flanders, and which was to continue after the Armistice for the British Army of Occupation in Germany. Detailed records of the Fleet's activities during the war are somewhat scarce, for example there is little mention of any enemy action against Army vessels, although they must have been at risk from mines, U-boats and, to a lesser extent, air attack (a steam launch named *Swale* was damaged in an air raid in 1918).

An interesting footnote to developments during the Great War is that, following the amalgamation of the Royal Flying Corps and Royal Naval Air Service on 1 April 1918 to form the Royal Air Force, another 'Navy' appeared on the scene. Within a few days of the creation of the RAF, a unit entitled the Marine Craft Section came into being, which as the Marine Branch was to survive until 1986, becoming the longest-serving branch of the RAF, operating a wide range of vessels including ex-RN minesweepers and in its final years commissioning new classes of long-range recovery and support ships and also an experimental laboratory ship for the Royal Aircraft Establishment. Well-known figures who served in the Marine Branch included the racing driver Sir Algernon Guiness, the novelist Alistair Maclean, the writer John Harris and T.E. Lawrence (of Arabia), the latter being involved in the development of high-speed armoured launches used as bombing targets. Several histories of the RAF fleet manned by 'airmen afloat' have been published, perhaps the best-known being *The Sea Shall Not Have Them* by John Harris about the air-sea rescue launches operated by the RAF in the Second World War (the same title was used for a film on the same subject). In later years, there was a degree of overlap between the Marine Branch RAF and the Army's Navy, as some of its ships and their duties were taken over by the Army Civilian Fleet owing to shortages of RAF crews in the Second World War and in the last years of the Branch's history.

At the end of 'The War to End All Wars' in 1918, the War Department fleet was at approximately the same strength as in 1914, and carrying out much the same duties. In the following inter-war years the Fleet was to undergo considerable change and expansion, as well as undertaking tasks that had not hitherto been envisaged.

Between the Wars, 1918-1939

During this period the Fleet was directed and operated by what was now entitled the Royal Army Service Corps, and the vessels were entirely manned by civilian crews who wore naval-type uniforms with War Department insignia. Officers' cap badges resembled those of naval officers, but with the Royal crown being contained within the laurel leaves rather than above them. The centre of the badge showed crossed swords with the letters W and D either side of the hilts. The uniforms of both officers and men had remained much the same as laid down in the 1890s, with minor changes in cut and cloth to keep up with alterations in naval dress. However, items such as the officers' caps and jackets, as well as the ratings' round hats, were still more suited to the nineteenth century, and certainly in the case of the officers altered at their own expense to more modern versions. Insignia of rank on jacket sleeves and shoulder straps now followed Merchant Navy practice, for example all engineer officers had a purple stripe between the gold.

Although the Fleet's principal role remained the same as always, there were tasks required of the Army's Navy particular to the immediate post-war period. Firstly, as soon as the war ended in 1918, the Fleet began to return surplus stores and ordnance to Woolwich following the standing-down of coastal defences, including the offshore forts guarding strategic estuaries. The removal of heavy guns from these sea-girt fortifications by War Department vessels called for skilful ship-handling, coupled with a close watch being kept for sudden changes in the tide or the weather. Nowhere was this more apparent than in the waters of the Humber Estuary where forts were situated at Spurn Point, Bull and Hale Sands. A base had been established at Grimsby to serve the area, and the target tower *Sir Herbert Miles* was based there, with the additional role of support vessel to the Humber forts. She was assisted by the *Lord Wolseley*, which had been fitted with extra water tanks for supplying the isolated forts. After their closure, she continued to ferry maintenance parties out to them so that the batteries could be ready for re-activation in case of any future outbreak of hostilities. The actual removal of the guns was carried out by men of the Royal Garrison Artillery, while on one occasion the gun barge *Gog*, towed by the *Katharine*, had to be brought up to the Humber for the removal of two 9.2in guns from Spurn Point. *Gog* then carried the guns to Grimsby for transhipment into the *Marquis of Hartington* which was to take them to Woolwich. This particular operation was complicated by the weight of the guns (29 tons each) and the fact that the strong easterly winds in these unsheltered waters could well have resulted in a dangerous situation. At Grimsby further difficulties were encountered as the guns could only be transferred from the barge to the ship by means of sheer legs, which meant that the receiving ship had to shift position repeatedly before the guns could be safely settled in her hold.

The second post-war task was the disposal of surplus ammunition and explosives in deep water. High explosives, often in a deteriorating condition, were dangerous enough, but poison gas shells and cylinders were even more so, as were deck cargoes of chemicals such as picric acid and calcium carbide, the latter highly inflammable when in contact with water. The ships used for the dumping were not specially equipped, barrels and crates of toxic chemicals simply being pushed over the side from makeshift platforms, while explosives were hoisted out of the hold, swung outboard on derricks and then slipped from the lifting hooks. Initially the dumping crews were supplied by soldiers from local units, but a high incidence of *mal de mer* amongst the military personnel meant that the job gradually reverted to the civilian seamen of the Fleet. Although an extra hourly payment was made to seamen for this job, it can well be imagined how hazardous it could be, especially in rough seas or a heavy swell. In fact at least one man was lost overboard in the course of these operations.

The routine supply work of the Fleet continued, and the wartime cross-Channel service was extended to German ports in support of British occupation forces. The steamer *Sir Redvers Buller* underwent modifications to her masts and funnel to allow her to sail up the Rhine to Cologne, while larger ships of the Fleet offloaded their cargoes at Rotterdam into smaller WD vessels for passage up the Rhine to Cologne and Wiesbaden.

It is not now widely remembered that following the foundation of the Irish Free State in 1922, the British Army maintained a presence in the new country which was to last until 1938, with responsibility for coastal defence at Berehaven, Queenstown and Lough Swilly, and of course wherever the Army went, the ships and boats of its Navy naturally followed. It was inevitable that British forces would be subject to IRA attacks during the Irish Civil War which ensued, and two attacks involved War Department vessels. In 1922 the steam launch *Cambridge* came under fire when approaching Queenstown: three unarmed British soldiers and the vessel's Master were wounded. A more serious incident occurred in 1924, again at Queenstown, when gunmen opened fire on a War Department vessel landing passengers. One soldier was killed and twenty others wounded. New agreements were signed between the British and Irish governments in 1938, bringing the Army's role in Eire to an end. All seven of the vessels of the Fleet based in Ireland were handed over to the Irish Army, including the already ageing *Wyndham*, built in 1903, which was to soldier on into the 1960s, only finally being scrapped in 1971. Many of the ships' crews were Irish, and transferred to the new Irish civilian-manned Maritime Service, while non-Irish Fleet personnel could volunteer for temporary service with this organisation under special agreements.

The Great War and After: 1914-39

Following the Armistice, there were major cutbacks in all the Services, and the Army's Navy did not escape the attentions of the committee headed by Sir Eric Geddes, whose recommendations for economies in all areas of government expenditure were known as the 'Geddes Axe' of 1922. Measures introduced included reductions in both ships and personnel, reductions in pay and a ban on overtime except in cases of emergency. Many of the target-towing vessels were either laid up in reserve or disposed of, with two of the steamers, *Sir Redvers Buller* and *Lord Wolseley*, being sold. Nonetheless, the 1920s saw considerable new building of major vessels, such as *Sir Noel Birch* (1926), *Sir Desmond O'Callaghan* (1927), *Lord Plumer* (1927), *General McHardy* (1928), *Sir Walter Campbell* (1928), *Geoffrey Stanley* (1929) and *Sir Cecil Romer* (1929). The IWT was also a victim of the 'Geddes Axe', being abolished in 1924, although it was revived in the Second World War, as we shall see.

During the 1920s and 1930s coastal artillery continued to achieve high standards of efficiency and accuracy and this was due in no small measure to constant practice firing at moving targets towed by the vessels of the War Department Fleet. The targets were of the 'Hong Kong' type, introduced some years previously and destined to remain in service almost until the end of coastal artillery itself. By joining two or more of these targets together, together with erecting fake superstructure on them and altering the length of tow, it was possible to represent a wide range of warships, from battleships and cruisers to motor torpedo boats and even submarines. The towing vessels' special winches enabled them to pull targets across the ranges at realistic speeds of up to 20kts, well in excess of what the vessels themselves were capable of. For target towing, the WD Fleet vessels would take aboard an Army range officer and a party of soldiers for communications and recording duties: as well as wireless, heliograph and lamp signalling, simple flag codes were also used to signal such information as whether the ship was on course and whether it was safe to commence fire and cease fire. To facilitate the range officer's task Henry Travis, Superintending Engineer and Constructor of Shipping, had invented a device which, because of its resemblance to a garden rake, was known as the Travis Rake, a manually-operated instrument for supplying fall-of-shot data. In later years an automatic version was developed which, geared to the towing winch, superseded the manual rake. It is interesting to note that during the inter-war years damage to ships and injury to personnel while target-towing rarely occurred, while only one death has been recorded, that of the engineer of *Sir Frederick Walker* who was killed when a shell hit the vessel's engine room.

Apart from a slight involvement in the Graeco-Turkish War in 1921-2 when the British occupying force at Chauak was under threat from hostile Turkish forces under Mustafa Kemal (later Kemal Ataturk), life for the War Department Fleet was relatively peaceful in the 1920s. There were, however, threats from Irish terrorists, as we have seen, and there were also a number of serious accidents involving vessels of the Fleet at this time. In 1923 WDV *Marquis of Hartington* was loading picric acid, a highly volatile substance used in the manufacture of high explosives, from railway wagons at Liverpool Docks, when one of the steam cranes being used broke an axle and toppled over, spilling red-hot coals from its firebox underneath the wagons, causing a serious fire. The ship was saved from serious damage thanks to the fire being quickly extinguished by dock workers, but the War Department was seriously taken to task by the port authorities for not having declared the hazardous nature of the cargo.

Another serious incident occurred in 1928 when the barge *Gog* managed to lose her cargo, a 52-ton converted naval gun, whilst being towed from Shoeburyness to Woolwich by the *Katharine*. Having missed the tide, it was decided to anchor the giant barge south of Canvey Island, but the deteriorating weather caused her to drag her anchor and put her in danger of colliding with a neighbouring anchored sailing barge, the *Royalty*. Gale-force winds prevented the crew of the *Katharine* taking the *Gog* in tow, and at the height of the storm, despite the crews' best efforts to keep them apart, the *Royalty* crashed into the *Gog* with considerable force. The giant barge immediately began to take in water and eventually sank, although the *Katharine* was able to save all of her crew before she went down. Next day, her cargo having rolled out of her stern gates, *Gog* resurfaced and was found half-submerged by the Trinity House vessel *Alert*. After being fully raised by salvage vessels, she was returned to Woolwich for repairs and went on to give many more years' service in both peace and war. A happier event took place in 1925 when the target tower WDV *Langdon* escorted a successful cross-Channel swimmer, the New Zealander Lieutenant-Colonel Bernard Freyberg VC DSO MC. A hero of the Great War, he was later to command New Zealand forces in the Middle East in the Second World War, was knighted and became Governor-General of New Zealand, rising to the rank of Lieutenant General.

The 1930s was to see a considerable increase in the number of vessels in the War Department Fleet, accelerating as the threat of war with

Nazi Germany grew ever more apparent. In 1930 the target tower *Sir Robert Wigham*, the motor barge *Katharine II* and the launch *Wuzzer* joined the Fleet, followed by the motor barge *Henry Caddell* and the launch *Raven* in 1931. In 1934 there was a substantial increase in the Fleet with the commissioning of WDVs *Crystal II*, *Vawdrey*, *John Adams* and *Sir Hastings Anderson*. The latter ship, specially built for the War Department by Harland & Wolff, Glasgow, was a graceful vessel with the appearance of a rich man's yacht, despite being designed for target towing and the carriage of freight and passengers. Often described as the finest-looking ship ever to fly the Blue Ensign with crossed swords, she was stationed at Singapore where she was to be tragically lost during the Japanese invasion of 1942.

By 1934 the War Department Fleet consisted of 23 steam vessels and launches, 23 motor ships and launches, 17 barges and tongkangs and 132 small craft. The Fleet was kept busy: in 1932 the steam target tower *Hurst II* was first on the scene when a flying boat coming in to land at Plymouth harbour collided with a dockyard craft, causing several fatalities. The gun barge *Gog* also suffered another accident at about this time. While under tow by *Katharine II* in Yanlet Creek off the Isle of Grain, she inexplicably surged forward on the tow line, striking the stern of the towing vessel and forcing her aground, but the crew of the *Katharine II* managed to free her and damage to both vessels was minor.

One of the vessels stationed overseas was the elderly steam target tower *Abercorn*, built in 1903. Despite her age, she steamed out to Jamaica in 1934 in what was then probably the longest deep-sea voyage ever made by a ship of the Army's Navy. Manned by local civilian crews, *Abercorn* was to live up to the Fleet's tradition of long service. A story is told of a senior officer visiting the ship who asked the Jamaican Master, who was very proud of his command, how old the ship was. 'About forty-five years old, Sir', was the reply. The VIP remarked, 'About the same age as myself then', to which the proud Captain replied: 'Yes, but she is good for at least another ten years' work'. Unfortunately this was not to be the case as the *Abercorn* foundered in a hurricane in 1951, although by that time she was no longer in Army service.

Following the acquisition of the motor passenger vessel *Fusee II* and the motor launch *Jackdaw* in 1935, a completely new class of high-speed target towers was built by British Power Boats in 1936-7. The 'General' class were necessary because even with their special winches, the Fleet's ageing steam towers could not pull their targets

31

at the speeds modern destroyers and torpedo boats could make (anything up to 40kts). Ten of these 57ft craft were commissioned, named *Allenby*, *Clive*, *French*, *Haig*, *Kitchener*, *Marlborough*, *Raglan*, *Roberts*, *Wellington* and *Wolseley*. The increased speed of targets and towers required the building of high-speed range clearance craft, and eighteen 45ft craft of the 'Bird' class were built in 1937, also by British Power Boats. In the same year a 47ft launch named *Wolf* was built and designated as a special launch.

Also in 1937 a motor coaster/barge *Blenheim* and a similar cargo-carrier *Ramillies* entered service, whilst throughout the inter-war years many small craft such as launches (*eg Phoenix* and *Titlark* in 1936) and dumb barges (such as *Arctic II*, *Forth II*, *Elm*, *Chestnut* and *Nippy* in 1931) appeared in Fleet lists, and many lighters and native craft, often unnamed and built locally, were taken into service on overseas stations. The final new-built ship to join the Fleet before the Second World War was the 528-ton coaster *Malplaquet*, the last seagoing ship to be built for the civilian-manned War Department Fleet. Although completed in 1939, she did not enter service until 1940 and was destined to have a busy war.

Despite the promise at Munich in 1938 of 'Peace in our Time', it became clear that war with Germany was inevitable. As Nazi Germany completed the annexation of Czechoslovakia in 1939, the pace of British rearmament increased, there even being the introduction of a form of conscription in peacetime, hitherto unheard-of. After the signing of the Nazi-Soviet non-aggression pact in August 1939, Hitler invaded Poland on 1 September, and two days later Britain and France declared war. The Second World War was to involve the Army's Navy in every theatre of the conflict, and, unlike the Great War, was to result in considerable losses of ships and men. The war also saw the reactivation of the Royal Engineers' Inland Water Transport Organisation, and both fleets were to play an essential part in the Allied victory over the Axis Powers.

Spritty sailing barge. This type of barge was in use by the Army's Navy, particularly for the carriage of explosives, throughout the nineteenth century and up to the Second World War.
(Painting by Major Bill Wynn-Werninck)

WDV *Wyndham*. Built in 1903 as a target tower, she was transferred to the Irish Army in 1938. (Author's collection)

The steam target tower *Gordon* (1907) served through two World Wars to 1947. (Reg Cooley collection)

The gun barge *Gog* (1886-1948). With her sister *Magog*, this huge barge was employed in ferrying large-calibre guns between Woolwich Arsenal and the Shoeburyness proving ranges. The bogies on rails to carry the guns can clearly be seen.

Miners of the Submarine Mining Service, RE, working on underwater mines in the early 1900s. (RE Library, Chatham)

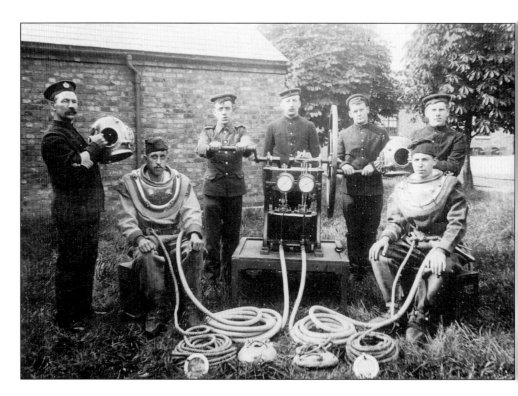

Divers of the SMS in 1904. (RE Library, Chatham)

Ensign flown by all ships of the Royal Engineers, *ie* the Submarine Mining Service and the Inland Water Transport. (Author's collection)

The Great War. Troops being transported by a barge of the IWT on the Furnes-Dunkerque canal, 4 August 1917. (Museum of Army Transport, Beverley)

Train ferries of the IWT c1917. Crewed by sappers and civilian seamen, these ferries operated between Richborough and French ports in support of the BEF. (RE Library, Chatham)

Stern-wheel paddle steamer *S.47* operated by the IWT in Mesopotamia during the Great War. Eleven vessels of this class were originally built in Great Britain and shipped out to India and Mesopotamia for assembly. (Museum of Army Transport, Beverley)

An officer of a Motor Boat Patrol on Lake Laganza during the Macedonian campaign, hailing a local boat, May 1916. These patrols were carried out by Army Service Corps personnel. (Museum of Army Transport, Beverley)

An ingenious improvised motor-boat of the RASC during the Allied intervention in Russia in 1919 in support of the White Russians against the Bolsheviks. The paddle-wheels are driven by the back axle of the truck. (Museum of Army Transport, Beverley)

The handsome WDV *Sir Hastings Anderson*, built by Harland & Wolff, Glasgow, for the War Department in 1934. She was lost at the fall of Singapore in 1942. (Author's collection)

The coaster *Malplaquet*. Commissioned in 1940 she undertook many long ocean voyages during the Second World War and after. (Author's collection)

Chapter 3

The Second World War (I):
1939-43

At the outbreak of war in 1939 the War Department Fleet numbered 70 vessels manned by some 240 civilian officers and ratings. Rapid expansion soon followed, with many new craft being built or requisitioned, and the Fleet began to undertake new and diverse duties which often required long voyages to strange waters. The Inland Water Transport organisation, Royal Engineers, was revived in 1939 and was to play a significant role in many theatres of war. Details of these activities can be found in Chapter 5.

During the first few months of the war it was assumed that the WD Fleet would simply continue with the tasks it had carried out in the Great War, *ie* support of the BEF in France, supplying offshore forts, shipping military cargoes between ports in the UK and target-towing and range safety duties. There was the difference, however, that this time the Fleet also had to deal with a large increase in ships and personnel. In January 1940 major organisational changes took place, resulting in the formation of Water Transport Companies RASC, which introduced military personnel to the manning of the Fleet's ships, although civilian crews continued to predominate. Each company was commanded by RASC officers, while an new civilian post, Master Superintendent, was created to serve as nautical advisor to the company CO, additionally carrying out duties of the sort undertaken by a Marine Superintendent in a commercial fleet. These officers were recruited from Senior Masters of the Fleet and the post proved to be a welcome addition to promotion prospects for the civilian officers of the Army's Navy. Four Water Transport Companies were initially formed in the UK, at Leith (covering Scotland), Portsmouth (Southern Command), Barry (superseded by Bangor, Western Command) and Woolwich (south and south-eastern coasts). A company was also formed at Malaya in 1940, with a small establishment.

In August 1940 a further innovation occurred with the creation of wholly military RASC marine units. These Motor Boat Companies RASC were tasked with providing military water transport in all theatres of war. Their name is something of a misnomer, since as the war progressed they were to be found manning far larger vessels than the small craft it implied. Further confusion came from the use of the name 'Water Transport Companies' which led to the belief, still extant today, that they were involved in transporting water to Army units. The first personnel for these units were volunteers with previous nautical experience drawn from all branches of the Army, not just the RASC. Two companies were formed, located at Salcombe and Falmouth, No.1 becoming a training unit while No.2 was the operational unit. Their initial strength was forty launches each, deployed in sections of ten.

There is a tendency to think of the first few months of the Second World War as a period of relative inactivity, the so-called 'Phoney War'. There may have been some truth in this as regards the land and air forces, but from the first day of the war all ships at sea were at risk from U-boats, mines, aircraft and surface attack. WD Fleet vessels ran the same risks as any others, but the first attack on a ship of the Army's Navy was not to come until 1940.

After the unsuccessful Norwegian campaign of April 1940, and the opening of the German offensive in the West on 10 May, the Luftwaffe had stepped up attacks on shipping in British waters. The first air attack on a vessel of the Army's Navy took place in May when the high-speed 'General' class target tower *Marlborough* was attacked by two Messerschmidt fighters. Her Master, Captain E.L. Beard and one of the gunners aboard returned fire with a Lewis gun and a Bren gun, and although the vessel was hit several times, wounding two crewmen, they put up such accurate fire that the fighters were forced to break off their attack.

By 24 May, the German onslaught into France had left the BEF and several thousand French troops cut off from the main French armies in northern France and falling back towards the Channel coast. The decision was made to evacuate them from the port of Dunkirk, in Operation 'Dynamo' that lasted from 27 May to 3 June. The 'Miracle of Dunkirk', in which over 330,000 British and French troops reached safety, involved a vast armada of ships of all shapes and sizes, several vessels of the Army's Navy being among them. Dunkirk was the WD Fleet's first large-scale military operation. Many of its ships had been armed with machine guns, and civilian crew members were being sent on gunnery courses. Later in the war, more sophisticated weapons such as 20mm Oerlikon cannon, were fitted to the larger craft, as well as 'novelties' like PAC (parachute and cable) anti-aircraft rockets and barrage balloons, while DEMS naval and army gunners formed part of the crews.

The following WD Fleet vessels took part in the Dunkirk evacuation: the range-clearance launches *Grouse, Pigeon, Teal, Swallow, Kestrel* and *Vulture*, the high-speed launch *Wolfe*, and the target-towing launches *Haig* and *Marlborough*. Over 1200 men were rescued from the beaches by WD Fleet craft, including 900 by *Haig* commanded by F.J. Wales. Their valiant work was recognised by the then Quartermaster-General Sir Walter Venning in Special Fleet Order No. 1, dated 8 June 1940. But all this good work was not achieved without loss of both vessels and personnel. *Teal* became a total loss, while *Swallow* continued to ferry troops from the beach to HMS *Impulse* and *Winchelsea* offshore despite being badly damaged and having only one propeller out of three in operation. On her second trip to Dunkirk, she also brought 68 men back to England. In addition to evacuating the largest number of troops, *Haig* also found herself escorting the destroyer HMS *Ivanhoe*, which was on fire. Steaming at 30kts, she fought off three waves of German bombers attacking the *Ivanhoe* over a half-hour period, despite being armed with only two Lewis guns. *Haig*'s luck ran out, however, when she was accidentally rammed by two French vessels at Dunkirk and sunk, although she was raised the next day and returned to Ramsgate. *Marlborough*, under Captain Beard, rescued 132 men in four trips to Dunkirk. On her last visit, she was ordered to pick up French naval personnel from Quai Felix Favré. Unfortunately, in the darkness she lost her rudder and propellers on underwater obstructions and had to be towed back to Dover. Her time of departure from Dunkirk was logged at 0200 hours on 3 June, making her the last vessel to leave the beaches at the end of Operation 'Dynamo', albeit not under her own power. In recognition of their excellent work, several Fleet members were Mentioned in Dispatches, and all the Masters received copies of Special Fleet Order No. 1 (mentioned above). Another WD vessel involved in the evacuation from France was the elderly coaster *Sir Evelyn Wood*. Although damaged, she rescued many soldiers from the port of St Valery, and distinguished herself by embarking the beach-master and his staff just before the town fell to the Germans.

Events now moved swiftly, with Italy declaring war on France and Britain on 10 June, Paris being captured on the 14th and France surrendering on the 21st. The last troops of the BEF, plus French and Polish servicemen who wished to continue the fight, were evacuated to Britain by 22 June. Great Britain now stood alone against Germany and Italy. It was believed that a German invasion of the British Isles was imminent, and consequently the war effort focused on home defence, although the Italian declaration of war meant that hostilities had erupted in the Mediterranean and in North and East Africa, theatres in which the Army's Navy was to play a major role. Hitherto peaceful ports such as Malta and Gibraltar were now in the front line and men of the Army's Navy came under attack from Italian bombers.

A major administrative change occurred in the summer of 1940, when the office of the Assistant Director of Military Transport was disbanded and replaced by ST1, a branch of the Supplies and Transport Directorate, which took over control of the water transport elements of the RASC, including the Water Transport Companies, the Motor Boat Companies and the Boat Stores Depots, but its responsibilities steadily increased as the war continued. In effect, ST1 was the Admiralty of the WD Fleet, responsible for ships and crews, plus construction of new vessels under the Superintending Engineer and Constructor of Shipping. At the request of the Admiralty it also became the co-ordinating office for all demands for Admiralty-controlled craft for military service, and maintained liaison with the Ministry of Shipping , which later became the Ministry of War Transport. ST1 was divided into three sections. ST1(a) was responsible for organisation, policy and operation of RASC water transport units, liaison with the Admiralty and MOWT, as well as provision of all marine stores; ST1(b) took care of provision and maintenance of RASC vessels, scales and issues of stores and equipment, pay, promotions and transfers of crews, preparation and issuing of Fleet orders, and navigation and general administration; and ST1(c) was responsible for design, construction and conversions of RASC vessels, machinery and equipment, and also for dealing with claims for compensation from owners of private craft requisitioned for service.

The threat of invasion lead to the WD Fleet taking on new roles. Launch patrols were established on estuaries and rivers, especially on the south and east coasts. Many of the craft employed had been requisitioned from private owners, and although the majority of the WD Fleet's vessels were still civilian-manned, more and more of the craft assigned to this type of operation received military crews. Port security patrols were also undertaken by WD vessels, while all the normal peacetime duties continued, though at an increased level. For example, the fortification of Flatholm and Steepholm in the Bristol Channel saw the transport of thousands of tons of cargo, as well as personnel, to the two islands by WD ships.

German air attacks on shipping in the Channel and off the east coast were commonplace during the period of the 'Blitz', as it was known, and WD Fleet ships were not to escape unscathed. The 'General' class target tower *Haig* was dive-bombed while leaving Harwich in November 1940. Two of her crew were badly wounded by machine-gun fire, one of them, the Chief Engineer, later succumbing to his injuries. Further damage was done to the Army's Navy during air raids, including the destruction of the building housing ST1 in Whitehall Place, and, more seriously, the loss of seven new 48ft launches, with three others badly damaged, when the builder's premises received a direct hit. In one incident, while lying at Shoreham the launch *Eagle* was hit by an incendiary bomb which failed to explode. The bomb had ended up in the engine room in a gradually growing pool of high-octane fuel leaking from pipes severed as the bomb had penetrated the engine-room hatch. The craft was only saved by Able Seaman R.E. Davey entering the engine-room recovering the bomb and throwing it onto the wharf. Davey was serving as AB-in-Charge of the launch *Pauletta*, and received the BEM and Lloyd's Medal for Bravery at Sea for his courageous act.

After the German victories in Europe, including the occupation of Denmark and Norway, it became vital for the British to secure the transatlantic 'life line' on which her supplies depended. Therefore in May 1940 the Faröes Islands and Iceland were occupied, while the USA took over Greenland. Although a Motor Boat Company was requested for Iceland in July 1940, its original craft were unsuitable for service in those waters, while attempts to use local craft were unsuccessful. Therefore, WD vessels were not involved in Iceland in this period, although as the British presence in the Faröes grew, the RASC became increasingly involved in providing water transport between the islands, mostly using local craft or Norwegian trawlers that had escaped the Germans, which were not actually part of the WD Fleet, being chartered by the Small Vessels Pool operated by the appropriate government ministry. One WD Fleet ship was to become a familiar sight in those waters, however, as the recently-commissioned coaster *Malplaquet*, complete with barrage balloon, made several cargo runs between the UK and the Faröes in the following months.

1941

The new year began with little change from the latter months of 1940 as regards the Army's Navy in the United Kingdom, enemy air attacks continuing as the work of building-up defences against possible invasion continued. In April the 'Bird' class launch *Falcon* was sunk by air attack whilst alongside Harwich Pier, and her Master, W.R. Clark, who had commanded the launch *Swallow* at Dunkirk, was killed.

Both the military-manned Motor Boat Companies were now taking up their allotted duties, with No.1 Company as the training unit, but No.2 Company was about to take on a new role. Because of a shortage of suitable personnel, the Royal Navy was unable to operate security patrols above high-water mark on rivers such as the Stour, Deben, Blackwater and Crouch, and on the Norfolk Broads. It was decided that No.2 Company should take over this role. Its tasks included reporting enemy aircraft laying mines, checking of all vessels entering special defence zones, and general security of rivers and estuaries. This resulted in an unusual chain of command for a British Army unit, because although it was administered by Eastern Command HQ, operationally it was controlled by the Royal Navy, as represented by the Commander-in-Chief, The Nore, through Flag Officer-in-Charge, Harwich. Although their craft consisted mostly of requisitioned small pleasure craft, the 'soldier-sailors' were nonetheless apparently held in high esteem by the Navy. No.2 Motor Boat Company was to continue in this role until 1942 when, despite strong objections from the Navy, it was sent out to North Africa. Also in 1941 No.3 Motor Boat Company RASC was sent to West Africa to provide water transport in Nigeria, Gambia, the Gold Coast and Sierra Leone. The Company was based at Freetown, but suffered many problems due to the distances to be covered, sickness among the crews (particularly malaria), poor facilities, including a chronic shortage of slipways, and the inexperience of locally-recruited personnel. The launches themselves were also at constant risk from attack by the teredo worm.

By the end of May, the Axis occupation of Yugoslavia and Greece was complete, with the final evacuation of British troops from Crete on 1 June. Although WD Fleet vessels had not been involved in this campaign, the local Greek sailing vessels, or *caiques*, used to evacuate many of the troops were later used in the *Caique* and Schooner Companies which were used, *inter alia*, for clandestine missions by the Army's Navy.

Back in the UK, the threat of invasion seemed to be lessening, and the normal activities of the Army's Navy continued as before, in tandem with their security duties, including target-towing for shore batteries. An innovation in this field was the introduction of the fast (20kts) radio-controlled target boat known as the 'Queen Gull', which had to be towed to the range and recovered after its run by other launches, which also maintained ship-to-shore communications. Being able to perform evasive manoeuvres at high speed like an MTB made the 'Queen Gull' a more realistic target for coastal batteries.

Malta, and to a lesser extent Gibraltar, were now coming under increasing Axis air attack. The ships of the WD Fleet at Malta were under constant threat, a situation that was to continue for many months. It soon became difficult to maintain the local civilian crews of the ships, resulting in increasing numbers of military personnel being employed. The 'General' class launch *Clive* had a very eventful career during her time at Malta under the command of Captain J.F. Cairns MBE, which has featured prominently in the official histories and in *The Unknown Fleet* by Reg Cooley. Her adventures included being seconded to the RAF as an air-sea rescue launch with an RAF crew under the command of Captain Cairns, accidentally sweeping mines with her cable while towing targets for a shore battery, clandestine operations and rescuing the survivors from a sunken Italian MTB. *Clive* suffered damage during the early air raids on Malta. Other WD craft damaged were *Thrush*, which suffered a direct hit, *Pike*, damaged beyond repair while on a slipway, *Trout*, sunk at her moorings (though later raised and returned to service), and *Snipe*, which was destroyed by fire.

The first active service for military-manned ships of the Fleet outside home waters was Operation 'Gauntlet' in August 1941, when No.1 Motor Boat Company RASC was involved in a combined operation against the island of Spitzbergen, lying close to the southern limit of the Arctic Ocean. The purpose of the operation was to land a garrison on the island, evacuate Russian miners and Norwegian civilians, destroy the coal mines and hunt German shipping in the area. The four launches of No.1 Company were to ferry troops from the liner *Empress of Canada* to the jetty at Barentsberg, a round trip of some 12 miles, and the keenness of the crews earned praise from all concerned.

The first of the new 48ft 'Derby Winner' class high-speed target towers entered service in 1941. A total of twenty-one were built up to 1944, named *Bahram, Blue Peter, Captain Cuttle, Coronach, Call Boy, Cameronian, Felstead, Flying Fox, Grand Parade, Humorist, Hyperion, Isinglass, Ladas, Lemberg, Manna, Minoru, Omonde, Spion Kop, Sunstar, Taigo* and *Windsor Lad*.

By the end of 1941 the WD Fleet had increased to more than 200 vessels, but this figure was to fall dramatically due to the greatest losses from enemy action in the history of the Army's Navy. On 7 December 1941 carrier aircraft of the Imperial Japanese Navy struck at the US naval base at Pearl Harbor in Hawaii, causing considerable damage. Simultaneously, attacks were launched against British possessions in the Far East, particularly Malaya and Hong Kong. The war had now truly achieved the status of a world war, and vessels of the WD Fleet were in the thick of it. The first major British defeat in the Far East was the fall of Hong Kong on Christmas Day, after several days of stubborn resistance by the garrison of British, Canadian and Indian troops against overwhelming odds and continuous air and artillery bombardment. In fact the decision to surrender was only taken after the main reservoirs had been captured by the enemy.

WD Fleet vessels had been involved from the beginning of the attack on 8 December. Mainly crewed by local Chinese seamen, who in the main behaved splendidly in the best traditions of the service, they carried out a variety of tasks, from ferrying patients and staff from the military hospital at Kowloon to Hong Kong Island to the delivery of pack mules to all parts of the Colony. The evacuation of all British forces from the mainland to the island on 11-12 December called for every available craft to be pressed into service. The ageing steam launch *Victoria*, under the charge of Major A.J. Dewar and Captain C.G. Turner, did sterling work in evacuating Indian troops, while *Oudenarde* ferried considerable numbers of men across the harbour to the island and was then finally scuttled. *Omphale* met a tragic end while recovering explosives from the Government Explosives Depot on Green Island. Several RN and civilian experts were on board when she received a direct hit. There were no survivors. The 'General' class launch *French*, commanded by her civilian Master Mr Holden (later killed in action), also did good work during the evacuation in which twelve WD vessels were lost. Although the majority of the local Chinese crewmen served well, there were some desertions prior to the final evacuation of the mainland, and in some cases craft had to be manned by volunteer Army crews and European civilians. By the fall of Hong Kong, all WD Fleet vessels were either sunk, scuttled or in enemy hands.

1942

The Japanese continued to chalk up victory after victory in the Far East in the early months of 1942, with Singapore falling on 15 February, Rangoon on 8 March and the Dutch East Indies at about the same time. April saw the occupation of most of Burma, threatening India, and attacks on Borneo and the Philippines, the latter being taken on 6 May with the surrender of the final US forces on Corregidor. Further seizures of strategic islands and landings in New Guinea meant Australia was now in great peril, and the whole Indian Ocean and South Pacific were under threat.

All of the vessels of the Army's Navy in areas taken by the Japanese were lost, the greatest number being at Singapore. A Water Transport Company had been created here in 1940, and brought up to strength by purchasing or requisitioning local craft. Problems were encountered in recruiting local crews because of the better rates of pay offered by commercial employers. Unlike at Hong Kong, there were mass desertions of civilian crewmen towards the end of the campaign and the vessels had to be manned by military personnel. The final task of the Singapore-based craft was the destruction of ammunition dumps on outlying islands to deny them to the enemy, and although several had left the harbour before it fell, all were subsequently sunk or captured by the Japanese. In all, thirty WD Fleet vessels were lost at Singapore, including the fine ship *Sir Hastings Anderson*.

Back in the UK, the Marine Stores at Woolwich had been temporarily transferred to Slough and, now known as the WD Fleet Store, became a group in an MT Stores Depot RASC, which organisation took over all marine stores previously held by the Royal Army Ordnance Corps. There was a further name change to Boat Stores Depot RASC, and the unit finally returned to Woolwich once again. It all tends to remind one of the well-known wartime expression 'Is your journey really necessary?'! The Boat Stores Depot now had responsibility for all marine stores for all arms of the Service whether at home or abroad, and also for the establishment and training of personnel for Boat Stores Depots overseas.

Following the formation of the Royal Corps of Electrical and Mechanical Engineers (REME) in 1942, there was discussion as to whether the new corps should take on the repair and maintenance of all vessels of the WD Fleet, or just of the military-manned Motor Boat Companies. It was decided that both should remain the responsibility of ST1, as before, which allowed for some repairs to MBC craft to be carried out by the workshop platoons of those units, while the rest was done in the Royal Dockyards under agreements made with the Admiralty.

Ever-growing demands were being made on the Army's Navy, all over the world. In the early months of 1942, the steam cargo ship *Sir*

Walter Campbell was stationed in Iceland for target-towing duties. Her work in seaward artillery practice, often in foul weather, was highly praised by the coastal batteries stationed along that bleak coastline. New water transport companies were formed, based at Plymouth, the Clyde, Grimsby and Sheerness, while a new class of General Service launches entered service. Designated High Speed Launches, nine of these 40ft craft built by the British Power Boat Company of Hythe had been transferred from the RAF which had used them as seaplane tenders. They were named *Grey Dame, Grey Dawn, Grey Girl, Grey Lady, Grey Lass, Grey Maid, Grey Mist, Grey Nymph* and *Grey Queen*. Built for service in quiet harbours, with open cockpits, they were clearly unsuited to work in heavy seas, as was tragically proved in October 1942 when *Grey Dame* was overwhelmed by a following sea and lost with all hands.

In January the elderly steam target tower *Lord Plumer*, which had been commissioned in 1927 and spent all her working life at Malta, came under air attack off Tigre Point. Despite a gunner being injured and her Chief Engineer mortally wounded, she managed to make it back to port, and her Master was awarded the MBE. Later the ship's civilian crew was replaced by military personnel and she was transferred to North Africa, where she remained for the rest of the war.

No. 3 Motor Boat Company was still holding the fort in West Africa, and in the early months of the year it was considered that an attack by Vichy French forces on British West Africa was more than likely. A feasibility study was undertaken to see if troops and supplies could be moved up the rivers of Sierra Leone to the borders of French territory, involving a programme of day and night reconnaissance of those rivers. The most ambitious river voyage by an Army ship was that undertaken by an ex-German twin-engined vessel called *Waja*. Transferred from Lagos, she was 120ft long and 25ft beam. She sailed from White Man's Bay on 2 February and arrived after a safe passage up the Great Skarcies river not far from the French Guinea border. Local opinion had been that such a voyage was impossible, and native chiefs revealed that not in living memory had any craft, even one half the size of the *Waja*, been seen so far up river. Further explorations were later carried out on the Little or Lesser Skaricies rivers.

In the Western Desert, the British 8th Army and the German Afrika Korps, with their Italian allies, continued to fight back and forth along the coast between Libya and Egypt. A German offensive in May led to the fall of Tobruk on 21 June, but Rommel's advance was checked at a little-known place called El Alamein, some 60 miles from

Alexandria. On 23 October the 8th Army went onto the attack and defeated the Axis forces at El Alamein, the first step in finally driving them from North Africa. This was a major boost to British morale after the disasters of 1941 and early 1942, and seen as a turning-point.

On 7 and 8 November 1942 a joint British and US force invaded French North Africa in Operation 'Torch', sandwiching the Axis forces between themselves and the 8th Army advancing from El Alamein. Although the Army's Navy had been little involved in the 8th Army's campaign, 'Torch' had required large numbers of vessels of all types and the WD Fleet was called upon to play its part. No.2 Motor Boat Company, now redesignated No.247 Motor Boat Company RASC, was sent to Algiers in the first overseas deployment of a Motor Boat Company in the war. A base was established and steps taken to acquire additional craft from local sources. These included launches, schooners and coastal vessels with a wide variety of engines, including steam, which caused considerable problems for the crews and the workshop staff. Nonetheless the Company played a vital role in the North African campaign, supplementing the inadequate roads and railways.

In November of 1942, a young soldier of the Queen's Royal Regiment, Jack Toft, was posted to the Water Transport Training Unit at West Mersea in Essex. He had first become aware of the Army's Navy during the summer while on a signals course at Maidstone, and volunteers were being sought for RASC Water Transport Units. Although his nautical experience was virtually nil, he managed to convince the selectors he was suitable to become an Army mariner and in due course arrived at West Mersea. The new intake, about forty men in all, paraded in a wide variety of headgear, badges, shoulder flashes and webbing, reflecting the different regiments they had come from. Likewise they all bore different titles, apart from private, such as trooper, fusilier, sapper and rifleman. All of them, apart from those who had achieved NCO rank, now became privates RASC, and the rest of the first day was spent sewing on RASC shoulder flashes and treating all webbing equipment with honey-coloured blanco. All ranks were issued with sea-kit consisting of oilskins, sou'wester, sea boots, two pairs of sea boot socks and a duffle coat, all of which had to be stowed in a separate kit bag from their more military uniform items. Under the supervision of a retired Master Mariner, training then commenced with the theory of seamanship and navigation, including knots and splices, coastal pilotage, chartwork, Rule of the Road, the international code of signals and principles of boat construction. These courses took place in classrooms ashore, and were followed by practical boat work afloat. Classes were embarked in harbour launches and taken out to deep water on the River Blackwater, where the pupils practised helmsmanship and making fast and casting off, using the derelict Tollesbury Pier for the latter purpose. Other drills involved the picking up and letting go of mooring buoys, the correct use of bends and hitches, and also the splicing of ropes and wires. The instructors ran a taut ship and every man took turns at every nautical skill until he became a proficient seaman. A small group of young officers and senior NCOs practised more advanced skills afloat in two old cabin cruisers, the officers naturally being allocated the twin-engined one! Meanwhile, those training to become marine Mechanics spent their days in the workshops at Osea Island. A highly-skilled team gradually came into being, consisting not only of engineers and mechanics, but also other trades such as shipwrights, electricians and welders. In fact, without the dedication of the workshop staff, the ageing fleet of training craft could not have survived the almost constant use they were subjected to.

The continuing gains in North Africa meant that 1942 ended on a much higher note than it had begun. This 'feelgood factor' was best described by Winston Churchill: 'Before El Alamein we never had a victory: after El Alamein we never had a defeat.'

1943

In this year the Inspectorate of Water Transport Services was inaugurated, with the task of advising commands in the UK and overseas on any problems relating to water transport. The honorary adviser to the Army Council on matters concerning the WD Fleet, Mr H.E. Chubb, who had been a Motor Boat Company commander during the Great War, was a tower of strength and the value placed on his wise advice was shown by the award of the CBE for his wartime services.

In North Africa, Anglo-American forces continued to make steady progress against the German and Italian armies, culminating in the total surrender of all Axis forces in Africa at Cape Bon in Tunisia on 12 May. No. 247 Motor Boat Company had been sent out to North Africa the previous year but by the end of 1942 only four out of the intended total of ten vessels had arrived in the theatre of operations. Although the plan was for the Company to operate local craft, the principal Sea Transport Officer, in urgent need of vessels to carry out coastal duties, suggested that the task be assigned to French vessels with civilian crews under Royal Navy control. As a result, serious consideration was given to returning No. 247 Company to the UK. However, a temporary reprieve was won when the Company was assigned to harbour duties at Algiers, which continued until the end of February, when the RN asked for assistance in manning two small coastal vessels, providing a service from Bone to La Calle and Tabarka in support of road and rail communications. The Company performed this task so well that they were asked to operate as many requisitioned craft as possible, which needless to say put paid to any idea of it being sent home!

Back in Britain, Jack Toft had successfully passed his trade tests and from February was listed as a Waterman Class III, signified by a plaited yellow ornamental lanyard on the right shoulder and a small circular badge of yellow cloth on the left sleeve of his uniform jacket. He also received a minute increase in pay and was transferred to an operational Motor Boat Company, where he found life much less hectic than at the Training Unit. However, on returning from a short leave, he found he had been posted to the newly-formed 624 Company at Inverary in Scotland, where the Army's mariners were to acquire new skills in tasks never before carried out by any water transport unit. For about a year, the Royal Navy had been training Allied troops in assault landings at Loch Fynne, but increasing need for their landing craft and crews in other operations meant that this training now fell to 624 Company, using a flotilla of new American-built LCTs. Many thousands of troops were trained in making opposed landings at Loch Fynne, one of the best-kept secrets of the Second World War, while the men of the Army's Navy engaged in this task were allowed to wear the coveted Combined Operations shoulder badge, a source of great pride for them. Toft's task aboard his LCT was to operate the large winch controlling the kedge anchor which was let go from the stern as the LCT approached the beach. Once the troops and vehicles were ashore, the kedge anchor was used to help pull the craft off the beach and back afloat, with the engines put full astern. This could be tricky, particularly during night exercises as, with the LCT riding high in the water after landing her tanks, the kedge anchor hawser could easily foul the propellers and cause damage. Close cooperation between the winch operator and the wheelhouse was essential to avoid such a mishap. By the end of September, with the nights drawing in and worsening wintry weather, the operation was run down and Jack Toft and his companions came ashore to await transfer back to West Mersea. Now 21 years old, he had been

upgraded to Waterman Class II, the extra pay helping him cele-
brate his coming of age. But due to family bereavement and a long
illness, it was not to be until nearly Christmas that he was able to
rejoin 624 Company.

During 1943 several new class of craft began to be commissioned
into the Army's Navy, such as the fourteen 69ft 'Battle' class built by
Thornycroft & Co. Ltd (final commissionings in 1945), the eight
72ft 'Battle' class which were ex-RN MTBs converted by
Thornycrofts (last craft commissioned in 1945) and the six 70ft
'Battle' class of converted MGBs built by Higgins of New Orleans
and transferred to Britain under Lend-Lease in 1940 (the last of these
did not enter Army service until 1946). Smaller craft also entered
service in 1943-6, these being the twenty-one 45ft 'Shakespearean
Males' class passenger launches, built by Philips, Anderson & Co. and
formerly operated by the RN and the 50ft 'Dickens' Series 1 general
service launches, of which twenty-three were built by W. Weatherhead
& Sons, R.A. Newman & Sons, and F. Curtis Ltd.

Stoutly-built Motor Fishing Vessels (MFVs) also joined the ever-
growing fleet in this year, comprising twenty-one of the 61½ft type
(final commissionings in 1945), and two of the 45ft type, both completed in 1945. Twenty of these MFVs were converted into fire boats
between 1943 and 1946, the result of a decision that the Army would
be responsible for the provision, equipping and manning of all fire
boats to be deployed during the invasion of Europe or in captured
ports. The boats would be organised as Fire Boat Sections under the
operational control of the Army Fire Service, which was to provide
the actual fire-fighting personnel while the boats would be operated
by RASC crews, although the fire-fighting crews did receive some
training as deckhands and the RASC men as fire-fighters. The 61½ft
boats had a crew of six fire-fighters and three RASC mariners, namely
a coxswain, 2nd coxswain and engineer, while the 45ft type had a
slightly smaller crew of five fire-fighters and two mariners.
Interestingly, after the end of the war in Europe the Army Fire Service
became part of the RASC, including its fire boats.

After the Axis capitulation in North Africa, the Allies then invaded
Sicily on 10 July, all resistance ceasing within thirty-nine days.
Landings on the Italian mainland followed on 3 September, leading to
the surrender of Fascist Italy, but German resistance was to continue
in northern Italy until 29 April 1945, in a very hard-fought campaign.
At the beginning of the Sicilian campaign, 247 Motor Boat Company
was based in Tunis and operated craft in North African and Sicilian

waters, shifting to Italian coastal operations in September. The Army's Navy was to benefit from the acquisition of numerous first-class schooners in southern Italian ports in the early stages of the invasion. Officers of the Motor Boat Company would locate suitable craft and notify the local Sea Transport Officer, who then chartered them. A committee, entitled the Allied Schooner Control Committee, was formed and included representatives of the Divisional Sea Transport Officer (DSTO), the Ministry of War Transport, the American War Shipping Administration, 'Q' (Movements) Transportation (US) ST HQ Allied Armies in Italy, the Allied Control Commission and the Italians. In practice, the DSTO was in operational control of all schooners and, in the case of vessels allocated to RASC units, the RASC acted as his agent, while surplus RASC craft were detailed by a Schooner Control Staff consisting of Sea Transport Officers. Some of these schooners, with Italian crews supervised by NCOs of the RASC, conducted special operations in support of partisans in areas still occupied by the Germans. However, in Yugoslavia the partisans flatly refused to have anything to do with Italians, so the schooners operating there were manned entirely by RASC crews. Further east, similar operations in support of the Greek resistance were being conducted, using local sailing vessels known as *caiques*, which blended into the Greek coastal scene perfectly, many of which had crossed over to North Africa in 1941 following the German invasion. They were crewed by RASC personnel, who received special training in handling sailing vessels in Egyptian ports. The Army's Navy had already had some experience of 'cloak and dagger' operations in the Mediterranean, with the civilian-manned launch Clive taking a group of Free French officers to Tunisia before the Allied landings in 1942 to make contact with Vichy officials there, but engine-failure half-way into the 200-mile voyage forced the abandonment of the mission, to the chagrin of all concerned, particularly the Frenchmen.

In both West and East Africa, expansion of Fleet activities was taking place. In West Africa problems were still being encountered because of the shortage of both personnel with engineering expertise and suitable berthing facilities. This led to a review of all water transport require-ments in the area, and the formation of 793 Water Transport Company, West African Army Service Corps (WAASC), replacing the existing services and based at Freetown, while water transport sec-tions were activated in the Gambia, Sierra Leone, the Gold Coast and Nigeria. For example, four launches were stationed in the Gambia mainly for ferrying personnel across the River Gambia. Also, the ports of Freetown and Takoradi lacked berthing facilities for large ships so Army craft were employed in loading and off-loading stores and personnel here. Similar duties were carried out by the Nigerian section of the WAASC at Lagos, including ferry services to places such as Apapa.

An identical situation had developed in East Africa, where from 1941 a loose collection of vessels had been operating under the control of various military units throughout this theatre of war. In May 1943 some fifteen vessels were placed under RASC control, but these had old engines which were suffering from lack of regular maintenance. Because of the enormous area of coastline involved, it was clear that a Water Transport Company was necessary, so plans were made for the commissioning of some fifty-seven craft, purchased from the UK and South Africa, and for a training cadre to be sent out to train local personnel. However, the implementation of these plans lay some time in the future and until delivery of the new vessels, which included MFVs for use as fire boats building at Simonstown Dockyard in South Africa, it was necessary to requisition local craft, and transfer men from all Army units in East Africa to man them.

A similar shortage of civilian crews at Gibraltar resulted in soldiers from other arms being asked to volunteer for service afloat, and these men were ultimately transferred to the RASC with subsequent remustering to appropriate trades. The WD Fleet at Gibraltar was tasked with inshore anti-sabotage patrols in requisitioned vessels manned by an independent Company. These patrols were of particular importance given the activities of supposedly neutral Spain in helping the Axis powers. At Algeciras, across the bay from Gibraltar lay an Italian tanker, the *Olterra*, ostensibly interned for the duration, but in fact used as a base by a flotilla of Italian two-man 'human torpedoes', which penetrated the harbour at Gibraltar on several occasions to attach limpet mines to the ships there. This constant threat required round-the-clock patrols, and the long hours of duty required of the crews had led to a falling-off of standards of general maintenance. In recognition of the demands placed on the WD Fleet in these conditions, a Water Transport Company with proper accommodation was established, reinforcements were sent out from the UK to bring the crews up to strength, while suitable facilities, including a slipway, were made available for a planned maintenance programme.

Meanwhile, in the UK, the lessons learned from the amphibious landings in North Africa, Sicily and Italy, as well as forward planning for the invasion of France, resulted in new units of the Army's Navy being formed. Among these were the military-manned Fast Launch Companies which were necessary for the control of the amphibian 2½-ton vehicles known as DUKWs, which were becoming increasingly important in amphibious operations transporting troops and stores from ship to shore and inland. Universally know as 'Ducks', the acronym DUKW translated as D = Model Year (1942), U = Amphibian, K = All Wheel Drive, and W = Dual Rear Axles. Purists of course will argue that DUKWs were not really vessels at all, merely land vehicles that could swim, but they were equipped with anchors, maritime life-saving gear and ship's navigation lights, so there is no doubt that at least while afloat they were indeed vessels. Their crews were drawn from RASC personnel. Seaborne control of DUKWs proved essential, and there had been problems during the Sicilian landings when the only craft available to the controlling officers were amphibious jeeps, which proved unseaworthy. In future, therefore, military crews in fast launches would carry out control of DUKWs, particularly during opposed landings.

A further innovation in the War Department Fleet was the setting up of two Military Oil Barge companies, to be included in the 21st Army Group for the forthcoming invasion of France. They were for the carriage of petroleum products and were to have military crews. Two types of barges were utilised for this, an 80ft converted dumb barge and a larger craft 104ft long. The smaller barges were difficult to handle and uncomfortable for the crews, while the larger ones were better seaboats and more manoeuvrable. The crew's quarters were quite dreadful: because of their flammable cargo no heating was possible and cooking was only permitted when the barges were in ballast, but nonetheless some crews actually lived aboard them for considerable periods of time.

During the second half of 1943 War Department Fleet activities in the central Mediterranean were expanding, and in October an additional Water Transport Company was formed to deal with the opening of more ports to Allied coastal traffic and the consequent increase in that traffic. Also at this time a Chief Inspector of Water Transport Services was appointed, with two assistant Inspectors, to examine and report on the state of vessel maintenance and stores control for both Motor Boat and Water Transport Companies in the UK and abroad, and to provide advice for officers commanding such companies.

Because of personnel shortages, it was still necessary for Water Transport Company vessels to be largely civilian-manned, although the Motor Boat Companies continued to be crewed by military personnel. It remained policy, however, for any War Department Fleet vessel carrying out security-sensitive or dangerous duties to have a military crew wherever possible. Of course, civilian crews often had to operate in dangerous situations and carried out their duties admirably, as was seen at Dunkirk, to cite but one example. Conversely, a shortage of civilian artificers for the maintenance of War Department Fleet ships lead to the authorisation of the employment of military artificers when suitable civilian personnel could not be found. In November 1943 the decision was made to militarise the Fleet with an initial establishment of 34 officers and 400 other ranks, but the continuing shortage of personnel meant that no great progress was made in the replacement of civilian crews until after the war, when approval was given for 25 per cent of units in the UK to be militarised, but even this was largely based on a continuation of training programmes for military mariners before taking up overseas postings.

As larger and more sophisticated craft were commissioned into the Army's Navy, it became necessary for military personnel to obtain higher marine qualifications than had hitherto been required. Furthermore, the tasks being undertaken by ships of the Army's Navy now required their commanders to possess superior navigation and seamanship skills. Although a soldier with the qualification of Waterman Class I was considered capable of taking charge of a 36ft launch, larger vessels required the skills of a Class I Navigator, equivalent to a Yacht Master's Certificate. However, this qualification required having a considerable period of sea time, which it was rare for an Army man to possess. For commanders of the 112ft motor launches, the oil barges and the MFVs, the qualification required was that of Navigator, Class II. Looming large in all planning was the knowledge that by the middle of the following year at the latest the invasion of France would take place, the largest amphibious landings on a hostile coast in history. Increased training for the landings was instituted, with vessels of the Army's Navy being assigned to the 21st Army Group, the British Army's main contribution to the assault on 'Festung Europa'.

Following a request for more vessels to serve in the Mediterranean and Middle East, the drifters *Ocean Breeze* and *Boy Phillip* sailed in convoy from Milford Haven on 4 December. Both vessels were manned by civilian War Department Fleet crews under the overall command of Inspector of Shipping G. Sparshott. Despite adverse weather conditions during the voyage, and the difficulty of transferring coal from the fish holds into the coal bunkers by hand in baskets, both ships reached 247 Motor Boat Company at Algiers on Boxing Day. During their stopover at Oran, the two vessels even managed to render assistance to a Greek merchant ship which had parted her moorings in a gale. For this action they earned a signal of appreciation from the Senior Officer, United States Naval Forces, Oran. Two civilian-manned trawlers, the *Lucien Goughy* and *Elizabeth Therese*, were similarly sent out to North Africa, while the coaster *Malplaquet*, also with a civilian crew, which had undertaken several voyages to the Faröe Islands while based in the UK, was also sent to serve in the Mediterranean.

In the Mediterranean, RASC water transport was becoming increasingly important as many small ports were becoming inaccessible by road or rail due to war damage, combined with the difficult terrain, and constant demands were being made for more men and vessels for Water Transport Companies. In November, 782 Company was formed at Alexandria and took responsibility for all small craft used by military forces in the Middle East, including the *caiques*. As crews training in the sailing of these vessels became available, they took up duties in the eastern Mediterranean. A common sight throughout the region, with a design little changed from Biblical times, they did not attract undue enemy attention and were thus able to be used in waters where there was constant surveillance from Axis-controlled territory such as Rhodes, Cos and Lemnos. Hazardous operations such as ferrying aviation fuel to forward bases, transporting stores to recently captured territory and brining back prisoners of war became routine tasks for these ubiquitous sailing vessels.

High-speed target towing launches also found themselves undertaking more exciting duties than usual, when it became necessary to establish a fast boat service from the island of Simi, some 350 miles north of Alexandria, to certain of the Dodecanese Islands. The target towing launches were the only suitable craft available, and all became involved in this operation, leaving Alexandria in the early evening and arriving at their destinations at about noon the following day, slipping past enemy-occupied Rhodes in the small hours of the morning, a constant speed of 20kts being maintained throughout the voyage.

In the latter part of the year No.3 Boats Stores Depot was formed at Tahog near Tel-El-Kebir in Egypt to support the Water Transport Companies. Staffed by Ceylonese personnel under British officers, the depot carried out its work very efficiently, becoming particularly proficient in the manufacture of fenders and cordage. The unit was also responsible for the design and construction of the 'Howard' spray target which superseded the heavier 'Hong Kong' target then in use. The unit relocated to Alexandria in 1944 and remained there until the end of the war when it moved to Port Said.

The year ended with the prospect of many more months hard fighting in Italy and the Far East, in which the Army's mariners would continue to play a vital role. Meanwhile, in the UK, the build-up for the invasion of France was accelerating rapidly.

Chapter 4

The Second World War (II): 1944-45

From the beginning of 1944, the build-up for the invasion of France, codenamed Operation 'Overlord', was in full swing. Four Motor Boat Companies, to be commanded by HQ, Commander RASC, Water Transport Units, had been assigned to 21st Army Group. Two were Military Oil Barge Companies, one was a Fast Launch Company for duties with Amphibian Companies (DUKWs) and the fourth was to act as a Harbour Launch Company. Additionally, there was a requirement for thirty-nine fully-manned fire boats, of which twenty had to be ready in all respects for D-Day.

Jack Toft had by now rejoined his unit, 624 Company, at West Mersea and in the New Year several ex-RAF 'Grey' class launches were taken on strength. These had an RASC crew of four, commanded by a corporal, and Jack Toft, now a Lance Corporal, remembered that these four-man crews tended to stay together, although hardly had they become used to the 'Grey' class boats when they were replaced by high-speed 45ft 'Bird' class range clearance craft and the newer 48ft 'Derby Winner' class high-speed target towers. According to Toft, the crews were aware that something big was in the offing, not least because now stores and repairs, hitherto virtually unobtainable, were now freely available. After being promoted to Corporal, Jack Toft found himself serving aboard the 'Bird' class launch *Swallow*, and the crew, as well as taking pride in keeping her maintained to a high standard, were elated to learn that she had given yeoman service at Dunkirk. A plaque commemorating her work in evacuating troops from the beaches was prominently displayed in her wheelhouse.

Although it was planned that the Army's Navy vessels directly involved in the D-Day landings would have all-military crews, this is not to say that the civilian-manned fleet would have no part to play in 'Overlord'. There were now ten Water Transport Companies in the

UK, operating over 500 vessels of all shapes and sizes, and with some 1400 men, mostly civilians. The companies based in the south in particular were working flat out in the build-up to the invasion. New tasks for the war Department Fleet included support of the 'Mulberry' floating harbours and PLUTO (Pipe Line Under The Ocean), and duties with pontoons and bridge-building equipment for the Royal Engineers. Normal duties also continued, with target towing, ferry services, exercising of coastal searchlight batteries, support of offshore forts and provision of transport for senior officers, including taking General Sir Alan Brooke on an inspection of the Mulberry harbours.

Although it was not until 1945 that the name of the War Department Fleet was changed to Royal Army Service Corps Fleet, in February 1944 a War Office instruction stated that in future vessels entitled WDV would have their prefix changed to RASCV. Nonetheless, it is generally regarded that this change did not in practice take place until 1945.

In April and June 798 and 801 Water Transport Companies took up duties with Central Mediterranean Force, while with the Middle East Forces small craft duties were covering an enormous area, including the whole coast from Tripolitania to Palestine and down to Aden in the south. This was obviously an impossible workload for one unit, so it was decided to disband 782 Company and replace it with 697 Company (Water Transport) to be based at Port Said and covering the Mediterranean coasts eventually as far as Piraeus in Greece, and 698 Company to be based at Suez covering the Suez Canal and ports in the Red Sea.

In East Africa, following arrival of a training cadre from the UK, 510 Company East African Army Service Corps (Water Transport) was established at Mombasa. Its area of responsibility was extensive, being divided into three sections: the islands, consisting of the Seychelles, Mauritius and Madagascar; the centre, being Mombasa, Tanga, Dar Es Salaam and Zanzibar; and the north, comprising Mogadishu and Berbera. Initially there was difficulty in raising local crews, but a recruiting drive in the coastal and lake regions of British East Africa brought in an intake of keen mariners, very ambitious to pass their proficiency tests and thus earn the coveted seaman's cap. Workshop personnel were also trained to a high standard, such that many large concerns in East Africa, *eg* government harbour departments, were anxious to employ ex-EAASC personnel on their discharge. An example of the efficiency of the EAASC water transport company was the 3000-mile unescorted voyage of four 46-ton motor fishing vessels from Mombasa to Alexandria, where the vessels were urgently required. Routed via Mogadishu, Cape Guardifui, Aden, Port Sudan and Suez, the trip took twenty-four days, the vessels taking on sufficient fuel, water and provisions at Mombasa for the whole journey. 510 Company EAASC (Water Transport) went on to earn an enviable reputation for excellent turnouts on parade, being reported as the smartest unit on parade on VJ Day by the *Mombasa Times*.

In the central Mediterranean, No. 247 Company (Water Transport) had set up its headquarters south of Naples, with responsibility for Sicily and the North African coast, while two of the newly-formed companies were based at Bari and Torre del Greco to cover the east and west coasts of Italy respectively. However, operations extended beyond the Italian coast and Sicily, including the occupied islands off the Dalmatian coast, Albania and Greece to the east, and Sardinia and Corsica to the west.

In 1943, a special mission, entitled the Lethbridge Mission, had been sent out to Southeast Asia to conduct a survey of the requirements for the organisation and equipment of the Army's Navy in that theatre of operations and to make recommendations accordingly. The mission reported in 1944, covering Burma, Malaya and the Dutch East Indies. Its recommendations were carefully studied and many were acted upon, but the early end of hostilities with Japan in 1945 meant that some never got beyond the planning stage. As regards water transport, the recommendations were as follows:

1. Operation of craft engaged in bulk distribution should be the responsibility of the Royal Engineers, while those engaged in detailed deliveries should be controlled by the RASC.
2. The RASC Water Transport service would consist of a River Regiment and a Coastal Regiment. The River Regiment would control inland waterway vessels such as local craft, amphibians, shallow-draught vessels and swamp craft, while the Coastal Regiment would have responsibility for landing craft and trawlers.
3. In both cases, provision should be made for maintenance of vessels, including floating workshops and appropriate personnel, while operational companies should be self-contained administrative units.

Until 1944 water transport in India had been of a somewhat haphazard nature, mostly operated by the Transportation Service rather than the Directorate of Supplies and Transport. S&T did control a few vessels in the larger ports but in general Army ships in India operated without any overall organisation or regulations, and with locally-recruited crews. However, as the campaign in Southeast Asia began to escalate, the importance of the Indian ports likewise increased, and there was seen to be a need for a proper water transport organisation, with a division of responsibility between Transportation and Supplies and Transport. To achieve this, and in particular to specify what types of vessel would be operated by the Royal Engineers and which by the RASC, the Directive issued by the War Office in June of that year (see Appendix V) was now to apply to India. Of course, the Indian Army was entirely independent of the British Army but the War Office Directive was accepted, with a few exceptions. For example, the Quartermaster General, India, ruled against the establishment of a Boat Stores Depot, arguing that the supply of marine stores should be the responsibility of the Ordnance. This somewhat strange attitude was balanced, however, by the provision of an RASC Boat Stores Depot for both RE and RASC vessels attached to Allied Land Forces, South East Asia Command.

As more vessels would now come under the control of S&T, a Water Transport Company was formed, to be part of the Royal Indian Army Service Corps, and to assist in its establishment the War Office seconded an experienced water transport officer for duty with the Indian S&T Directorate and sent out a cadre of similarly experienced personnel. About ninety craft were eventually operated by the Company at six ports from Karachi to Calcutta, a coastline of over 4000 miles. As in other theatres of operations, this area was found to be too large to be administered by a single company, but plans to divide the organisation into four companies were overtaken by the end of the war.

In the UK, preparations for Operation 'Overlord' continued apace. Motor Boat Companies Nos. 571, 624, 625 and 626, assigned to 21st Army Group under HQ, CRASC, formed 42 Water Transport Column. 571 and 625 Companies operated Military Oil Barges, in five divisions of five barges each. Support craft included a TID (Towing In Dock) tug, Division Officers' craft, Minca barges and MFVs. The Harbour Launch Company (626) had forty 36ft launches, mostly new construction, with two MFVs for backup. The fast launches of 624 Company were for control of DUKW units and consisted of thirty 40ft, 45ft and 48ft craft, in four divisions of seven launches, each with an MFV as 'mother ship'. The two remaining launches were assigned to the Company HQ, along with two MFVs, one as company headquarters and the other as a workshop. Each division worked with a beach group.

The two Fire Boat Companies were to operate fifteen boats each, in single-boat sections. The need to crew these vessels with RASC personnel put a strain on manpower supplies from April 1944. They were supposed to have eighteen of the converted 61½ft MFVs and twelve converted LCVs, but in the event conversion was slow and by May only three MFVs had been delivered while the Admiralty had released only ten LCVs. In order to get the fire boats needed for 'Overlord', as a stop-gap measure 75ft and 45ft MFVs, as well as some Thames fire boats, were pressed into service until such time as they could be replaced with the intended vessels.

During May the hundreds of ships taking part in the invasion began assembling at their ports for departure to France, and 624 (Fast Launch) and 626 (Harbour Launch) Companies were ordered to proceed at full speed from their base in Essex to the Isle of Wight. The voyage would not be without some risk, as the Straits of Dover were notorious for attacks on shipping by the Luftwaffe and heavily-armed E-boats. However, Corporal Toft, who was aboard the fast launch *Swallow*, recalls that the only alarm came when they had passed Deal and entered Dover dummy darkness. They had just passed the boom defences when a destroyer appeared from nowhere and passed through the incoming formation at full speed, scattering the launches in all directions, but fortunately there was no damage. They resumed their passage to the Isle of Wight the next morning and completed it without further incident, taking up their various assembly points for the invasion. *Swallow* found herself berthing at the little-used Newton Creek near Fishbourne, where she lay hidden by the tall reeds and cow parsley that lined the banks. The operation was not without its unintentionally comic side - two of the units received orders to proceed to positions that were actually inland on the Sussex Downs! - but all the launches had reached their allotted rendezvous by 25 May, and as with the scores of other ships assembling there, come under the operational control of Royal Navy Command, Portsmouth.

Meanwhile the Military Oil Barge Companies, by agreement with 21st Army Group, had been assigned to supplying water to the vast armada of ships assembled on the south coast for 'Overlord', under the control of the Admiralty and the Ministry of War Transport. It had initially been agreed that this employment would last for thirty days after D-Day, but in the end, to the crews' great chagrin, they remained on the south coast until September, missing the landings in France completely.

Despite their small size, the Fast Launches and the Harbour Launches were to make the Channel crossing under their own power, and their equipment had to be increased accordingly. Extra fuel was loaded in jerrycans for the voyage, life-saving equipment was increased and medical supplies issued. The crews would have to spend days at sea aboard their launches so hammocks or stretchers were embarked for sleeping along with food and water for four days and portable stoves to cook it on. Each mother ship of the Fast Launch Company also embarked artificers with tools and spares for repair work. Corporal Toft also recalled that each launch was armed with a pair of Bren guns on a swivel mount at the stern.

Security for 'Overlord' was very strict. No written orders were issued to any vessel from the beginning to the successful conclusion of the landings, all instructions being passed by personal contact. While *Swallow* was in Newton Creek, the crew were not allowed to go ashore, and supplies were brought to her along a narrow creekside track from the nearest road several hundred yards away. A few days after their arrival, the commander of *Swallow*, Sergeant Lister, and his opposite number aboard the 'Derby Winner' class launch *Hyperion* were suddenly whisked away without warning for a secret briefing on the invasion. On Sergeant Lister's return, Jack Toft recalled that he would say nothing about what was to come, but after another briefing the following day, he was more open with his second-in-command. Having sent the rest of the crew below to their quarters, Lister and Toft went to the cabin they shared below the wheelhouse, where the sergeant explained to him that it had now been authorised for seconds-in-command to be briefed on what was planned for their vessels, in case anything happened to the commander. He explained, with the use of coastal charts, the details of the plan including the proposed landing sites in France and the methods by which the landings were to be accomplished. He also revealed that *Swallow* and *Hyperion* would be crossing in the first wave, ahead of the rest of the company. Of course he did not know the date and time the invasion would be launched, as this was entirely dependent on the weather.

In the event, the two launches began their cross-Channel voyage in the mid-afternoon of 5 June. As they emerged from the creek, Jack Toft vividly remembers how the Solent was a mass of ships of all shapes, sizes and descriptions, all making their way towards the English Channel. The ships were being shepherded into separate convoys and eventually the two launches were ordered to join two lengthy columns of Royal Navy assault support ships heading slowly towards Spithead. They were to take up position on the quarters of the leading ships, and as they approached they saw that the two leaders were each towing a large metal pontoon, later identified as components of the 'Mulberry' floating harbour to be built off Gold Beach at Arromanches. The pontoon being towed by *Swallow*'s leader had not been properly secured and was yawing some 20 degrees out of line, causing problems with the tow and also making it difficult for the next ship astern to keep station. *Swallow* was signalled to investigate, and the launch made a cautious approach to the pontoon until it was seen that the problem was caused by the bight of the heavy steel towing hawser, which had somehow developed an extra turn around one arm of the bitts, thus causing the yaw.

Sergeant Lister steered the launch as close as possible to the pontoon to allow Jack Toft to board it and free the fouled turn from the bitts. Although the height of the launch's deck above the pontoon should have made what the Navy would call a 'wash deck transfer' relatively easy, the pitching and rolling of the launch, plus the wild yawing of the pontoon, described as being larger than an average room, made it a much more hazardous undertaking. Although Corporal Toft made the leap from *Swallow* to the pontoon successfully, he found that he could not cast off the foul turn single-handed, so the launch's engineer, Lance-Corporal Watson, joined him, bringing with him a jemmy to lever the offending part of the hawser off the towing bitts. They eventually succeeded, taking advantage of a moment when the hawser went slack. The leap back aboard *Swallow* was more difficult, now being lower than her deck, but both men made it safely despite the encumbrance of their lifejackets, but just after Jack Toft was pulled aboard by his crewmates, the launch collided violently with the pontoon. Holed just below the forward cabin, *Swallow* began to take in water, but despite the risk Sergeant Lister decided to carry on across the Channel and organised repairs and the bailing-out of the bilges. Luckily the launch had been equipped with the means of making repairs in case of small-arms damage or collisions, but it had not been anticipated that it would be needed so early in the voyage. Toft said that if they had been travelling at their normal speed the hole in the bow would have been raised clear of the water but their speed was restricted by that of the slow-moving convoy.

With daylight on D-Day, 6 June, *Swallow* and *Hyperion* began work off Juno Beach, guiding loaded DUKWs from the ships of the convoy to the beach and back again. Speed was of the essence in the landings and once a ship had discharged its cargo into the DUKWs and smaller landing craft it vacated its position to make way for another ship arriving fully-laden from the UK. The two launches also sometimes ferried senior naval and army officers from ship to ship or from ship to shore. Fighting was still going on just inland from Juno Beach, and at dusk a single Stuka dive bomber attacked the anchorage, but was driven off by a storm of anti-aircraft fire from the ships. *Swallow* joined in with her Bren guns, although the bomber was nowhere near in range, but firing back probably boosted the crew's morale. On D-Day +1 the rest of the Fast Launch Company arrived, followed a day later by the mother ship and the Harbour Launch Company, some of which were later to be used on the Rhine.

There is no doubt that the RASC DUKW companies played a vital role in the D-Day landings, ferrying stores from the ships offshore or from 'Mulberry' to dumps ashore, and also evacuating casualties from the beaches, while the overall success of their operations was in no small part due to the control exercised by the Harbour and Fast Launch Companies. The DUKWs brought 11,000 tons of supplies ashore on one alone, one company losing three officers on D-Day, while by D-Day +5 thirty-six DUKWs had been put out of action by enemy fire. The amphibious vehicles were at constant risk from mines drooped during the night by enemy aircraft, as well as from E-boat torpedo attacks on the 'Mulberry' harbours. There were occasionally lighter moments, such as the time when a DUKW crew received an unexpected award from the Admiral commanding the beach sector in which it was operating. A DUKW triggered a mine near a marker buoy, but escaped damage. The Admiral commanding the beach had seen this, and signalled to the Commander, RASC that the crew were due the customary reward of a bottle of whisky for sweeping a mine, which they picked up from Naval HQ. And there were also moments of glory, when on 12 June an RASC DUKW brought ashore the Prime Minister Winston Churchill and the Supreme Allied Commander General Eisenhower. Two days later King George VI landed in France also from an Army DUKW.

Some of the 'Derby Winner' class launches were allocated permanently to the Port Commander and other senior officers. Among these was the launch *Bahram* which was given the prestigious assignment of personal barge of Vice-Admiral Sir James William Rivett-Carnac, Flag Officer British Naval Assault Force. During an inspection of *Bahram*, the Admiral expressed his disapproval of her flying the Blue Ensign with Crossed Swords, the flag of all Army vessels, thinking that the only appropriate flag for an Admiral's barge was the White Ensign.

His request for the ensign to be changed was politely but firmly refused and so it was that an Admiral's barge, with the Flag Officer aboard, was seen flying the War Department ensign. The admiral was so impressed with the Army crew that he showed his appreciation by borrowing the RASC crew to instruct the naval crew of his later White Ensign barge in the art of fast motor boat handling.

In the early days of the invasion, before the completion of the 'Mulberry' harbours, conditions for the smaller craft were very bad, with their being forced to lie a mile offshore at night. The crews of the open launches suffered particularly badly. Some made fast along-side merchant ships. *Swallow* spent the night of D-Day moored to a merchantman for shelter, only for Jack Toft to find the next morning that their 'shelter' was fully loaded with ammunition! Eventually accommodation was found for the RASC crews in the unsubmerged part of one of the scuttled blockships and once 'Mulberry' was completed the launches could take shelter there. Many craft sustained heavy damage during 'Overlord', particularly to propellers and rudders striking the mass of floating debris that had collected off the beaches. With no slipways or docks available, makeshift repairs had to be carried out afloat, often requiring considerable ingenuity. One technique was to use the derricks of merchant ships to lift launches clear of the water, allowing repairs to be carried out from dinghies, a difficult and dangerous operation even in a calm sea.

Although Operation 'Overlord' had been deemed so hazardous that only military-manned vessels of the Army's Navy could be used, not long after the landings civilian-crewed WD ships were carrying stores and ammunition across the Channel to the landing areas. Among these was the ageing coaster *Sir Evelyn Wood*, built in 1896. A veteran of Dunkirk, she had suffered a serious fire while shipping bombs to Belfast and only the staunch efforts of her crew had pre-vented a catastrophic explosion. She was to have another narrow escape carrying munitions to the Normandy beaches, when a V1 flying bomb barely missed her mainmast. Other civilian-manned vessels were deployed to south coast ports for Movement Control in support of the vast number of ships crossing the Channel to France.

It was not only enemy action that was inflicting damage on the ships of the invasion flotilla. Rough weather took its toll, and the Army's Navy was not to escape unscathed. The crews of launches and MFVs were to distinguish themselves in assisting vessels in difficulties, a prime example of this being the coxswain and crew of a harbour launch the author has only been able to identify by a number - *HL*

278. The coxswain was Sergeant A.E. Smith RASC, and his launch took part in three separate rescue operations, the last of which sadly resulted in the launch being lost. On 10 June, *HL 278* saved three men from a launch that had struck a mine. The following day, another launch hit a mine 1½miles offshore. Despite being engaged in gearbox repairs, Sergeant Smith and his crew improvised a gear lever from a Stillson wrench and proceeded to the site of the explosion, picking up six men. The end for *HL 278* came on 21 June, when trying to pass a line to the destroyer *Fury* which had been mined, set ablaze and had drifted onto rocks. High seas prevented her getting the line across and unfortunately she herself was blown onto the rocks and became a total loss, although all her crew were rescued safely.

The storm which began on 17 June did severe damage to the 'Mulberry' harbours and to many of the vessels off the Normandy beaches. On the first day of the storm, a group of eight launches of 626 Company were on their way across to France. On voyages such as these, some launches were towed by their companions part of the way to conserve fuel. Only one launch had to turn back, due to engine failure. A minesweeper took her in tow, the commanding officer of which was highly impressed by the steadfast behaviour of the crew of the launch, who refused to abandon ship despite the extreme conditions. This launch was the only one not to reach France under her own power. The storm reached its peak on 19-21 June, wrecking the American 'Mulberry' harbour off Omaha Beach and severely damaging the British one at Gold Beach, putting many vessels in danger. Many small craft of the Army's Navy carried out numerous rescues during the storm, the most outstanding being that achieved by Sergeant R.J. Yeabsley and his RASC crew aboard *MFV 610*. No Royal Navy vessel was in any position to come to the aid of 180 anti-aircraft gunners stranded in a section of 'Mulberry' harbour being pounded by waves which were threatening to break up the floating harbour. Yeabsley immediately volunteered to make a rescue attempt and for five hours he and his crew battled against the storm. By now the gunners were clinging to the rocks, and as the MFV approached them, Corporal K. Popperwell jumped across and made a line fast. More than 100 men were saved in the first attempt, the rest being got off on the second trip. For his part in the rescue, Sergeant Yeabsley received the British Empire Medal for Gallantry, one of ten decorations for bravery won by the Army's Navy at the Normandy beaches.

A total of forty-eight harbour launches of 626 Company were deployed to the invasion beaches, and on 22 July one of these had the honour of conveying the Prime Minister Winston Churchill, who was visiting the beaches, from the small boat pier to his ship offshore. A message of thanks was received from the Prime Minister, complimenting the crew on the smart appearance and excellent handling of their launch. Later four of these launches were sent up the Canal de Caen to work under the Port Commander of Caen.

By September the Allied armies had reached the Seine and it was considered that the work of the motor boat companies off the Normandy beaches was finished. All of 624 Company and half of 626 Company were to return to West Mersea to refit, and the plan was to then deploy them to Antwerp once that port had been captured. The deteriorating weather as winter approached was another factor in the withdrawal of the small craft. French and Belgian ports were also finally falling to the Allies, meaning that the beaches need no longer be used. Cherbourg had been taken on 27 June but German demolitions had been so skilful and thorough that it was late September before the port became fully operational again. Dieppe fell on 1 September, Antwerp on 4 September and Le Havre on 12 September.

Both Military Oil Barge Companies had now been relieved of water supply duties and had reverted to ferrying fuel to ships at south coast ports. On his return from Normandy, Corporal Toft had been given command of one of these MOBs. Engaged in supplying fuel to destroyers at Harwich, he found the barges very uncomfortable, with excessive noise, diesel fumes, poor accommodation and bad handling characteristics. It had been planned to transfer the MOBs to the Belgian waterways to supply fuel to Allied forces there, but by the time the Scheldt had been cleared for shipping and the Ghent Canal opened at Ostend, large numbers of commercial barges had fallen into Allied hands, which were more suitable for the waterways and had greater capacity than the MOBs. So once again the MOB Companies were denied the chance to serve in the European theatre.

In other overseas theatres, more water transport units were entering service, one of these being 899 Company (Water Transport) RASC, which was formed in July 1944 to operate all Army vessels in north Caribbean waters. Based in Jamaica, the Company, among other duties, ran a long-distance (650 miles) cargo and passenger service between Kingston, Jamaica and British Honduras, for which it acquired a 250-ton American fleet auxiliary via Lend-Lease. Commissioned as the *Catania*, she was taken over by a WD Fleet crew at Boston, Massachusetts, and sailed to Kingston. The *Catania* was to make many long passages, for as well as the Honduras run, she also made trips to Nassau in the Bahamas and the Turks and Caicos Islands. It was during one of these voyages that the ship's cook went mad and jumped overboard. A British Army corporal who was on board immediately dived into the shark-infested waters and rescued the man, an act of bravery for which he was later decorated.

In the southern Caribbean there was no real need for Army water transport services until after the end of the war, when the winding-up of Lend-Lease meant that supplies now had to come from British sources. Tasks such as the operation of harbour launches for the inspection of shipping were also undertaken. The base for the Army's Navy in these waters was Port of Spain, Trinidad, and the commissioning of another ex-American fleet auxiliary under the name *El Alamein* meant long-haul voyages to British Guiana, Barbados and the lesser Antilles could begin.

With the bulk of Army vessels having returned to the UK now that beach operations in France were concluded, planning was beginning for the recapture of territory lost to the Japanese in the Far East. The scale of the operation required large numbers of Army vessels capable of long voyages, and vessels would also have to be provided for tasks which hitherto the Army's Navy had not undertaken. Floating workshop companies, coaster companies and ambulance launch companies would all have to be set up and personnel trained to man and maintain these craft. In September HQ, CRASC, 56 Water Transport Units was established at Stranraer in Scotland to administer the proposed water transport requirements for the Far East, which far exceeded those of 21st Army Group for Operation 'Overlord'. The recommendations of the earlier Lethbridge Mission were not fully adopted and the final establishment for water transport was as follows:

Two HQ CRASC Water Transport units.
Two Fast Launch Companies (reduced to one).
Two Harbour Launch Companies (increased to five).
Two Military Oil Barge Companies (reduced to one).
One Ambulance Launch Company.
Two Coaster Companies (not required).
Two Floating Workshops (reduced to one).
Two Boat Stores Depots (reduced to one).

In the event, however, the surrender of Japan meant that even the reduced establishment was not needed.

During the autumn of 1944 the Allied advance in Italy required a

71

further reorganisation of water transport arrangements with 247 Company taking responsibility for southern Italy, Sicily and Malta, 797 Company for the northern Adriatic, 798 Company for the northern Tyrrhenian Sea and 801 Company for the southern Adriatic, Yugoslavia, Albania and Greece. The invasion of the South of France, on 15 August, placed even greater demands on the water transport services, and to co-ordinate all the operations in this theatre a special water transport office was set up at Allied Headquarters.

As the end of the war in Europe seemed to be approaching, planners' thoughts were turning to the Herculean task of invading Japan as the year came to a close.

1945

The last months of the Second World War saw major changes to the War Department Fleet, not the least of which was a change of title to Royal Army Service Corps Fleet, with vessels' names now being prefaced with RASCV instead of WDV. In time also the uniforms of the civilian crews were altered in line with this change: officers' cap badges now bore the lettering RASC, while the War Department insignia on ratings' round hats was replaced by the same lettering, while in due course all ranks were issued with naval battledress bearing shoulder flashes of a blue ensign with crossed swords. The same flashes were worn on the khaki uniforms of military personnel manning RASCVs.

Throughout 1945 the fleet steadily increased as newly-built vessels, those transferred from the USN and RN, and those purchased or requisitioned came into service. Commissioning continued of 69ft 'Battle' class high speed target towers, the 72ft 'Battle' class ex-RN MTBs, and the 70ft 'Battle' class American-built ex-MGBs. The 40ft 'Barracks' and 'Barrack Lines' classes of General Service Launches continued to enter service as did the 44½ft 'British Rivers' class fast launches, and the 45ft 'Shakespearean Females' class General Service Launches and the 45ft 'Shakespearean Males' class of ex-RN passenger launches. New classes included the 'Dickens' class Series 1 and 2 General Service Launches, while MFVs were taken over, some for conversion to fire boats.

By January a review had been carried out of the requirements for RASC craft for operations in Belgium and Holland, and subsequently only 624 Company was dispatched to Antwerp, with ten Fast Launches, twenty Harbour Launches and two MFVs, all delivered as deck cargo. Later some of the launches were employed in the Rhine

One of the numerous *caiques* used for clandestine operations by the Army's Navy in the Mediterranean from 1941 on. Note that the censor has blacked out the name of the ship. (Museum of Army Transport, Beverley)

Soldier-sailors of No. 1 Motor Boat Company RASC (a training unit) learning boat pulling in the summer of 1940.

During 1941-2, No. 2 Motor Boat Company RASC was tasked by the Royal Navy to undertake security patrols on rivers and estuaries on the east coast of England.

Launches of No. 2 Motor Boat Company RASC taking up station for a review before a senior officer, c1941.

A launch of No. 2 Motor Boat Company passing in review. Most of these vessels had been requisitioned from private owners.

A fast target towing launch manned by civilian War Department seamen passing one of the Spithead forts off Portsmouth during the Second World War. Their uniforms gave them the look of First World War U-boat crews. (By permission of the Trustees of the Imperial War Museum: H15034)

A 'Queen Gull' radio-controlled target boat. They entered service in 1941, and provided a far more realistic simulation of an MTB target for coastal batteries. (Author's collection)

The early type of Military Oil Barge, *c*1943. These vessels were very unpopular with their soldier-sailor crews.

The 69ft 'Battle' class target towing launch, which entered service beginning in 1943.

Military-manned cargo-carrying 61½ft MFV *c*1943. (Museum of Army Transport, Beverley)

A 90ft MFV converted to a military-manned firefighting vessel, 1944.

An African recruit to a Water Transport Company receiving instruction aboard an East African Army Service corps vessel *c*1943. Overseas elements of the Army's Navy made wide use of local personnel as well as vessels.

Original wooden-built ramped cargo lighters in Burma during the Second World War.

WDV *Oma* leading the liberation fleet into St Peter Port, Guernsey, on 12 May 1945.
(John De La Haye collection)

A DUKW coming ashore in the Solent. During the Second World War these amphibious vehicles, crewed by RASC personnel, did sterling work during the D-Day landings in June 1944. (HMSO/Crown Copyright)

A TID (Towing In Dock) tug, of a type used by both the RASC and IWT Fleets during the Second World War. Note the Oerlikon gun abaft the funnel.

The IWT launch *Karmala* on the River Euphrates, Iraq, 1942. This vessel may have been requisitioned from the Calcutta Port Commissioner. (RE Library, Chatham)

crossings. Once the civilian barges had been handed over to Inland Water Transport control, the HQ CRASC, 42 Water Transport Units was withdrawn from Antwerp where it had been sent in September 1944 after the end of the Normandy campaign.

On their return to the UK, forty-two Water Transport Units would now be re-equipped for service in the Far East. Headquarters Allied Land Forces Southeast Asia was now urgently demanding these units and by January 1945 men and vessels were being sent out by sea. Among the units were 856 and 884 Companies.

The men of 856 Company, who had arrived in February in advance of their vessels, were dispatched to Akyab in Burma to assist the Inland Water Transport organisation of the Royal Engineers. Taking over eight tugs, they were based at a former rice mill on a most insalubrious and desolate creek. They now found themselves undertaking tasks far beyond their previous experience or training, such as helping to moor up freighters in strong currents and towing heavily-laden lighters through dangerous and uncharted waters.

The second company, 884, also arrived before its craft and was put to work in the same way, operating tugs from Chittagong in support of the IWT. They worked on the river Chindwin between Kalewa and Myingyan, a swift-flowing, largely unbuoyed river with the constant risk of grounding on the numerous sandbanks. Navigation was 'by guess and by God', the channel markers of bamboo poles often having been washed away. Shifting sandbanks were an additional danger, and the time-honoured means of refloating stranded craft was to persuade excess passengers, usually large bodies of Indian troops, to disembark in the shallows and push!

A detachment of DUKWs manned by RASC personnel from 2 Divisional RASC also served in Burma, being used to maintain communications on the River Yu when all the road bridges from Tamu to Kalewa had been swept away by flooding. Apart from the strength of the current (a trip of 30 miles downstream took 4 hours, the same distance upstream could take anything from 16 to 19 hours), floating debris and logs caused much damage to shafts and propellers. Maintenance problems were exacerbated for the workshop platoons by the shortage of spares for DUKWs in the Far Eastern theatre.

In April 856 Company was withdrawn to Calcutta where it was re-equipped with its own 36ft harbour launches, and then was sent to take part in the recapture of Rangoon in May. The liberation of the capital of Burma after three long years of war marked the virtual end of the Burma campaign. After the city had fallen, 856 Company based itself at a former iron foundry and undertook a range of harbour duties such as boarding and helping to moor vessels, while also maintaining a weekly passenger and dispatch boat service between Rangoon and Bassein.

In the UK, February saw the RASC take over fifteen LCVs from the Royal Navy. These craft, manned by RASC personnel after conversions had been carried out under ST1 arrangements, were assigned to working with the Royal Engineers on beach mine clearance around the coasts of Britain, being redesignated BMCs (Beach Mine Clearance). In another sign that the end of the war in Europe was nearing, preparations began to be made for the disposal of unserviceable and captured ammunition in deep water, as had happened after the Great War, and in April two LCTs were provided by the Admiralty for this work, with the RASC to provide the crews. These first Ammunition Dumping Craft (ADCs) were manned by civilian crews from 616 Company RASC (Water Transport), while further ADCs, commissioned after the fall of Japan, had military crews, eventually totalling some 100 converted LCTs world-wide.

But the priority was still the provision of vessels for the war with Japan, and problems were encountered in meeting the requirements of Allied Land Forces, South East Asia Command. For example, the existing 80ft Military Oil Barges were entirely unsuitable for service in the Far East, given their many shortcomings, so, following consultations with the Admiralty, the Ministry of War Transport and ST2, a new class of coastal tankers was built. Numbered MOB 1 to 16 (which presumably must have lead to some confusion as the original MOBs, also numbered from 1 on, were still in service), they were built by various shipyards to the order of the Admiralty, Director of Contracts (MS). Their dimensions varied but they were generally 100ft long and between 136 and 167grt. It appears that on completion they took up duties with various Admiralty civilian departments, *eg* Victualling Stores Department, Naval Stores Department, etc. Only MOBs 3 and 9 were completed before VJ Day (15 August), and although MOBs 8, 13 and 14 are recorded as being built in 1945, no exact dates can be found. Only four actually joined the RASC Fleet, MOBs 7, 8 and 9 being sent to 630 Company (Water Transport) at Ipswich in December, while MOB 13 joined the fleet in the same month.

The Lethbridge Report's recommendation for the provision of 100 floating workshops to service small craft and amphibious vehicles was to be met by the conversion of LCT Mark IIIs which were redesignated LCT(E). These were of 305grt and 192ft long, with a range of 1460 miles, but these vessels had been chosen more for their availability and speed of conversion than their ability to make long voyages. However, the early end to the war with Japan meant that the floating workshops never really got under way.

But the Ambulance Launch Company did come into being. Designated 395 Company RASC (Ambulance Launch), it was commanded by Major Archie Campbell, an ex-RN destroyer officer. Intended for casualty evacuation during combined operations, and for ferrying the wounded from minor to major ports, the company was equipped with converted 112ft Fairmile Type 'B' motor launches with a capacity of twenty stretcher cases or forty 'walking wounded'. Two Hall Scott Defender petrol engines gave a maximum speed of 23kts, while wing fuel tanks on deck gave extended cruising range. Twelve of these were commissioned, named after locks on the River Thames: *Chartsey, Boveney, Abingdon, Clifton, Benson, Bray, Goring, Cleeve, Boutlers, Cookham, Culham* and *Caversham*. Details of the conversions to ambulance launches are given in Appendix VII, while crew complements are in Appendix VIII.

It was intended that the ambulance launches should make their way to Rangoon under their own power. For this long voyage, the company was divided into three divisions, two of which would set sail in mid-September to avoid the worst of the weather in the Atlantic. The boats of the third division would not be ready by then, and would have to have made their way to the Mediterranean via the French inland waterways. Forward planning for the voyage included scheduled stops for overhauls and hull inspections, and replacement engines were to be available when the launches reached Bombay. Each division would be accompanied by a Royal Navy liaison officer, and the programme included a flexible timetable to take account of delays due to adverse weather or delays in port, supply problems, and very importantly in these small craft, crew fatigue. Smaller craft of the Harbour Launch companies would be sent out east as deck cargo, invariably meaning that the crews would arrive before the launches did, as has been seen earlier. The danger of pilfering of 'attractive items' from the craft while on passage meant that they had to be accompanied by a small party of ship keepers. After experience in Africa, all small craft heading to the Far East, whether as cargo or under their own power, were treated against teredo worm.

The commissioning of larger vessels capable of long voyages meant that the military personnel who were to man them needed to be better qualified and more skilled than previously. New Army trades of

Navigator and Marine Engineer were introduced, and corporals previously rated as watermen could become the former after obtaining appropriate qualifications, while similarly barge engineers could become the latter. It was now necessary for improved training facilities to be provided, with special officers appointed as instructors, with higher standards applied to other ranks being trained in the new trades. Officers selected for advanced training in navigation were sent to a Sea School at Warsash, run by Captain O.M. Watts, a retired Master Mariner. Many of the officers went straight from OCTU to the Waterborne Training Centre at Yarmouth on the Isle of Wight, and after an eight-week course gained practical experience with water transport units. Those who showed especial aptitude for this kind of work were then sent to the Watts Sea School. These officers, after obtaining the qualification of Navigator, Class II, were particularly needed for service with the Ambulance Launch Company.

A veritable armada of Army ships and craft for the war against Japan was now being assembled at Yarmouth on the Isle of Wight. Personnel were accommodated in requisitioned holiday camps on the island, and three Victorian coast defence forts were also used. Support facilities at Yarmouth included a navigation and engineering school, workshops and other ancillary services. Sea training was carried out aboard *ML171* commanded by the Sea Training Officer, Captain C. Gill RASC, whose second-in-command was Captain (later Major) Bill Wynn-Werninck RASC, who in later years became a well-known and respected marine artist, specialising in paintings of Army ships and mariners. There is evidence that *ML171* may have been named *Richmond*, but Bill Wynn-Werninck has no recollection of this launch being designated other than by her number. Jack Toft, having relinquished his command of his MOB without any regrets, arrived at the Isle of Wight for a navigation course, which would lead, after passing his examination, to a qualification equivalent to that of Mate, Home Trade, except as regarded knowledge of cargo-handling. As part of the practical tests, he took an 90ft MFV from Weymouth to Cherbourg at night, and having passed, earned his third stripe.

In Italy, following the capture of Venice by New Zealand troops on 28 April, among the many boats and craft requisitioned there (excluding gondolas!) was the floating 'Black Maria' formerly used by the Venetian police, which was taken over by the Corps of Military Police. This was not, however, the first vessel of this kind to be operated by the Army's Navy. One vessel of 647 Water Transport Company, stationed near Dunoon in Scotland at Sandbank, Holy Loch, for service on the

Clyde, was seconded to the Military Police for the transport of prisoners. These were mostly deserters who had absconded rather than board their troopships in the Clyde.

By VE Day on 8 May, the RASC was operating a large fleet of vessels, both civilian and military-manned. Stationed at various ports in the British Isles were Water Transport Companies, some dedicated to training. Motor Boat Companies were operating in liberated or occupied territory in Europe and the Far East, while other units were engaged in the Mediterranean and Middle east, but by far the largest concentration of activity was at the Isle of Wight, where the build-up for the continuing war with Japan was taking place.

One of the most enjoyable tasks given to the British armed forces after VE Day was the liberation of the Channel Islands, the only British territory to be occupied by the Germans in the Second World War. Although small parties of British troops had accepted the German surrender on 9 May, it was not until three days later that the main body of the liberation forces landed, first on Guernsey, then Jersey, followed by Sark, while the final German surrender was on Alderney on 16 May. Operation 'Nest Egg', as the liberation was code-named, was carried out by Task Force 135, of which 841 Company (Water Transport) RASC was an integral part.

Among the civilian-manned craft in 841 Company, the crew of the 38ft launch *Oma* had a vested interest in the liberation of the islands. *Oma* had the distinction of being the smallest vessel in Task Force 135. Powered by two 100-horsepower petrol engines, she had a top speed of 23kts, and was rather luxuriously appointed for her size, having been requisitioned from the Hon. A.E. Guinness, a fact recorded on an engraved plaque in her wheelhouse. Her commander, Ralph Palmer, was a native of Guernsey who had begun his wartime adventures by joining the Guernsey-owned and registered merchant ship *Sarnia* as an Ordinary Seaman in May 1940. In the third week of June, the *Sarnia* received orders to proceed to Guernsey and evacuate as many women and children as she could carry. After an uneventful trip she landed her passengers at Newlyn, one of the last ships to escape from the Channel Islands, which were occupied by the Germans on 1 July. Ralph Palmer joined the War Department Fleet in January 1942 and after a few months' service was appointed Acting First Mate on WDV *Haslar*. Two years later he was made Master of *Oma* and joined her at Cowes. While meeting his new crew (which consisted only of an Engineer and a Boy so *Oma* probably also had the smallest crew in Task Force 135 as well), he was agreeably surprised to find another

Channel Islander aboard. Boy John de la Haye, aged fifteen, was a native of Jersey and had been evacuated with his family prior to the invasion. *Oma* was his first ship, and the launch could claim yet another distinction in having what was believed to be the youngest participant in Operation 'Nest Egg' aboard.

Task Force 135 sailed on 12 May, with *Oma* being assigned to the fast convoy, the last to depart from Plymouth with an ETA of 0800 hours off St Peter Port, the intention being that the launch would proceed under her own power. However, following a final briefing at Devonport, Ralph Palmer, while in conversation with his fellow RN and USN commanding officers, was surprised when a British Admiral came up to them, demanding to know who was in command of *Oma*. When Palmer introduced himself, the Admiral told him that because *Oma* was so small it had been decided she would go over as deck cargo. This so incensed Palmer that he actually told the Admiral, who was not used to being contradicted, that he could not possibly do this as he was returning to liberate his home town and his vessel could not suffer the indignity of arriving as deck cargo. Purple in the face and stunned into silence, as were Palmer's fellow officers, the Admiral recovered himself and eventually agreed that *Oma* should have a try. The general consensus amongst the naval officers was that this was the first time anyone had crossed swords with the Admiral and lived to tell the tale! Boy de la Haye was sent ashore to buy white and green ribbons, the colours of Guernsey, to be displayed from *Oma*'s masthead. He could only find white ribbon, so some of it was painted with green enamel from the engine room stores. Incidentally, John de la Haye's most important duty aboard *Oma* was the making of tea and toast to the satisfaction of his commanding officer!

During the crossing, *Oma* steadily fell astern of her convoy, so Palmer took a short cut through what were familiar waters to him, but this caused great alarm in the convoy as the launch was heading into unswept waters. An American MTB was sent back to advise Palmer of this and see him back onto a safer course. With Guernsey in sight after five years away, and his most pressing task being to make the rendezvous on time, Palmer thought it was a bit silly to worry about the possibility of a few stray mines, but he complied with the MTB's instructions.

All the ships made the rendezvous off St Peter Port on time, and much to Ralph Palmer's delight he was hailed by an American warship, whose CO obviously remembered his argument with the Admiral, with the message: '*Oma* ahoy! As you are going home you had better

lead the way.' *Oma* sped into St Peter Port leading the whole of the
task force, her green and white ribbons fluttering at her masthead, the
first vessel of the liberation force to enter port. Shortly afterwards
Palmer was appointed acting Master Superintendent of the Water
Transport Company, the incumbent having suffered an accident.
Later reassigned to command another launch, he was demobilised in
December and took up civilian work ashore. But what of fifteen-year-
old John de la Haye, who was making his first voyage aboard *Oma*?
He was to go on to greater things, in 1961 co-founding Caledonian
Airways with Sir Adam Thomson with the incredibly low capital of
only £54,000. Later Caledonian became British Caledonian, with
John de la Haye holding a directorship.

Once Burma had fallen to the British in May, preparations were being
made for attacks on Malaya. Following three months of operations on
the Chindwin, 884 Company returned to Calcutta to take delivery of
their own craft and prepare for the Malayan operations. The Japanese
surrendered before the landings took place, but the Company did go
to Malaya in September and at Port Swettenham formed the basis for
future RASC operations in the area. A third military-manned
Company, 626, had meanwhile been reformed in the UK following
service at the Normandy beaches, and was also dispatched to
Calcutta, arriving in June.

Sergeant Toft was likewise getting ready for his transfer to the Far
East, having been assigned to a new fast launch company. He and his
fellow 'soldier-sailors' were taken to a boatyard in Southampton to
inspect the new launches that in fact they would never sail in. Then
they were sent to Scotland with their stores and equipment to await
further orders, eventually moving to Irvine in Ayrshire for embarkation
in a fast troopship once their launches had sailed from Southampton
as deck cargo. There then followed a period of uncertainty, resulting
in a series of orders to stand-by shortly followed by their cancellation.
During one of these stand-down periods Toft attended a selection
board in Edinburgh, and was accepted for officer training and entry
into an OCTU in Kent. While completing the initial stages of officer
training, Japan suddenly surrendered after the dropping of atomic
bombs on Hiroshima and Nagasaki. Cadet Toft was then presented
with an ultimatum: he could not continue officer training unless he
gave a firm commitment to serve for a minimum of two years, probably
in Borneo; alternatively he could revert to Sergeant with the prospect
of demob within six months. His decision was required within twenty-
four hours. As he had recently become engaged and was sure his

fiancé would not welcome a two-year separation, he turned down the chance of a commission and reverted to his NCO rank.

A group of Fairmile 'B' launches additional to the 'Thames Lock' class were commissioned before VJ Day: *Hambledon, Hurley, Iffley, Maple, Durham, Marsh* (i), *Marlow, Molesey* (i) and *Shepperton*. Although they were intended for conversion to ambulance launches, *Iffley* and *Shepperton* remained as MLs, while MLs 557 and 884 appear never to have been named so probably were not converted either.

The Japanese capitulation on 14 August, followed by the formal signing of the articles of surrender aboard USS *Missouri* in Tokyo Bay on 2 September, finally brought the greatest war in history to an end after six years. In that time the War Department/RASC Fleet had grown from a modest establishment of seventy vessels, mostly ageing and manned by civilian crews, to a fleet of some 1400-1600 vessels of all types, many modern and sophisticated and capable of long ocean voyages, mostly with military crews, all fully trained as seamen. The uncertainty about the total number of ships in the Fleet is due to the fact that many overseas units, particularly in the Mediterranean, the Middle East and Far East frequently requisitioned or chartered local vessels, and only for short periods of time for urgent tasks. Many of these transactions were paid for out of unit funds, and records of hirings may never have made it back to the War Office. It may therefore even be the case that the Fleet actually exceeded the higher figure of 1600 vessels given above.

In conclusion, the men and ships of the Army's Navy, whether civilian or military-manned, had given sterling service worldwide, service which had been acknowledged by the many decorations and honours awarded to the men who sailed under the Blue Ensign with Crossed Swords.

Chapter 5

The Inland Water Transport RE: 1939-45

The outbreak of war in 1939 saw the revival of the Inland Water Transport, Royal Engineers, and like the War Department/ RASC Fleet, it was to reach its peak in both ships and men during the Second World War. Although the duties of the IWT and the WD/RASC Fleet were demarcated as shown in the June 1944 War Office Directive (see Appendix V), in practice the work of the two services very often overlapped, especially in overseas theatres.

The initial plans for the maritime activities of the RE were based on its operations during the Great War, *ie* that it would act as an adjunct to the French railway network on the canals and rivers of the Western Front. There would also be a requirement for craft for the building and maintenance of military ports. The first vessels acquired by the RE after the declaration of war were specialised types for this latter task, such as hoppers and dredgers, and it was not until the winter of 1939 that the IWT proper was reactivated with two operational companies, a workshop company and a group HQ. By January 1940 it was clear that the shortage of rolling stock on the French railways made water transport vital for moving essential bulk cargoes such as coal, fuel oil, construction materials for defensive works, ammunition and other military stores. It was envisaged that the need for water transport would increase as the war continued, with the introduction of specialised vessels such as refrigerator and ambulance barges, as in 1914-18.

The newly-appointed Director of Inland Water Transport, with the rank of Lieutenant-Colonel, was able to establish a good working relationship with his opposite number at French GHQ, and also with the authorities in Paris controlling the movement of petrol tanker barges on the inland waterways. Additionally, a liaison officer from the French Sapeurs du Navigation was attached to the Inland Water Transport Directorate. Although the French were able to supply conventional cargo barges, they were only able to provide specialised petrol tanker barges temporarily for moving fuel from Dunkirk, so it would be up to the British Army to provide these for service on the canals of Northern France. A request was therefore placed with the War Office for twelve powered and twenty-four dumb fuel barges for operation by the IWT. In the event, only two motor barges had been deployed to Dunkirk, with a third plus a dumb barge at Calais, before the German blitzkrieg brought the war in France to an end until 6 June 1944. Shortly after the evacuation of the BEF from Dunkirk and other ports, the IWT Group HQ and Workshop Company were disbanded, while the operational companies were absorbed into the dockside and stevedoring activities of the RE in the British Isles.

The Middle and Far East, 1940-43

Although the IWT's activities in the West had been brought to an end, overseas it was a very different matter, particularly in the Middle East. In early 1940, a small cadre of IWT units had been set up in Egypt to operate and maintain vessels on the Nile, and to land cargoes from ships in Egyptian ports. The Italian entry into the war in June 1940 led to an acceleration of activities and soon the HQ Staff at Cairo found themselves controlling nearly all powered craft, tugs and barges on the River Nile and the Delta. Services from Alexandria, Port Said and Suez to the barge berths on the Suez Canal, Ismailia and the depots at Cairo were run in the Delta, and, together with the Sudan Railways Steamers, services were maintained in the Nile Valley, while some cargoes were directly shipped up the Nile by the IWT from Wadi Halfa in the Sudan to the Delta without transhipment onto the railway. As the war in the Western Desert swung back and forth, the capture of ports in Libya brought more work for IWT craft and personnel. As with the WD Fleet, wherever possible the IWT chartered or requisitioned local craft with civilian crews, which was both efficient and economical, but it was also responsible for the construction of new vessels for a variety of purposes, and this period saw the introduction of the 'Z Craft' powered lighters. Built in great numbers, and with both military civilian crews, these were prefabricated in India and shipped to the Middle East for assembly, an became very popular for a broad range of tasks, able to carry vehicles, freight and passengers, and also having the capability to undertake short ocean voyages, if in ballast and in fine weather. They were later to be used in other theatres of the war, as will be seen, and became renowned for their longevity, many still being in use long after the end of the war. The IWT also built concrete pontoons, lighters and motorised craft for use on the Suez Canal.

In 1941, IWT units began to be formed further afield, in India and the Far East. A unit was established in India in the summer of that year, a group of officers arriving from the UK to recruit other ranks from those locals whose peacetime experience suited them for the job. The Port of Calcutta Authority proved a fruitful source of recruits, as did similar organisations throughout the Raj. In Malaya, the authorities opposed the militarisation of the ports and railways, and it was decided that the Singapore Harbour Board and the Federated Malay States Railways should retain control. Their civilian personnel were trained in civil defence, and it was only after the dock workers fled Japanese air raids that Army units took over work on the docks. An identical situation existed in Burma, with Army units again taking over work after air raids beginning in December had caused heavy casualties among civilian workers.

In April 1941, events in Iraq and Persia had caused a massive increase in IWT operations in the Middle East, when insurgents attacked British bases in Iraq, urged on by that country's pro-German government, lead by Rachid Ali (quickly nicknamed 'Wretched Ali' by the British press). By virtue of a treaty signed in 1930, British troops were stationed near Basra, and there were RAF bases both there and at Habbaniyeh. The initial attacks were quite serious, but troops from India were quickly sent to Basra, from where they relieved the besieged airfields. A hastily-assembled force then marched on Baghdad, leading to the collapse of the rebellion by the end of May and the occupation of all key points in Iraq by British forces.

The lack of roads and an adequate railway system in Iraq meant that the only reliable lines of communication were via the rivers Tigris and Euphrates, ensuring that the IWT would be heavily involved in the same theatre of operations as it had been in the Great War. Initially it was agreed that the agents for the Euphrates and Tigris Steam Navigation Company, Gray Mackenzie, would make suitable river craft available for military operations, which would be crewed, maintained and operated by the Company. However, the majority of these vessels had in fact arrived in the country with the previous IWT organisation in 1914-18, and time was beginning to take its toll on them. More modern craft were being used by the Anglo-Iranian Oil Company, but these could not be used as they were all based in nominally neutral Persia.

The IWT's first operation came in June, when British troops

advanced up the Tigris to capture Amara and Kut, towns that had been household names during the Mesopotamian campaign in the Great War. Codenamed 'Regatta', the operation was successful, but the water transport was beset with problems, principally the potential refusal of the local crews to serve in dangerous conditions. Although they received double pay, there was a danger they would desert if they encountered enemy opposition, or even bad weather. Because of this, the local British Commander, who as part of the 10th Army was under Indian Army control, sent a message back to India for backup crews. Unfortunately, a misunderstanding due to poorly-composed signals lead to this request ending up with the Ministry of War Transport. To compound the error, the crews were designated for service with Gray Mackenzie & Co. Ltd, Basra, although the Army had given them the title of First IWT Contingent. Therefore, the crews which arrived in Iraq were recruited from the lowest stratum of the Calcutta workforce, effectively unemployable misfits who from the outset flatly refused to serve under military orders, and the majority of them, apart from a few who did agree to work for the IWT, had been returned to Calcutta by May 1942, having done no work whatsoever for the whole time they had been in Iraq.

In July 1941, a committee had been set up to make recommendations for implementing an IWT presence to operate military shipping between Basra and Baghdad. The chairman was a Mr Berry (from whom the committee took its name), who had previously worked for the India General Navigation and Railways Company Ltd. Information on the viability of IWT operations in Iraq was hard to come by, owing to the shortage of reputable officials with recent experience of the Tigris, and the absence of up-to-date and accurate hydrographic surveys of the river. The committee's work was given further impetus when in August, following Persia's refusal to expel Axis representatives who were negotiating for landing rights for German and Italian aircraft, the Allies acted to secure the vital Persian oilfields. British forces occupied the oilfields and adjacent areas in the west of the country, while the Russians crossed the border into north-west Persia. This takeover brought the welcome bonus of access to the Anglo-Iranian Oil company's modern fleet of vessels based at Khorramshahr and other ports. The Berry Committee now found its remit extended to a possible IWT service from Khorramshahr to Ahwaz, and by September the Quartermaster-General, India, was convinced that it was not only possible but highly desirable. The Committee was therefore ordered to return to India and put its recommendations into effect, completing the planning for an IWT organisation to cover Iraq and Persia, and for appropriate personnel, craft and equipment to be supplied from India as a matter of urgency.

A nucleus of IWT officers and other ranks had been established in Iraq by October, from IWT officers sent from India, personnel from other Army units in Iraq with IWT experience, and even some troops who had been enjoying some leave in a rest camp. As the old saying goes 'Great oaks from little acorns grow'. Within a year the strength of the IWT in this theatre had grown to 10,000 men. The hired vessels were surveyed, and extra ones chartered, the rivers were inspected, accommodation provided, proper arrangements made for paying and feeding the native crews, and the IWT formally took over control of all water transport from Gray Mackenzie.

The increased volume of harbour lighterage and river traffic meant that further assistance from India was now required. At the end of November the recently-appointed Director of Inland Water Transport paid a fact-finding visit to Iraq. He concluded that the implementation of the Berry Committee's recommendations was so far behind that the following year would see no vessels or equipment being supplied from India. Indeed, the only vessels likely to be available were a few paddle-steamers and barges, being prepared for the voyage to Iraq. With India written off as a source of supply for the IWT in Iraq and Persia, alternatives had to be found. The Americans were able to offer some assistance in the shape of Higgins barges and Eureka tugs. Despite being somewhat unsuitable, they were accepted as a stop-gap in the absence of anything better. Furthermore, all local craft were to be requisitioned, chartered or purchased, whatever condition they were in, and local workshops commandeered, with plans to build new workshops also. Four principal IWT departments, Marine, Traffic, Engineering and Administration, had begun to function by the end of the year.

There had been no training for RE officers in IWT duties between the wars, and the 200 officers required for service in Iraq had to be recruited directly from appropriate civilian employments. Time being of the essence, these officers were not able to undertake basic military training, their technical skills, experience and administrative acumen being the basis of their selection and eventual promotion. Doubtless 'old sweat' senior NCOs must been have horrified by this new officer intake's complete ignorance of such hallowed military customs as being smartly turned out on parade in the correct uniform, and the ability to march and salute properly! As regards the crews, it was accepted that the local personnel recruited would have no military experience, so British IWT troops were requested to be sent as a Group to Iraq to supervise and train these crews. This Group arrived in January 1942, and was split up, with officers and other ranks being sent to the different companies, achieving a high level of success. By the end of 1941, the IWT was operating 180 vessels, over 50 of them powered, and a training centre had been set up in Bombay, sending drafts of 400 men to Iraq twice a month.

With the outbreak of war with Japan on 7 December 1941, as with the WD Fleet the IWT organisations in this theatre of operations had to be rapidly expanded, but the rapid fall of Malaya and Burma forestalled much of this work. At Singapore, which fell on 15/16 February 1942, no IWT units had been formed, although a scratch docks operating company attempted to keep the harbour in operation. However, the mass desertion of civilian dock workers as the fall of the city approached meant that they could do little except arrange the evacuation of troops.

Similarly no IWT units had been activated in Burma by the time of the Japanese occupation, river transport being undertaken by the commercial Irrawaddy Flotilla Company. However, the crews had been unwilling to continue services downriver from Prome to Rangoon, fearing attacks not only from the Japanese but from Burmese rebels also. Although the civilian crews were replaced by British officers of the Irrawaddy Flotilla guarded by British troops, with men of the Burmese Auxiliary Force being trained as deck and engine room hands, it was really a case of too little, too late. Rangoon was finally evacuated on 7 March, the vessels left behind being disabled by demolition parties in river steamers which were then themselves scuttled. Three days later the surviving river craft reached Prome, where further trouble occurred with the crews who were reluctant even to sail upstream to places well to the north of Mandalay. All eyes were now on the Chindwin River as a means of escape to India, but low water levels denied this route to deep-draught vessels, while some craft were captured by the Japanese at Monywa. Most of the remaining Irrawaddy Flotilla craft were scuttled at Mandalay and other river ports, while by early May the IWT personnel had set out on foot from Katha for India. The final evacuation of troops via the Chindwin River was from Shwegin to Kalewa together with an infantry brigade from Shwegin to Sittaung.

In Persia and Iraq, 1942 saw further expansion of the IWT organisation, though in common with the rest of 10th Army it was principally concerned with maintaining lines of communication for shipping vast quantities of war material to Russia rather than in actual operations against the enemy. 'Aid to Russia', which had begun in September 1941, was jointly run by the Army and the Ministry of Supply, and the IWT supplemented road and rail transport by moving cargoes north through Persia on the Karun River, especially from Khorramshahr. In January 1942 the fleet of the Karun Navigation Company had been purchased, providing tugs, barges and ancillary machinery, while the Iraqi government passed legislation allowing the requisitioning of river vessels for service with the British Army. At about this time, 10th Army was transferred from Indian Army control to Middle East Command, but day-to-day administration remained with Army HQ in Iraq and Persia, the name 'Paiforce' (Persia and Iraq Force), being applied to British forces in this theatre.

Services were being maintained on the Tigris, where problems arose with the arrival of large towing steamers and barges from India. Firstly, the steamers had to be converted to burn oil fuel, which was done as they arrived at the Gray Mackenzie dockyard, now under the control of the IWT Engineering Department, and secondly these deeper-draught vessels required the introduction of a traffic control system to cope with the low-water periods on the river. The river was divided into four sectors for vessels of different draughts: the stretch from the main base at Basra to El Azir was suitable for large paddle steamers and twin-screw crafts drawing up to 8ft, the Narrows from El Azir to Amara could take only twin-screw tugs of up to 4ft draught, the Middle sector from Amara to Kut could take medium vessels of 4ft 6in draught, while the final leg from Kut to Baghdad, the Upper sector, was limited to vessels drawing no more than 3ft. The area of greatest difficulty was the Narrows, where the navigable channel was only 120 yards wide, and several control towers had to be built to regulate traffic to prevent strandings and collisions. Further refinements to traffic control came in May, with the Gulf and port operations being controlled by Base Area while Forward Area, based at Kut, ran river traffic. The reactivation of IWT base at Dockyard Island, Ashar, was a further reminder of the 1914-18 War. This entailed the eviction of all civilians, raising the island 3ft with dredged earth, and building jetties, roads and workshops. Gray Mackenzie's workshops were coming under increasingly pressure, despite new equipment from India and the UK, as the arrival of the new Eureka tugs from the USA and the Higgins barges which were assembled in Kuwait increased their workload. By August 1942 the

IWT was operating 661 vessels, more than a third of them powered, and by the end of the year inland water transport in the area had been fully organised (see Appendix IX).

Throughout the year recruitment and training of IWT personnel in India had been steadily increasing, boosted by the influx of experienced officers and crews who had escaped from Malaya and Burma, particularly the Irrawaddy Flotilla. It was now possible to raise companies for service in India itself and in preparation for the recapture of Burma as well as supplying men to Iraq. Group HQ was at Calcutta and in March 1942 the IWT was given the job of providing military-manned craft to patrol and defend the Mouths of the Ganges. This involved a flotilla of requisitioned river steamers and tugs armed with machine guns and in some cases an anti-tank gun to patrol countless creeks and rivers. The crews were somewhat mixed, consisting of Indian Engineers, contracted to serve in Bengal only, while the officers were drawn from the Royal Engineers, Indian Engineers, the infantry, artillery and the Royal Indian Navy. The flotilla was stood down in October and although it had not seen any action, nonetheless it had provided valuable experience for its crews which would stand them in good stead in the forthcoming Burma campaign.

As the liberation of Burma got under way in the latter part of 1942, the port of Chittagong assumed greater importance as a maintenance base. Originally supplies for the forces fighting in Burma from Chittagong were landed at an anchorage at Cox's Bazaar, then shipped several miles upstream by small native craft before transhipment to road vehicles for transport to forward areas. The IWT craft used for the voyages from Chittagong to Cox's Bazaar were quite unsuitable for even this short coastal voyage. They were, with the exception of some Eureka tugs and Higgins barges, all ancient underpowered steamers and even launches fitted with converted road vehicle engines! The barges, although in some instances capable of carrying up to 1000 tons of cargo, had all been requisitioned from the river trade and their shallow draught made them extremely hard to handle in anything but a flat calm. The situation was not to improve until the capture of the ports of Maungdaw and Buthidaung on the Rivers Naaf and Mayu in the closing weeks of the year allowed two convoys to sail directly from Chittagong to Maungdaw.

In January 1943 an attempt was made to capture the Japanese-held town of Akyab in Burma, and three IWT paddle-steamers together with naval-manned landing craft transported an infantry brigade for the attack. Although good progress was made down the Mayu to within four miles of the landing site, bad weather prevented the tanks getting ashore from the landing craft and the operation had to be abandoned. Then in April the Japanese went on the offensive, out-flanking British forces by taking control of the Rivers Mayu, Kaladan and Kyauktau, forcing the abandonment of Maungdaw and Buthidaung, supply operations shifting back to Cox's Bazaar and Chittagong. This, coupled with the onset of the Monsoon season, made further operations in the Arakan impossible, and although the offensive was resumed after the rains, the Arakan was to remain a tough nut to crack. During this period IWT strength was increased with two Groups deployed, one operating between Chittagong and Cox's Bazaar and the other on the Naaf river.

By June 1943 the IWT presence in Iraq and Persia had reached its peak, with over 10,000 men employed. A breakdown of nationalities shows some 800 British, including 200 officers, 6000 Indians of all ranks and 400 Chinese, the balance being made up of locally-recruited Iraqis, Persians, Kurds and Arabs. An IWT school was operating at Kut, and this trained personnel who were able to be sent back to the UK in time for D-Day. The total number of vessels had reached 1300, slightly less than the 1634 the IWT had had at its peak in Mesopotamia during the previous war. But from this point the IWT was to decline, as new road and rail links took over the transport of supplies to Russia. Already twenty-two steamers and twenty barges had been recalled to India. Although the American-controlled barge construction site in Kuwait closed down in June, at the end of 1943 the IWT reactivated it for the assembly of prefabricated vessels which continued to arrive there. Between its opening in August 1942 and its closure, 365 barges had been delivered from Kuwait to Basra.

More prefabricated vessels from America, Britain and Canada began arriving in India in the autumn, with more planned for 1944-5. Also, with the end of the North African campaign, 'Z craft' were being returned to India in preparation for the next offensive in Burma. This increased load on the Indian shipyards led to the estab-lishment of a new facility at a disused jute mill some twelve miles from Calcutta, although its construction was not complete until 1945. Assembly work on the prefabricated vessels had begun long before then. With an IWT Group already concentrated at Chittagong and the Arakan, a second Group was based at Calcutta with responsibility for several IWT units being trained in Bengal, and also for the requi-sitioning of launches for use on the Chindwin river. In April 1943 it moved to Narayanganj, where several units were training, and in the autumn did sterling work transporting emergency food supplies during the Bengal famine, until it too was sent to Chittagong at the end of the year. By the spring a third group was based in Assam operating on the Brahmaputra river, while also in 1943 the port of Vizagapatam began to come on stream as a base for the forthcoming Arakan campaign, lessening the load on Chittagong, although it was not to reach its full potential until January 1945 when the final operations against Akyab were set in train.

D-Day and Europe 1944-45

In 1943, those planning Operation 'Roundup' (later 'Overlord'), the invasion of France, realised that a considerable IWT presence would be needed in the British Order of Battle for the liberation of France and Belgium, and preparations began to be made in the UK. IWT workshops in the London docks began converting approximately 400 sailing barges into craft with loading/discharging ramps. Some of these were fitted with engines and were known as Powered Barges, Ramped (PBR), the remainder being classified as Dumb Barges, Ramped (DBR). New units were formed, comprising five IWT companies, five workshop companies and three Group HQs. Deliveries also began of prefabricated Canadian Minca barges, which were assembled in various locations in the UK.

As well as their traditional task of providing transport on the inland waterways of France and Belgium as those countries were liberated, the IWT was to have another role in Operation 'Overlord'. As early as 1942 the need for artificial harbours to be built off the landing beaches had been identified, and Prime Minister Churchill had asked for designs for floating piers, apparently even carrying out his own experiments in his bath! Two artificial harbours, known as 'Mulberries' were to be built, one for the British and one for the US forces, and the Royal Engineers were to be closely involved in the towing out and construction of 'Mulberry B' off the beaches at Arromanches in the British sector. The floating harbours had to be protected from heavy seas by a line of scuttled obsolete ships and concrete caissons. The ships, codenamed 'Gooseberry', were to be the responsibility of the Royal Navy, while the caissons ('Phoenix') and other floating equipment were to be towed out to 'Mulberry B' by RE vessels. Of course the actual construction of the harbour was the responsibility of the Royal Engineers Port Construction Force and the Port Floating Equipment Companies. The main difficulty in the construction of 'Mulberry B' was its sheer size. For example, at high water, the area it enclosed was three times the size of Dover Harbour. Erecting extending legs know as 'spuds' on the seabed, siting the concrete caissons and assembling the floating roadways and connecting them to the pierheads was a mammoth task.

As the preparations for the invasion continued, a considerable number of ramped craft lighters (RCLs) were shipped over in sections from the USA for assembly. They were to be used both in the initial landings and later on the waterways of France and Belgium, but in the event they were not ready for D-Day and nor did they serve in Europe at all, the majority being dismantled again and sent to India. Similarly, small prefabricated tugs known as 'Sea Mules' were also imported and put out to contract for assembly, but there were problems in putting the sections together. Further responsibilities for the IWT arrived in December 1943 with the delivery of thirty-nine large ferrys, named 'Rhinos', from the USA. Built from pontoon equipment, it was originally planned that they would be assembled and operated by the Americans, but they were then transferred to the Royal Engineers.

As with the WD Fleet, IWT craft and personnel began to take up their 'jump off' positions on the day prior to 6 June 1944. The principal tasks for the mariners of the RE on D-Day were operating 'Rhino' ferries to transfer vehicles from ship to shore, ramped powered barges at 'Mulberry B' and Courseulles (later some would be based at Port-en-Bessin after the capture of that small port) and tugs, mainly of the TID (towing in dock) class, for towing the 'Phoenix' sections of 'Mulberry B' across the Channel. This armada of tugs was commanded by Captain Luck RE. Unfortunately, bad weather on 6, 7 and 8 June caused considerable problems, particularly for the ramped powered barges, and by 8 June most of the 'Rhinos' had been driven onto the beach by heavy seas and strong winds, although work began at once to get them back afloat with a remarkable degree of success. But the weather on the first three days was a gentle zephyr compared to the storm of 19 June, in which both 'Mulberries' were severely damaged, the American one being put out of action completely. Later, with hindsight, some historians have questioned whether the enormous cost and manpower required for the 'Mulberries' was worthwhile, given that records show that prior to its destruction, more cargo was being landed directly onto the beaches than was coming through the American 'Mulberry' at Omaha Beach. Be that as it may, this author believes the 'Mulberries' served well, particularly in the early days of the invasion, and fully deserved Winston Churchill's congratulatory signal that 'This magnificent port has made possible the liberation of Europe'. Furthermore, it should not be forgotten that the revelation of these artificial harbours was a great morale booster for the civilian populations in Great Britain and the USA, becoming a part of the history of the Second World War. Perhaps a parallel could be drawn with the news in the Great War that 'tanks', rather than being just big water containers, were in fact the armoured 'wonder weapon' that was going to force a breach in the hitherto impregnable German trenches.

Only one Light Aid Workshop had been assigned to support the 'Rhinos', but with the extensive storm damage to the ferries from the outset of the landings, a second company had to be deployed, with a third being sent to support the ramped powered barges. A Heavy Workshop Company arrived in July, planned to be based at Courseulles, but could not be operational until August.

It seems surprising that in the midst of all the intense activity taking place on the Normandy beaches in June 1944, the War Office took the time to issue a Directive regarding Waterborne Craft, setting out the different responsibilities of the Directorate of Transport (IWT Royal Engineers) and the Directorate of Supply and Transport (RASC Fleet). See Appendix V for details of this Directive. However, in practice on numerous occasions activities of the IWT and the RASC Fleet tended to overlap and this continued throughout the war, despite the Directive. Furthermore, during the Normandy landings and the building of the 'Mulberries' similar overlap occurred between the IWT craft and those of the RE Port Operating Companies. The Directive's guidelines and instructions were intended only as a wartime interim measure and were eventually superseded by postwar policy.

By July, with all storm damage repaired, the 'Rhino' ferries came into their own transporting cargoes ashore from ships. A further use for these versatile craft was in carrying POWs from the beaches to ships off-shore for passage to the UK. Likewise most of the PBRs had been salvaged and repaired. However, by September, with the prospect of winter storms looming, the 'Rhinos' were declared unsuitable for further service and their crews were transferred to some seventy LBVs taken over from the Royal Navy. The IWT presence was further reinforced when a further twenty-four French LBVs were allocated for work on the Normandy beaches under the control of the Royal Engineers.

With the Allies now advancing well inland, it was time for the IWT to take up its planned role of supplying transport and services at the captured ports and on the canals and rivers of France and Belgium. It had been anticipated that the retreating Germans would do considerable damage to the canals, probably to such an extent as to deny their use by the IWT for some considerable time. However, inspection of the waterways from the French coast to the Valenciennes and Cambrai districts showed that the damage, *eg* from demolished bridges, was far less than expected. Similarly in Belgium, apart from the approaches to Antwerp, the port itself and the Albert Canal, the damage was nowhere near as serious as the planners had expected. The main obstacles to the opening of Antwerp were the large numbers of sunken ships both in the port and the Albert Canal. The speedy reopening of the inland waterways was also helped by the great efforts made by the French and Belgians themselves, and the organisation of local craft and crews by the IWT. Thanks to this, the French and Belgian canals were operating by October, and Antwerp was opened to traffic in November. The Belgian authorities' initial lack of resources, however, necessitated the RE sending three IWT groups to Brussels, Antwerp and Ghent. But it was not long before the Belgian Regulating Authority for Inland Waterways was able to resume control of operations on the country's canals, and also control local civilian-crewed vessels on the Dutch and German waterways, allowing the IWT to transfer control to Q (Movements). Movement Control personnel were seconded to IWT for an interim period in January and February, the full handover taking place in March.

At this time, bad weather including severe flooding after the thaw in February, was hampering the Allied armies' advance across the Maas and the Rhine. There was, however, a continuing increase in canal traffic, and the IWT provided vessels for the river crossings as well as maintaining military traffic using Dutch vessels on these water-ways. Plans were being formulated for IWT services to operate in western Holland as and when it was liberated, and for the control of German inland waterways as the British Army continued its advance, particularly in the area of the Hamburg and Munster conurbations, but the sudden surrender of Germany in May 1945 meant all plans had to be hurriedly revised.

Following VE Day, the IWT's immediate priority was transporting food supplies by water to alleviate very serious shortages in western Holland. To that end, a Group HQ, an Operating Company and a Light Aid Workshop Company were sent to Rotterdam. Also, because eastern Holland had adequate supplies of food and barges available to move it, another Group HQ and Operating Company were based at

Zwolle to oversee the transfer of food within the country. Later both of these IWT groups administered the removal of large quantities of German military stores and equipment from the Low Countries. With the cessation of hostilities in Europe, the IWT, like the British Army as a whole, concentrated on what was expected to be a long, drawn-out campaign against the Japanese.

The Far East 1944-5

By mid-1944 the preparations for the recovery of Burma were gaining momentum in India and by August a massive programme for the assembling of prefabricated craft shipped from Great Britain, the USA and Canada was under way. The Arakan campaign had resumed after the monsoon, resulting in the recapture of Maungdaw and Buthidaung by the end of November. By December an IWT Fleet had been established for operations on the Chindwin. Kalewa was taken on the 2nd of that month, affording another foothold for the reconquest of Burma, and it was selected as a forward base for the assembly of suitable craft, and initially ten Unicraft tugs and twenty Unicraft barges were flown there from the Arakan. The advance continued down the Mayu and Kaladan rivers, with the IWT playing a full part in the operation, and Akyab was finally captured in early January 1945.

As the build-up continued, the IWT Group based at Gauhati on the Brahmaputra river in Assam moved down the Chindwin to operate river communications. By the middle of 1945 the new site for the assembly of prefabricated craft at Fort Gloster near Calcutta had been completed. It now had railway links to and from the facility, slipways, machine shops, stores, workshops, fitting-out basins, office buildings and the capacity to receive and store large numbers of craft awaiting assembly. IWT personnel there comprised a Workshop Company, a Craft Erection Company, two Riveting Companies and a Stores Section, while almost 2000 civilian staff were also employed there. With the capture of Mandalay in March, IWT activities on the Chindwin increased considerably. The Japanese had done serious damage to the facilities there, but by mid-April the dockyard was back in working order, and also that month a workshop had been set up at Myingyan to service craft at the end of their voyage from Kalewa.

The Burma campaign came to an end with the liberation of Rangoon in May, with all Japanese forces west of the Irrawaddy now trapped and those to the east forced to fight their way through thick jungle to seek sanctuary in Siam. At the end of May the IWT fleet on the Chindwin was made up exclusively of craft assembled at Kalewa, consisting of 128 Unicraft barges, 97 Higgins barges, 73 tugs of varying designs and 45 ramped cargo lighters. Also, many salvaged and repaired large flats and barges were in use, with a total capacity of some 12,000 tons. Once Rangoon was recaptured, however, the facility at Kalewa began to be run down, with stores and personnel being relocated to Alon, Myingyan and Rangoon itself, while the dockyard at Mandalay had recovered to such an extent that by June its repairs to salvaged craft were running at three times its pre-war figures. In view of this the Chindwin L of C decreased in importance and was closed down in December. A similar situation occurred in the Arakan following the defeat of the Japanese there, with IWT men and material being transferred to Rangoon as quickly as possible, though the last units did not leave the area until early 1946.

On their arrival in Rangoon, the British found the port was in very bad shape, due more to neglect by the Japanese than their demolition attempts. No cranes had survived, and several of the deep-water berths were useless because there had been no dredging during the Japanese occupation. Access to the quays was hampered by sunken craft and the floating pontoon jetties for lighters were either sunk or so badly damaged that in many cases complete reconstruction was required. The task of getting the port back into operation was afforded high priority, with control gradually being handed back to the civilian authorities in the person of the Port Commissioners. River services on the Irrawaddy and throughout the Delta also had to be restored, with the vessels and dockyard of the Irrawaddy Flotilla Company needing to be back in service as soon as possible. An interim service between Rangoon and Pegu, with country craft being towed by IWT tugs, was under way by July, but had to be suspended in August due to falling river levels. Passenger/cargo services also came into operation between Rangoon and Bassein, but were severely curtailed when it was discovered that many of the launches believed to be available in the Delta were in fact in a sorry state and prone to constant engine failures. This shortage of suitable vessels meant that there were few sailings upstream on the Irrawaddy in May and June. The situation began to improve in early July, when a Landing Ship (Dock) arrived in Rangoon with a cargo of river steamers, tugs and launches, in the first of three such trips. These new craft enabled regular services to begin between Prome and Myingyan, and later from Mandalay to Bhamo. The end of the monsoon meant that many more vessels could be sent from India, either towed or under their own power, and by

September the agreed numbers of vessels requested by the Burma government had been delivered.

This was not the end of the story because by early 1946, more vessels were being requested for the export of rice from Burma. The Irrawaddy and Delta river services underwent rapid expansion from the end of the war, as did harbour lighterage at Rangoon for rice exports. This growing demand lead to problems in finding sufficient men to both crew the vessels themselves and also work in the dockyards. Irrawaddy Flotilla Company personnel were steadily returning to work and within two months of the liberation of Rangoon over 1500 civilian workers were employed in the Company's dockyard at Dalla. But this dockyard's workload had increased so much that another repair facility had to be established at a disused foundry elsewhere in the city. Many craft unsuitable for such heavy work had to be used and coupled with inexperienced crews this led to many breakdowns, while further problems were caused by attacks of teredo worm. By 1 January 1946 the port of Rangoon had been fully handed over to the control of the Port Commissioners, although the final RE Port and IWT units did not leave until October. Similarly, the Irrawaddy Flotilla Company had taken over from the military by 15 January 1946, except in the Arakan and Moulmein.

In August 1945, following the occupation of Moulmein and the Tenasserim coast, and IWT operational company supported by a workshop detachment arrived at Moulmein to operate a ferry service between there and Martabran, and also maintain the harbour and services on the neighbouring creeks. The area was infested with magnetic mines, ruling out the use of steel-hulled craft, forcing the company to use captured Japanese wooden craft. The poor state of these vessels imposed a heavy maintenance burden, and several wooden schooners had to be chartered to supplement them. However, 'Z craft' could be used during the good weather season from Rangoon to Tavoy and Mergui, south of Moulmein, discharging their cargoes onto the beach. Five LCTs with naval crews supported these operations until IWT personnel took over in February 1946. By May all the mines had been swept, and coasters were able to sail direct from Rangoon to Moulmein, with offloading into lighters at Tavoy and Mergui, and all IWT units were withdrawn in July 1946 when civilian control was restored.

Final deployments of IWT units in the Far East were to Malaya and the Dutch East Indies after they had been liberated from the Japanese. In Malaya Port Swettenham and Port Dickson received assistance, as did Batavia, Sourabaya, Semarang, Makassar, Medan, Padang and Palembang in the Dutch East Indies. In all these ports native labour and Japanese POWs were employed, and the civilian authorities were encouraged to take over as soon as possible. By the end of 1946 the majority of IWT units had been withdrawn.

With the end of hostilities, the IWT organisation at home and overseas began a phased rundown as had happened at the end of the Great War. But unlike the last time, when the whole IWT was disbanded by 1924, this time inland water transport activities were to continue for many years to come. That this was planned for by the powers that be is shown in the post-war policy review of February 1946 regarding the control of water transport services (see Appendix VI), replacing the hostilities-only War Office Directive of 1944 (see Appendix V). Although strong arguments were presented by both the RASC and the Royal Engineers that they should be solely responsible for all Army water transport services, in the end the status quo was preserved with both branches retaining control of their own fleets, In September 1947 an Army Council Directive laid down in more exacting detail the parameters of responsibility for each corps.

As with the RASC Fleet, the IWT had reached its peak by the end of the Second World War. Units were deployed in the UK, liberated Europe, occupied Germany, the Middle East and the Far East, fully living up to the RE motto 'Ubique' ('Everywhere'). Much work still lay ahead, however, for the IWT, including responsibility for bulk transport on lines of communication and assisting in the repair of war-damaged ports overseas. It would also supply, man and operate such classes of craft as tugs, barges and lighters (except those specialising in carrying fuel), pontoons, inland ferries such as those on the Rhine, craft required for port and inland waterway repairs, and coastal craft when used for bulk cargoes to army lines of communication.

The author has had some difficulty in researching some elements of IWT activity. For example, a retired RE officer spoke of Port Repair Vessels manned by sappers during the Second World War, but actual evidence of this could not be found. A Port Repair Ship was at Rangoon during its reoccupation (see above) and another retired sapper told of another active during the Italian campaign, but the names of these ships could not be discovered, and nor could it be confirmed that they were manned by RE crews. It may be that these ships were Merchant Navy, with RE units embarked to carry out the actual port repair work, or that they belonged to the Port Repair Companies, which although part of the RE were separate from the IWT. For example, during the Normandy landings, there were special Port Floating Equipment Companies associated with the 'Mulberry' harbour and these, together with Port Construction and Repair Groups, would also have had their own craft. The considerable overlap of tasks between the various marine branches of the RE and indeed between them and the RASC Fleet, has made researching the IWT's wartime role somewhat difficult. The written history of the IWT in this period is rather sparse, and practically no input from former IWT personnel was available, unlike from RASC veterans.

It was however possible to ascertain that at least in one instance an IWT mariner shared the longevity often found in the RASC Fleet. An obituary in 1997 recorded that the last naval survivor of the Gallipoli landings in 1915, Jack Gearing, had died aged 102. He had tried to rejoin the Navy in 1939 but was told he was too old at 45. The Royal Engineers accepted him into the IWT, however, making him a sergeant, and during the Normandy landings he found himself second-in-command of a vessel towing a heavy-lift crane to the invasion beaches. When his CO was taken ill, he was put in command, and although unable to read a chart, he brought his tow safely to its destination by following a destroyer. Jack had indeed proved himself a worthy seagoing Sapper sailing under the Blue Ensign with a Winged Thunderbolt held in a Clenched Fist.

Chapter 6

RASC to RCT: 1945-65

Now officially titled the RASC Fleet, sweeping changes were to affect the ships and personnel of the Army's Navy with the end of all hostilities in August 1945. The first of these was of course the cancellation of the sailing of the Army's 'armada' gathered in the Solent to the Far East which had been scheduled for mid-September. However, before this fleet dispersed, an Army Fleet Review was held shortly after VJ Day in early September 1945.

The venue was the Western Solent, and some 200 Army vessels sailed past the Reviewing Officer, Major-General Sir Reginald Kerr, Director of Supplies and Transport, who took the salute from the parapet of Fort Victoria, a nineteenth-century fort on the Isle of Wight, affording an excellent view of the Solent from east to west. The fort's signal station and radio room were also used to control the Review. The participating craft were all military-manned, with a total of some 1600 officers and men of the RASC on board. No civilian-manned vessels of the Fleet took part, and officially neither did any IWT vessels, although one eye-witness stated that a TID tug was present. This may have been an IWT ship, as they certainly did use these, and furthermore the skipper was a staff sergeant who had been a Thames tugman in civilian life! According to the then second-in-command of *ML171*, Captain Bill Wynn-Werninck, weather conditions were perfect, with a slight sea and very good visibility. His vessel, as Training Ship of 935 Company RASC (Ambulance Launch), had the honour of leading the column of these launches past the Reviewing Officer, presenting the most eye-catching appearance of all the Army vessels. Photographs show the Company in a faultless line-ahead formation with their soldier crews fallen in smartly fore and aft. Sadly this Review was to prove the swan-song of the Ambulance Launches, as although the converted Fairmile 'Bs' were to continue in RASC service, and indeed more would be commissioned, their ambulance role was at an end. The DST must have been very impressed by this excellent display, but not only was this Review the largest in the history of the Army's Navy, it was also to be the last on that scale. Incidentally Major-General Kerr was to have a new RASC vessel named after him the following year. RASCV *Reginald Kerr* was one of a class of LST Mark IIIs transferred from the Royal Navy in 1946.

Although the plans to send the Fleet out to the Far East had been scrapped, nonetheless RASC craft had to be sent from India for service in the newly-liberated territories. For example, a section of 626 Company with ten harbour launches was sent to Java, while another went to Hong Kong. The rest of the Company, equipped with fast motor launches and harbour launches, arrived at Singapore with HQCRASC 56 Water Transport units. The pre-war WD Fleet base at Pulau Brani was re-established amid joyous celebrations by the locals. Gradually, things returned to normal in all the former occupied countries, except in the former Dutch East Indies, where there was strong agitation for independence. An urgent need for two Army fire-boats in Singapore meant that the halt on sending ships out to the Far East from the UK had to be lifted. Two converted MFVs were selected, commanded by Captain A. Barr RASC and Captain Tom Wood RASC, both experienced seamen and navigators. These fire boats were to make the first long voyage crewed entirely by Army personnel and arrived safely at Singapore, after calling at Gibraltar, Malta, Port Said, Suez, Aden, Karachi, Bombay and Colombo.

Meanwhile, back in the UK, Jack Toft, a sergeant once more, had rejoined the Ambulance Launch Company and was coxswain of RASCV *Benson*. However, due to a shortage of subalterns, he was promoted to staff sergeant and made second-in-command of the launch. *Benson* was undertaking escort duties for ammunition dumping craft (converted LSTs) dumping surplus ammunition off the Channel Islands. The launch made regular trips to Poole, from where the ADCs would be escorted to Hurd Deep, a underwater trench near Jersey the depth of which made it ideal for dumping explosives. On one occasion the *Benson* carried out an all-night search and rescue operation for an ADC which had lost contact, but all was well, the ADC having taken shelter in Cherbourg but being unable to inform base of the fact. By now demobilisation was under way, leading to the loss of many qualified Army mariners. The CO of *Benson*, Captain Jameson, was directed to take over a flotilla of fast launches and take them up the west coast to Lancashire for paying-off, and much to Staff Sergeant Toft's surprise, command of the launch passed to him. This is believed to be the only case of an ambulance launch being commanded by an NCO. Although he was pressed to accept promotion to Warrant Officer, this would again have been conditional on serving for another two years overseas, and as he would be getting married soon, he decided to take his demob as soon as possible. His final duty as CO of *Benson* before he left the Army was to hand her over for final disposal to the Directorate of Surplus Craft Disposal at Chichester, a fate shared by other ambulance launches. This was not to be the end of *Benson*, however, as she was to cross the author's path in the not too distant future.

Despite the demise of the ambulance launch companies, other Fairmile 'B' launches were to enter RASC service between VJ Day and the end of 1947. Two companies were operating in Egypt at the end of the war. Based at Port Said and Port Fuad were 697 Motor Boat Company and 698 Landing Craft Administration Company, with a total of 140 craft, supported by workshops and a floating dock. There were six Fairmile 'Bs', some of which had been built locally or in India, named *Sonning, Sunbury, Iffley, Mosley, Marsh* and *Shepperton*, the latter being adapted for the use of the Commander-in-Chief, Middle East Land Forces. *Shepperton* was therefore quite luxuriously fitted-out and had communications equipment so that the C-in-C could maintain contact with his HQ. She was to make many voyages to Greece, Crete, Cyprus and the Dodecanese Islands, as well as Tobruk, and must have been greatly appreciated by the VIPs embarked. This was borne out by Major Bill Wynn-Werninck (Retd.), who had commanded the ambulance launches *Cookham* and *Clifton* in the UK after VJ Day and then gone out to Egypt. During his time there he commanded *Shepperton* for a while and remembers taking the Chief Signals Officer MELF, his wife and daughter to Piraeus.

Surprisingly the Army's Navy was to experience growth after the end of the war as, although the numbers of military personnel were to decrease due to demobilisation, there was a dramatic increase in the numbers of civilian crewmen, as a number of large vessels came into service between 1945 and 1947. To meet these requirements, a recruiting drive for qualified ex-MN or RN officers and ratings began in 1945.

Various launches from existing classes were to be commissioned during 1945 and 1946. These included 69ft 'Battle' class, 72ft 'Battle' class, 70ft 'Battle' class (ex-RN MGBs), 40ft 'Barrack' and 'Barrack Lines' class GS launches, 44½ft 'British Rivers' class fast launches, 45ft 'Shakespearean Females' class GS launches, 45ft 'Shakespearean Males' class passenger launches, 50ft 'Dickens' class GS launches, Series I and II, 61½ft, 75ft and 90ft MFVs and some hundred LCTs modified as ADCs for ammunition dumping in the UK and overseas. Four of the newly constructed Military Oil Barges, *MOB 7*, *MOB 8*, *MOB 9* and *MOB 13*, joined the RASC Fleet in 1945, with *MOB 8* and *MOB 9* leaving the service in 1946, while *MOB 7* and *MOB 13* were to carry on until 1957, albeit spending several years in Permanent Reserve. Although the majority of these craft would be civilian-manned, military crews would still be required for certain tasks, while indigenous personnel, whether military or civilian, would be employed overseas. Of course many craft were also disposed of between 1945 and 1950, including the Fairmile 'Bs' and the unmourned original Military Oil Barges, while scores of vessels either chartered or requisitioned during the war were returned to their original owners.

However, the greatest boost to the civilian-manned RASC Fleet was the seven LSTs commissioned between August and December 1946. Transferred from the RN, they displaced 2310 light tons, making them the largest vessels ever to fly the Blue Ensign with Crossed Swords. They also had the largest crews, comprising civilian Fleet personnel serving under special Merchant Navy articles, of any Army vessels before or since. They were named after senior Army officers as follows (former RN designation and date of commissioning in the RASC Fleet in brackets); *Maxwell Brander* (ex-*LST 3024*, 31 August 1946), *Charles Macleod* (ex-*LST 3021*, 31 August 1946), *Snowden Smith* (ex-*LST 3028*, 5 September 1946), *Evan Gibb* (ex-*LST 3037*, 10 September 1946), *Reginald Kerr* (ex-*LST 3009*, 24 October 1946), *Frederick Clover* (ex-*LST 3001*, 31 October 1946) and *Humphrey Gale* (ex-*LST 3509*, 10 December 1946). All of these ships were constructed in UK yards except *Humphrey Gale*, built in Canada, and all were to serve overseas. *Maxwell Brander* and *Charles*

Macleod were originally allocated to SEAC, the remainder to MELF, although as the years passed they were to interchange between commands, especially during the Korean War. Also in 1946-7 the following trawlers were taken over from the RN. Their class and date of acquisition are given in brackets after the names, which are in alphabetical order; *Copinsay* ('Isles', 3 June 1946), *Foxtrot* ('Dance', 31 July 1946), *Inchcolm* ('Isles', June 1946), *Mull* ('Isles', 27 April 1946), *Oxna* ('Isles', 16 July 1946), *Porcher* ('Isles', 11 March 1947), *Prospect* ('Isles', 15 August 1946), *Sheppey* ('Isles', 25 June 1946) and *Valse* ('Dance', 21 May 1946). *Inchcolm* was on loan from the RN while *Sheppey*, although originally on loan, became permanently RASC on 31 December 1947. These were to serve for several years in the RASC Fleet, performing various tasks at home and overseas. Some were to provide escorts to ADCs disposing of ammunition, and in that role embarked additional medical personnel in case of accidents.

Ammunition Disposal

A major task confronting the RASC Fleet in the immediate post-war period, and indeed for many years to come, was the disposal at sea of thousands of tons of surplus ammunition in all former theatres of war. This had already begun to happen before VE Day, as shown above, but after the cessation of hostilities more and more craft came to be employed on this task. The Ammunition Dumping Craft (ADCs) were both civilian and military-manned, with the actual dumping personnel coming from a wide variety of the armed forces, German and Italian POWs, and local recruits in the Middle and Far East. Operations were supervised by technical personnel of the Royal Army Ordnance Corps.

In the UK the biggest dumping programme was based at No.2 Military Port, Cairnryan, in Scotland, while other ADCs operated from St Helier in Jersey. Eight LCTs were used for ammunition disposal at Port Said, nine craft in Italy, and others in the Far East. ADCs from Cairnryan discharged their cargoes into the Beaufort Dyke, a deep undersea rift approximately midway between Scotland and Northern Ireland, while the Channel Islands craft used Hurd Deep near Alderney, which had been a dumping ground after the 1914-18 War. The first three LCT Mk IVs taken over from the RN were used for this duty, with RASC Fleet civilian crews. Although they followed

111

more or less the same procedures as after the last war, the LCTs were far better suited for the work than those used a quarter of a century previously. They were easily adapted to the task of dumping ammunition, especially when boxed. A network of 'railways' formed by rollers of the type used to move boxed ammunition ashore was laid down in the cargo space, and the procedure was for the boxes of ammunition to be rolled off the bow ramp as the ADC went slowly astern. Further modifications to the LCTs included removal of armament, provision of accommodation for the dumping parties in the hold, and the fitting of lifeboats for emergencies. They were considered good sea boats, but uncomfortable for both crews and dumping parties alike, although conditions aboard were a considerable improvement on those of the earlier ships. The work could be dangerous, for example if the sea surged up the lowered ramp the men were not just at risk of a soaking, as the dumped ammunition could be washed back on board also. At particular risk were the crews dumping RAF 5-ton bombs.

The LCTs were later joined by the veteran coasters *Marquess of Hartington* and *Sir Evelyn Wood*, while the newer *Sir Walter Campbell* and *Malplaquet* were also based at Cairnryan. These ships would normally only dispose of stable items such as small-arms ammunition, smaller-calibre shells and rockets, also boxed. The procedure for getting these over the side was the same as had been used after the Great War: a platform was loaded, then hoisted by steam derrick to the same level as a similar platform secured outboard over the sea. There then followed the time-consuming transfer, by hand, from the first platform to the outboard one, and then the boxes were put overboard, again by hand. This operation could take anything up to seven hours and was of course entirely dependent on the weather.

Given the hazards of explosions, fire and toxic fumes from cargoes such as phosphorous flares, it is amazing that so few accidents occurred during the disposal of over a million tons of munitions. The most serious incident was when a fully-loaded ADC disappeared with all hands off the Isle of Man, although whether this was due to an explosion or being overwhelmed by heavy seas has never been ascertained. Men were also killed in accidents, as when a faulty tin of detonators exploded killing two soldiers. More dangerous was the discovery that boxes of rockets were failing to sink when dumped, no holes having been drilled in the boxes, drifting away from the disposal site and washing

Illustrations for Chapter 6

Director of Supplies and Transport Major-General Kerr
taking the salute from Fort Victoria on the Isle of
Wight at the largest review of Army vessels held shortly
after VJ Day 1945.
(Bill Wynn-Werninck collection)

The ambulance launch *Benson*. Converted from RN Fairmile 'B' class launches for casualty evacuation in the planned invasion of Japan, in fact they never saw service in their intended role.
(Museum of Army Transport, Beverley)

An LCT Mk IV converted to an ammunition disposal craft, just after the end of the war. In fact, disposal of surplus and captured munitions had begun even before VE Day.

Soldiers preparing ammunition for disposal from an ADC (LST Mk. IV) of the RASC Fleet.
This could be a hazardous job!

Soldiers of the RASC Fleet being inspected ashore in the late 1940s. Note the Fleet shoulder flashes worn by officers and other ranks.

A civilian seaman of the RASC Fleet receiving an award, late 1940s. Civilian officers and men were now issued with Royal Navy battledress. (Museum of Army Transport, Beverley)

The civilian-manned LST *Evan Gibb*, 1947. This class were the largest vessels the Army's navy ever operated. They were in service from 1946 to 1952. (Author's collection)

The redoubtable Captain Marr and LST *Maxwell Brander*, beached at Inchon during the Korean War 1950-2 <u>without</u> the assistance of a US pilot! (Author's collection)

The 'Derby Winner' class launch *Isinglass* at a ceremonial function on the Thames. In June 1950 *Isinglass* had carried the body of the late Field Marshal Earl Wavell from the Tower of London to Westminster Pier for his funeral in Westminster Abbey.

The Admiralty-type trawler RASCV *Mull*, which served as a ferry between the missile range on St Kilda and Benbecula during the winter months. (Author's collection)

The LST MK. VIII *Audemer* beached at Village Bay, St Kilda. Heavy winter seas made the beach unusable for the LSTs, which could therefore only serve St Kilda between March and October.

RASCV *Arakan* leaving Portsmouth at the beginning of her long voyage to Singapore and Borneo, 1963. (HMSO/Crown Copyright)

HMAV *Audemer* berthing at Marchwood in the 1960s. Her built-up superstructure was fitted in 1961 to accommodate HQ staff. (Author's collection)

up on beaches. To avoid this, men of the Pioneer Corps were issued with braces and bits to bore holes in the boxes prior to their being loaded aboard the ships. This was a slow job and the men began using crowbars to punch holes in the boxes. Unfortunately this lead to an entire trainload of rockets exploding at Cairnryan when a soldier stuck his crowbar through the top of a box and into one of the rockets inside, setting off a chain reaction that destroyed the train. A disaster was only narrowly avoided as two fully-laden ADCs were alongside at the pier by the disintegrating train, and it was only by the good luck that it was low water and the ships were lying below the edge of the pier so that the exploding rockets passed harmlessly over them. If both of these craft had exploded, there could have been devastating consequences over a large area around Cairnryan.

The most hazardous materials, chemical weapons such as bombs or cylinders containing mustard or phosgene gas, were deposited much further out to sea, in the deep Atlantic beyond the edge of the Continental Shelf. Between 1945 and 1947 considerable amounts of these dangerous substances were disposed of, either in the RASC coasters which dumped them in the usual way, or in old merchant ships which were manned by volunteer skeleton crews. These were on a one-way voyage, as once they had reached the designated very deep waters, their crews would be taken off by an escorting destroyer and the ship scuttled. Handling these cargoes was very dangerous, both for the loading crews and the actual scuttling parties, borne out by photographs showing personnel wearing protective clothing and heavy-duty respirators. These operations were completed by the end of 1947, except for one final scuttling in 1955. The 5500-ton *Empire Claire* was the subject of great speculation as to the nature of her cargo, the Press having a field day printing rumours of a 'mystery' cargo possessing unimaginably horrendous properties. Although the official line was that the ship contained old bombs, suspicion lingered in the minds of the public, as it did over the exact nature of some of the other cargoes dumped from Cairnryan.

Greece 1945-50

In the Mediterranean, the RASC Fleet was involved in supporting British forces in Greece, which had been assisting the Greek government since they first landed in October 1944 to liberate the country from the Germans. Almost immediately, the Greek communists, up until then staunch allies in the fight against the Germans, began to attempt to seize power from the legitimate government, if necessary by forces, using their large ELAS guerrilla forces. The situation deteriorated until open warfare broke out between ELAS and government troops, the latter now supported by British troops. Fighting was to continue well into 1945, with the Communists being driven out of Athens but regrouping in the mountains and some outlying islands. As the conflict became more sporadic and desultory, the role of the British shifted from anti-guerrilla operations to famine relief, in which the RASC Fleet was to play a full part.

An RASC Fleet presence was to be maintained in Greek waters until 1950, but although some vessels were actually based there, *eg* two Fairmile 'Bs' and an MFV were usually to be found at Piraeus, all operations in this area were the responsibility of 697 Motor Boat Company based at Port Said. The craft were under the operational control of the British Military Mission to Greece, while personnel comprised RASC officers and men, Greek civilian seamen and some-times even German POWs awaiting repatriation. In addition to the MLs and MFVs, several high-speed target towers came out from the UK to assist in the delivery of fresh food to the recently-liberated Greek islands. This service, know facetiously as the 'Spud Run', had previously been carried out by the Royal Navy. One of the ships involved was RASCV *Lord Plumer*, which had done excellent work at Malta during the war with a civilian crew. The 250-ton ship, built in 1927 and still battered and scarred from her wartime career, took up the duties of an inter-island ferry shipping mail, food and cargo, up to 100 passengers at a time and an unrecorded number of sheep and goats! Water transport was vital in supplying not only the islands but also coastal areas whose inland communications had been destroyed during the Communist uprising. The motor launch *Sunbury* provided transport for the senior officer commanding the British Military Mission, and together with another ML, RASCV *Marsh*, carried out a number of operational and intelligence tasks, frequently visiting isolated areas of the coastline with Military Mission officers acting as advisors to the Greek army. Frequent voyages between Piraeus, Salonika and Crete were also carried out by MFVs *221* and *210*.

Sadly it was during this period that there occurred one of the worst disasters in the history of the Army's Navy. The military-manned RASCV *Lucien Goughy* (or *Govey*), variously described as a drifter or trawler, was a 160-ton vessel which had sailed out to the Mediterranean under her own power with a civilian crew during the war. Now operating with the Military Mission, she had a crew of eleven commanded by Sergeant Trewhearne, and was on passage from Salonika to Piraeus with a single passenger, a Brigadier Hands. Approaching Skiathos, the vessel encountered a blizzard which reduced visibility considerably. Not having a clear idea of his position, and knowing that the Skiathos Inner Channel was mined, Sergeant Trewhearne posted extra lookouts, but then visibility cleared and he realised he had entered dangerous waters. He immediately reversed course, but it was too late. The ship struck a mine and sank very quickly, so quickly in fact that no one below decks survived. Corporal Corrigan, who was to be the only survivor, found himself in the water with Sergeant Trewhearne and the cook, Private Hardy, who was only semi-conscious with a severe head wound. Corrigan, a strong swimmer, managed to grab a spar and a damaged Carley float, and attempted to save the other two men, but regrettably both Trewhearne and Hardy perished, probably due to hypothermia, while Corrigan was washed ashore and found unconscious on the beach the following morning. *Lucien Goughy* was the last RASC vessel to be sunk with heavy loss of life, and also the last casualty of the 1939-45 war, albeit after the lessation of hostilities.

The last two units engaged in support of the Military Mission, MLs *Sunbury* and *Marsh*, left Greece and later returned to RN service at Malta in 1950. However, before this, on Christmas Eve 1948, *Sunbury* was to take part in a search operation involving a crashed air-craft, a Dakota carrying sensitive documents, which had come down near Kalamata in a mountainous region of the Peloponnese. The ML was ordered to take an officer of Naval Intelligence to Kalamata, the nearest harbour to the scene, in blizzard conditions. One of *Sunbury*'s officers, Second Lieutenant Hughes RASC, proceeded to the crash site escorted by a party of Greek Army soldiers. His task was to recover secret papers together with personal and identifying items from any bodies at the scene. Regrettably inspection of the debris and bodies of crew and passengers disclosed the fact that insurgent forces had got to the scene beforehand and looted valuables from the dead men.

However, they failed to discover a cache of gold sovereigns and, more importantly, documents of great value to British Intelligence, including details of membership of the Greek Communist party. Hughes retraced his steps through the mountains back to Kalamata and *Sunbury*, where he handed over the rescued items to the Naval Intelligence Officer still embarked aboard the ML. Subsequently Second Lieutenant Hughes was awarded a commendation for his good work.

The RASC Fleet in Peacetime

In 1946 overall administrative control of the RASC Fleet was transferred from ST1, which had run it during the war, to ST3 Branch of Supplies and Transport, which directed the Fleet through a Fleet Administrative Unit, headed by a Fleet Superintendent, based at Kingston-upon-Thames.

The following year saw the acquisition and conversion of the seven ex-RN LSTs which gave such a boost to the numbers of the civilian-manned Fleet. The author was one of those recruited to in this period, when experienced personnel were being sought, and it is felt that a few observations on life in the RASC Fleet at this time would be of interest to readers.

Having seen an advertisement for qualified deck officers in the *Daily Telegraph*, the author submitted an application and was duly interviewed at his nearest Water Transport Company RASC, at Menai Bridge, North Wales. Following a successful interview and a medical examination, he was appointed to RASCV *Maxwell Brander*, undergoing conversion at HM Dockyard, Portsmouth, as second officer.

From the outset the newly-appointed second officer became aware that service in an Army ship was going to be vastly different from conditions then prevalent in the MN or RN. The first thing that struck him was that, although the crew were entirely civilian, notwithstanding being employees of the Army, all ranks were in uniform. In fact his first task, after reporting to the Master Superintendent at HM Gunwharf, was to proceed to the fleet stores to draw his uniform. As an officer he was issued with an officer's cap and badge, the cap being a standard naval officer's type, while the badge, although somewhat resembling that of a naval officer, had slight differences; the Royal Crown was contained entirely within the laurel leaves, with a gold embroidered on crimson plush centre supported by the letters RASC. The uniform consisted of naval battledress, bearing insignia of rank on shoulder straps, also shoulder flashes of a blue ensign defaced by crossed swords. These shoulder flashes were also carried on khaki uniforms worn by officers and other ranks serving in Water Transport Companies RASC. Insignia of rank for officers of the civilian-manned craft of the RASC Fleet comprised rings of gold lace, the numbers of these according to rank, but the upper ring was broken in the centre and formed an inverted V. In the case of a second officer, rank was indicated by two rings, with the upper one broken as described above. Other items of uniform issued to the author consisted of a greatcoat, oilskin, sou'wester and seaboots together with other clothing, all of which had to be signed for. Petty officers and ratings were issued with similar naval battledress, but petty officers received a peaked cap and ratings naval pattern blue round caps with black cap tally inscribed with the letters RASC. Like the officers, they also received other items, including foul weather gear and working rig.

The officers, most of whom had seen wartime service in the RN, RNR or MN, also usually had their uniforms from their past service and although no compulsion was applied, it was universally the custom to change their braid to RASC Fleet marks of rank. POs and ratings had normally served in the Royal Navy, and consequently the majority of crew members had a rather more disciplined demeanour than those who had served only in the Merchant Navy, especially in their uniformed appearance. There was a fair sprinkling of long-serving civilian RASC Fleet personnel transferred from smaller vessels of the Fleet and in continuation of a time-honoured Fleet tradition several boy seamen were borne on the ship's books. Although classified as Boy 'Seamen' they carried out duties as cabin boys and in the galley as well as on deck. The crew was considerably larger than would be normal in ships of equivalent tonnage under the Red Ensign, although of course falling far short of manning scales for ships of the Royal Navy.

In Portsmouth, in addition to *Maxwell Brander*, another LST, *Evan Gibb*, was also undergoing conversion. However, *Maxwell Brander* was considerably behind her programme. This was due to a serious fire which had occurred shortly before the author joined the ship. The fire had tragic consequences as, apart from heavy structural damage, two engineer officers lost their lives having been trapped on a mess deck where they had been working. Both succumbed due to smoke inhalation. Because of this, the ship's company was very alert to the danger of fire and all hands, including officers, took a course in fire-fighting at HMS *Phoenix*, the Royal Navy's fire-fighting and damage control school, at that time located at Cosham. This course was a tough physical one, beginning with an opening introduction by a super-fit Royal Marine Commando Sergeant who, after getting the class fitted with heavy protective clothing and respirators, the latter being part of Salvus gear which at the time was standard equipment in the RN for shallow diving, then began putting the class through its paces. Salvus gear was quite heavy, with a solid metal plate and air bottles, while once the respirator was donned, the air supply had to be constantly controlled by a valve which admitted air to a rubber collar fitted around the neck. This in turn had to be frequently deflated by a manual control or the pressure built up in the collar and breathing became difficult. Once dressed in the above, the class was then issued with enormous canvas sausages containing lead weights to be carried under the left arm, fallen in and marched off. Hardly had they got on to a long concrete path than they were given the order to double, which almost immediately resulted in breathing difficulties due to failure in balancing the two valves, while the eyepieces began to fog up, severely limiting visibility. Needless to say, most of the class having been at sea continuously for many years were shockingly unfit, especially those who were ex-MN, and a couple of runs up and down the long path quickly took the wind out of their sails! Over the next couple of days, worse was to follow with the class having to fight fierce petrol fires using only water hoses. The course culminated with being locked into a darkened three-decked mock-up of a ship, filled with smoke, on a first run with white smoke which afforded some visibility, then a second run with black smoke which gave no visibility whatsoever. Togged up in oilskins and wearing Salvus breathing apparatus, the class then had to climb down into the dummy engine room and extinguish a raging fire again using only water hoses. Other courses were undertaken by officers and ratings, and the author, in company with navigating and electrical officers from both LSTs in dockyard hands at Portsmouth, being sent to the Sperry factory for a course lasting several days in the operating and maintenance of gyro compasses.

There were lighter moments of course, with several `in-house' examples of humour within the 615 Company RASC (WT), both afloat and ashore at the Fleet Base at HM Gunwharf. Several changes of commanding officer of the Company took place during the few months the author served in *Maxwell Brander*, usually with the rank of Major although the last one was a Lieutenant-Colonel, who was also a Master Mariner who had served many years in the Merchant Navy pre-war. One CO, who shall be nameless, had a reputation for heavy drinking and it was widely believed, no doubt scurrilously, that his office contained a large filing cabinet holding dozens of bottles which dispensed spirits, wines, liqueurs and beers. All were filed alphabetically, starting with Advocaat and with bottles following for every letter of the alphabet, ending with Zupa, a red wine from Yugoslavia.

To use the Army telephone exchange, manually operated by women telephonists, one had to speak the number required and the hello girl would put the caller through. However, there were two numbers allocated to 615 Company which were never actually spoken. In the Company HQ at the Gunwharf, the Company Office was usually manned by two civilian clerks, named Frost and Winter. Callers wishing to phone this office never asked the telephonist to get number so-and-so but would request to be connected with `Stormy Weather'! The other section of 615 Company that was never asked for by name or number on the telephone was the boat and clothing store, which was located in several arches supporting the railway link viaduct between Portsmouth Town and Harbour stations. The nickname for this store was 'Flanigan and Allen', the names of a well-known stage and cinema duo during the 1930s and 1940s and who also formed part of the Crazy Gang, a top-of-the-bill comic group in variety theatres. Why the nickname Flanigan and Allen? Their signature tune, a catchy piece of music to which they performed a novel dance while singing the words, was 'Underneath the Arches'!

Although the author was to remain with the RASC Fleet for only a few months, this was not to end his acquaintance with the Army's Navy. Upon deciding to join the Royal Fleet Auxiliary Service, but having to wait a few weeks before appointment to his first RFA, he undertook a delivery voyage for the Arabian American Oil Co. (ARAMCO) in order to better his finances. The voyage was to deliver a personnel launch for use by ARAMCO as a small ferry between Ras Tannurah and Bahrain. Registered as a yacht named *Aramco 201*, the launch had to be sailed from the UK to Ras Tannurah via the Mediterranean, Suez Canal, Red Sea and Persian Gulf, with several stops for fuel en route. The delivery crew consisted of a Master, Mate (the author), Chief and Second Engineers, two ABs and an AB cook, while acceptance of the vessel from the Directorate of Surplus Craft Disposal took place at Chichester. The author was quite pleased to discover the launch's previous existence was as an RASC ambulance launch (converted from a naval ML) and was still fitted out as such, including the cots for patients still in place. Additionally its name when an Army craft was RASC *Benson* and as readers will recall this was the very same AL that Jack Toft had handed over for disposal at Chichester as his final duty before demobilisation some months previously. Apart from appalling weather conditions being experienced almost throughout, the voyage from the UK to Ras Tannurah was accomplished free from any untoward events with *Benson* (*Aramco 201*) proving an excellent sea-boat. Calls were made, mainly to top up fuel and carry out necessary maintenance, at Lisbon, Gibraltar, Malta, Port Said with passage through the Suez Canal, Aden, Masirah Island (courtesy of the Royal Air Force which in those days had a small aerodrome there) and Ras Tannurah. The voyage took fifty days and after delivery to ARAMCO the crew returned to the UK in a BOAC flying boat from Bahrain to Poole.

The years following the end of the Second World War saw the granting of independence to many parts of the British Empire, in most cases the new countries choosing to remain part of the British Commonwealth. In 1947, full independence was granted to India, which was partitioned into the predominantly Hindu India and the predominantly Moslem Pakistan. Both countries took over defence responsibilities from the Raj, and the water transport companies of the Indian Army Service Corps, along with the rest of the armed forces, were shared out on a religious basis between them. The last British soldiers left the subcontinent in 1948. Ceylon and Burma also gained their independence, the former staying in the Commonwealth, the latter not. However, the handover in the mandated territory of Palestine was not to be so amicable.

In the run-up to the creation of the State of Israel in 1948, British forces came under attack both from Jewish underground fighters and Arab guerrillas opposing the foundation of the Jewish state, while also having to try and keep the peace between these two factions. As it was clear that Israel was not going to become part of the Commonwealth, it was decided to evacuate all military stores and equipment to other British bases in the Mediterranean such as Port Said, Cyprus and Malta. It was in this operation that the recently-acquired LSTs would come into their own, with RASCV *Humfrey Gale* and *Evan Gibb* transporting 26,000 tons of stores and vehicles from Haifa to Port Said, each LST making a total of fifteen trips.

Changes were also taking place in the UK regarding the administration and operations of the RASC Fleet. The Fleet Repair Unit, later to be the responsibility of REME, had moved to Portsmouth, while No. 1 Boat Stores Depot was now located at Barry, South Wales. An organisation for training ex-officers of the RN and MN, now being commissioned into the RASC, was attached to No. 1 Training Battalion, RASC, at Aldershot, also being responsible for Deck and Marine Engineer training.

With the end of the war, many offshore and coastal military installations were now surplus to requirements, and RASC vessels were employed ferrying workers out to these sites to dismantle guns and equipment, and carrying these items back to the mainland. Some coastal batteries were kept in service, however, both in the UK and overseas, so there was still a need for the target towers and range safety vessels of the Army's Navy.

A new type of target had been developed and was now being used to exercise anti-aircraft batteries on the coast. These were 'Queen Bees', small radio-controlled aircraft, which were flown over seaward target ranges. Certain RASCVs, in addition to range safety duties, were deployed to recover the Queen Bees which had fallen into the sea due to running out of fuel or from other causes.

High-speed target towers also carried out trials with the Royal Navy, the Army launches pretending to be MTBs in action with destroyers. This led to exciting moments and even damage being sustained when 'battles' were being fought in rough seas, which resulted in rules of engagement having to be redrafted to take this into consideration.

The training element of the military-manned units was enhanced in 1947 by the conversion of a 90ft MFV fire boat into a sea training vessel. This was RASCV *Yarmouth Navigator* which was to serve in this role for many years to come, being transferred in 1959 to the civilian-manned Fleet. Sea training was also carried out by a smaller converted MFV *Yarmouth Seaman*. *Yarmouth Navigator* finally left Army service in 1988 when, in company with the remnants of the civilian Fleet, she was transferred to the Director of Marine Services (Naval) and in fact led the formation of the RASC civilian Fleet passing in their final review before the Director General of Transport and Movements.

Malaya and the Korean War

After the war, there was growing unrest in Malaya as independence approached. This spreading insurgency was mostly engineered by the Malayan Communist Party, supported by the United Chinese Party of Malaya, to ensure that the future government of an independent Malaya would be communist. In 1948, ever-mounting Communist terrorism, including murderous attacks on the managers and loyal workers in the rubber plantations and intimidation of the Chinese community, led to the declaration of a State of Emergency, which was to last until 1960, with the British Army fully committed to the campaign against the insurgents. The RASC Fleet presence included three LCT Mk IVs of Southeast Asia Command carrying supplies to the Prai River near Penang and also to other coastal locations on the Malay Peninsula. The defeat of the Communist insurgents in 1960 was a triumph for British military and diplomatic skills, not only crushing the terrorists but also 'winning the hearts and minds' of the Malay Chinese population. This was in fact the only successful campaign against Communism in Southeast Asia, a fact rarely remembered today, and resulted in Malaya achieving democratic independence within the Commonwealth.

But far more seriously, on 25 June 1950, without warning North Korea, a Communist dictatorship supported by Russia and China, invaded South Korea. The UN Security Council condemned North Korea and demanded that its forces withdraw back north of the 38th Parallel, the dividing line between the two Koreas. This did not happen and on 27 June the Security Council called on all UN member states to support South Korea under the UN Charter. Twenty-two nations answered this call, and of these allies, after the United States, Britain and the Commonwealth made the largest military contribution. The RASC Fleet formed a new unit, entitled LST Control, following an

Australian request for four of the civilian-manned LSTs, to administer these largest ships of the Fleet in the Korean campaign.

The commanding officer of LST Control, the late Major Norman Vincent RASC, recalled that just before Christmas 1950 he (then having the rank of Captain) was sent for by the DDST, FARELF, at Singapore and ordered to proceed at once to Kure in Japan to take command of the new unit. He was promoted to Major and told to find himself a good clerk, and it was impressed upon him that despite his grandiose title, he and his clerk would be the entire military complement of what turned out to be the smallest British unit in the Korea War. Major Vincent, in his search for the other member of his team, luckily remembered a Corporal Peter Robinson whom he had served with before, and who was in Malaya waiting to go home after fighting the terrorists up-country. He interviewed the Corporal and satisfied that he had the qualifications for the post, ie being able to drive and run an office, as well as being a good mixer, necessary when having to deal with civilian seamen and diverse nationalities, offered him the job.

Both men flew to Kure and immediately ran into problems. The Americans also ran an LST Control unit, somewhat more heavily manned with five officers, twenty-five enlisted men and nine master pilots, and it was with this last group that difficulties arose. The Americans had issued an irrevocable ruling that all LSTs, including the newly-joined British ones, could only be beached if one of these American pilots was actually carrying out the beaching. The first British LST to arrive in theatre was RASCV *Charles Macleod*, commanded by Captain John Marr, a redoubtable shipmaster who stood no nonsense. When informed by Major Vincent that no LSTs were allowed to beach without an American pilot, Captain Marr made it quite clear that this procedure was certainly not going to be implemented on his ship and furthermore no so-and-so Yankee pilot would ever set foot on his bridge!

On Captain Marr's first mission, an American pilot duly joined the ship for the beaching operation, but never got anywhere near the bridge. Captain Marr carried out a faultless beaching and, observing the pilot hanging about on the upper deck with nothing to do, politely invited him into the saloon for a drink. But the pilot, in high dudgeon, stormed down the gangplank and reported the incident to US LCT control. Considerable diplomatic exchanges followed, with the

Americans first complaining to the Australians, who had requested the LSTs in the first place. They replied that the LCTs were not in their command structure, being under the control of GHQ, Far East Land Forces, who in turn told the Americans that the ships were under the direct orders of the War Office in London, which finally referred them to 'On the Spot Officer i/c', that is to say, Major Vincent. Major Vincent was equally as forceful and dogmatic as Captain Marr and fully supported his attitude and that of the other LST captains that US pilots would not be allowed to beach British LSTs. The Americans then gave in gracefully and all involved became the best of friends.

Following *Charles Macleod*, the other three RASC LSTs were *Maxwell Brander*, *Frederick Clover* and *Reginald Kerr*. Although based at Kure, Major Vincent and Corporal Robinson made frequent trips in the LSTs to Korean ports, which both men thoroughly enjoyed, Corporal Robinson in particular as he had been offered honorary membership of the Officers' Mess, which included messing in the wardroom, a rare distinction for an Army NCO. No doubt it was deserved, however, as the Corporal was charged, *inter alia*, with ensuring prompt delivery of the ship's mail, a very important factor in keeping up the morale of any ship's crew and a duty that Robinson took very seriously indeed.

Sadly, however, in the latter part of 1952 all seven RASC LSTs worldwide were handed over to the North Atlantic Shipping Company and later transferred to the British India Shipping Company. This meant that although continuing to be tasked by the Army, the LSTs were no longer part of the Army's Navy, now flying the Red Ensign and manned by Merchant Navy personnel. In retrospect it seems strange that in the middle of what had developed into the biggest war since 1945 and in which the Army LSTs were playing such a vital part, the decision was taken to 'privatise' these ships and crews. One can only surmise that the reason for this must have been at the behest of the Treasury, who saw it as a cost-cutting exercise. Be that as it may, the result was, at a stroke, a huge cut in ships and men of the RASC civilian fleet, and it also brought about the demise of the LST Control unit.

However, the closing down of the British LST Control in Korea did not mean that it was to fade from memory completely. At the time of writing this book, ex-Corporal Peter Robinson was doing good work as co-ordinator of the Stamp Appeal for Guide Dogs for the Blind. He was directing this Appeal to members of the British Korean Veterans Association and in June 1996 he celebrated the naming of his sixth dog for this worthwhile task. The dog was named Major Vincent after Peter's old CO and, thanks to the Stamp Appeal, in a few more months enough money had been raised for two more dogs. At the suggestion of Major General Peter Downward, President of the BKVA, in recognition of the excellent work done by Peter Robinson with the Stamp Appeal, the eighth dog was called Robbie after him. So the memory of LST Control in Korea lives on with Guide Dogs Major Vincent and Robbie proudly honouring the `smallest unit of the British Army in Korea'.

At this time, the Army's Navy continued its broad range of duties elsewhere. A unique role was played by RASCV *Isinglass* on 7 June 1950 when the 48ft 'Derby Winner' class high speed target tower was given the honour of carrying the body of the late Field Marshal Earl Wavell from the Tower of London to Westminster Pier for his funeral service in Westminster Abbey. This was the first occasion that a national figure would be transported on the River Thames for his funeral since Nelson in 1806. The coffin was carried from the White Chapel in the Tower of London, where the Field Marshal's remains had lain in state for some days, by soldiers of his old regiment, The Black Watch. On arrival at Tower Bridge Pier the coffin was laid on the after deck of *Isinglass*. Major D.E. Cuff, RASC, the Commanding Officer of 632 Company RASC (Water Transport), was commanding the launch, his crew consisting of a staff-sergeant coxswain, watermen and engineers. Dignitaries embarked on *Isinglass* were Lord Keren, the only son of the late Field Marshal, the Lieutenant of the Tower and the Resident Governor, while a Yeoman Warder in full ceremonial dress was positioned at the bows. Three launches provided an escort, a Port of London Authority vessel stationed ahead of *Isinglass* and on each quarter the barge of the Commander-in-Chief, The Nore and a launch representing the London Division, Royal Naval Volunteer Reserve. Upon arrival at Westminster Pier the coffin was ceremoniously transferred by the bearer party to a gun-carriage and the cortege then proceeded to Westminster Abbey for the memorial service.

In 1951 the responsibility for repairs to the ships of the RASC Fleet was transferred to a new organisation, the Fleet Repair Unit, REME, commanded by Lieutenant-Colonel D.M. Wright REME. Upon this appointment the existing Superintending Engineer and Constructor of Shipping, Rear-Admiral R.C. Boddie RN (Retd) and the holder of the post since 1936, retired and the office was to lapse for ten years. The newly-formed unit now joined the Fleet Administrative Unit RASC at Kingston-upon-Thames. The Fleet Repair Unit was to carry out its duties until 1961, commanded by a succession of Lieutenant-Colonels, until October 1959 when the post was held by a Major REME, who proved to be the last REME commander of the unit.

By 1951 the RASC Fleet presence at Cairnryan had fallen to twenty vessels, all civilian-manned, including the four coasters *Marquess of Hartington, Sir Evelyn Wood, Sir Walter Campbell* and *Malplaquet*. Also on station were two ADCs and two trawlers, *Mull* and *Prospect*, employed as escorts to the dumping craft. Although nominally `on the strength' at Cairnryan, the veteran coasters were often employed on tasks other than dumping ammunition, examples being *Sir Evelyn Wood* undertaking such diverse duties as freighting stores from Aberdeen to Stromness, then south to the Thames to load an ammunition ship strike bound by a lighterman's industrial dispute and later returning to Cairnryan. The coaster *Sir Walter Campbell* also took part in exercises at Appledore with Territorials carrying out loading stores into landing craft and then discharging on to beaches. In this task she was accompanied by *Sir Evelyn Wood*. Both coasters remained for some time at Appledore, periodically sailing to Barry and loading further stores for the training of the part-time soldiers. Two RASC 'River' class launches were also in attendance. *Sir Evelyn Wood* additionally carried out voyages to Cherbourg and Brest, followed by freighting cordite from France to Felixstowe. *Marquess of Hartington*, the other 'oldie' at Cairnryan, carried out training exercises with Royal Engineers at Marchwood, which included two voyages to the Channel Islands to familiarise RE sailors with navigation and ship handling. A further Channel crossing involved visits to the D-day beaches at Arromanches and to the port of Le Havre. She also undertook the towage of a large naval target from Portsmouth to Dover and when back at Marchwood embarked cadets from Southampton Nautical College for sea training. The newest coaster, *Malplaquet*, built in 1939, was sent out to Singapore, while the trawler *Mull*, after conversion to an oil-burner, together with alterations to increase cargo capacity, also ceased her duties as escort to Cairnryan ADCs and made the long voyage to the Far East. On arrival at Singapore, both ships were engaged in carrying stores to Penang, Mull now manned by local civilian seamen with RASC officers and NCOs.

There was still a number of Mk III LCTs in service throughout the UK and overseas but these were being phased out and replaced by Mk IV LCTs, but not in the same numbers. It was policy not to give the Mk IVs names, although apparently some crews were in the habit of painting birds on the funnel representing those used as call-signs. However, the last Mk IVs in service, all military-crewed, bore names: these were *Augusta, Arno, Arakan* and *Akayab*. The last two, together with an unnamed ADC, were not sold until 1961, but in 1952 records show the Fleet included four Mk IIIs and three Mk IVs.

In January 1953 the UK was hit by hurricane-force winds which, coupled with high tides, led to serious flooding on the East Coast together with extremely rough seas in most waters around the British Isles. The ferry *Princess Victoria* was caught in this storm between the west coast of Scotland and Northern Ireland on 31 January. Her stern doors were breached by heavy following seas and she foundered with the loss of 128 lives. Urgent calls for assistance were broadcast to shipping in the Irish Sea and among those which took part in search and rescue operations was *Marquess of Hartington*. The only vessel berthed at Cairnryan with a full head of steam, the sixty-seven year-old coal burner, commanded by Captain Corvan, immediately put to sea despite appalling conditions. Regrettably by the time the elderly coaster had reached the scene, all hope for rescuing any survivors was lost, but nonetheless the ship recovered nine bodies and brought them back to shore. It is interesting to note that a previous rescue had been carried out by *Marquess of Hartington* in 1896, also coincidentally in the Irish Sea but on that occasion with happier results. On passage to Woolwich the then much younger War Department vessel, while some 26 miles off Cork, observed distress signals flying aboard the ketch *United Friends*, registered at Plymouth and bound for Cork with coal. The ketch had lost all her sails in a gale on the previous day and could no longer be steered. Furthermore she was leaking badly due to heavy seas straining the hull. Her crew, following a day of continuous hand pumping, were in an advanced state of exhaustion and the only course of action for the master of *Marquess of Hartington* was to transfer the men of the stricken ketch to his ship. This was done, with the saved seamen being fed and given fresh clothes, while the War Department vessel made an unscheduled call at Plymouth where the men were put into the care of the Shipwrecked Mariners Society. It was indeed fortuitous that the *Marquess of Hartington* had been in the vicinity and rescued the crew of *United Friends*, as shortly afterwards the ketch foundered. The coaster therefore had more than lived up to the traditions of the Army's Navy in rescue work, while also maintaining the history of longevity in Army ships. Another vintage Army vessel was to be involved in that month in relieving a community cut off by the flooding on the East Coast. The Isle of Sheppey was completely isolated by flood water, and the motor barge RASCV *Katharine II* (built 1930 and often used for towing the gun barge *Gog*), was used to carry medical supplies and food to the island, including a daily delivery of 2000 gallons of fresh milk, sailing between Chatham and Sheerness until the flood waters receded and the roads were passable again.

A more pleasant duty awaited the veteran *Marquess of Hartington* later in 1953. This of course was the year of the coronation of Queen Elizabeth II and to commemorate the great occasion various events were taking place throughout the year. One of the most prestigious of these was the Coronation Fleet Review held at Spithead in June and which involved hundreds of ships from the Royal Navy, Commonwealth navies, foreign navies, the Merchant Navy and fishing fleets, together with ships representing the various UK government departments, these of course including the Army's Navy. According to available information, the sole representative flying the Blue Ensign with Crossed Swords was our indomitable veteran of the RASC Fleet, the civilian-manned coaster *Marquess of Hartington*, now well into her twilight years. Certainly one of the oldest vessels present, she displayed a splendid appearance, largely due to the efforts of her crew. Many spectators at the Review have testified to her spick-and-span turnout, dressed overall with shining brass and gleaming paintwork, while because of her iron construction the hull was in uniquely good condition. Of course her general aspect, with teak decking, companionways and bridge, was reminiscent of an earlier era, augmented by a tall, thin funnel in buff with black top and open wings to the bridge. Her raking masts revealed to the knowledgeable that here was a steamer that could be rigged for sail and this further added to her silhouette as being that of a product of the nineteenth century. Needless to say, the crew were inordinately proud of having the honour of being the only Army ship present at the Fleet Review.

One addition to the Army's fleet in 1953 was the water carrier *Spalake*, of 600 tons displacement and a maximum speed of 10½kts. Of wartime construction, she was one of a class of six, all with names prefixed with 'Spa'. Built for the RN and originally manned by RFA personnel, although crewed later by HM Dockyard personnel under the direction of the Naval Victualling Department, they were named *Spa, Spabeck, Spabrook, Spaburn, Spalake* and *Spapool*. All had chequered careers; one (*Spapool*) flew the White Ensign for a short period of time as a temporary naval vessel, while *Spabeck* carried out special, and hazardous, duties with experimental submarine fuel. However, two were to be transferred to the RASC Fleet when Army bases in the Mediterranean experienced severe water shortages and the *Spalake* and *Spapool* carried out water runs, for example between Tobruk and Malta. *Spalake* served as an Army ship from 1953 to 1958, but the author has been unable to confirm the dates when *Spapool* was with the RASC Fleet.

By the end of 1953 the Fleet had decreased significantly in terms of vessels and tonnage, as well as in personnel, both military and civilian, and this trend was to continue over the next three years. The biggest factor leading to this was the transfer of the seven LSTs, together with their large crews, to commercial ownership the previous year. However, there were other reasons to account for the decline of the RASC Fleet, including the withdrawal of the British Army from overseas commitments as former colonies became independent.

Suez

1956 was to prove an eventful year for the Army's Navy, beginning with a rather gloomy outlook for the future of the RASC Fleet. On 17 February the Minister of Defence announced in Parliament that Coastal Artillery was to be abolished. This branch of the Royal Artillery had been wound up by January the following year, bringing to an end the RASC Fleet's role in target towing and range clearance duties. Also, ammunition dumping operations were coming to an end, resulting in further cuts in the Fleet. Sadly these cutbacks resulted in two newly designed units for the Army's Navy being scrapped. To support dumping operations, the Fleet Repair Unit REME had designed a special 65ft fire boat, fitted with a dedicated pump to operate monitors and foam spreaders. Now no longer required, the vessel ended up with the Kent and Essex Fire Brigade. Another successful invention was a 20ft radio-controlled target craft named 'Queen Gannet', which there was no longer a role for and was scrapped.

There were now only seven coasters and ADCs stationed at Cairnryan, supported by two 28ft diesel launches and RASCV *Bumble*, a 'Dickens' class launch. *Malplaquet*, having returned from Singapore the previous year, was one of the coasters based there and in January provided the setting for the presentation of awards for bravery to two of her seamen. The two men, Able Seamen McCubbin and Mylchreest, had at considerable risk rescued Second Officer Ashburn who, while the vessel was berthing, had fallen overboard and was rendered unconscious by striking his head on the side of the pier. Both seamen jumped on to a floating piece of timber and, at risk of being crushed between the pier and ship, pulled the officer to safety. The GOC, Lowland District, Major General R. Delacombe, presented Silver Palm Leaves and a Queen's Commendation for Gallant Conduct to both seamen and shortly afterwards the ship sailed again to Singapore.

Events in Egypt and the Middle East were now to provide more work for the Army's Navy. On 13 June 1956, in accordance with the terms of Anglo-Egyptian treaties, the last British troops were withdrawn from Egypt, including the Suez Canal Zone. On 26 July, the Egyptian President, Colonel Nasser, took advantage of this and seized the canal and all its assets. Although not supported internationally, Britain and France took strong objection to what they saw as the illegal seizure of an international waterway, the property of the Anglo-French Suez Canal Company. Plans were begun for retaking the canal with a combined task force, but there were problems for the British contingent owing to a shortage of suitable shipping. In view of this, the Chiefs of Staff Committee decided in September that for future operations, including the invasion of Suez, the Army must operate its own LCTs and that these, when engaged on operations, should be military-manned, continuing the further militarisation of the RASC Fleet as begun in 1943. But shortage of ships made this difficult to achieve. New Mk VIII LCTs were planned to replace the remaining

Mk IV LCTs, but to date only one, *L4086*, to be named RASCV *Arromanches*, had joined the Fleet. Other Mark VIIIs were to be taken up from the RN's 'mothballed' fleet, but the lack of military personnel and unexpected problems in restoring the ships to operational status prevented the success of the plan. Similar delays were being experienced in assembling the other elements of the task force, including RN and MN ships, and it was not until October that a cohesive invasion fleet began to take shape at Cyprus and Malta.

On 5 October, 76 Company RASC (LCT) was formed at Yeovil to operate the new Mk VIII LCTs, but their were insufficient military crews to man even the few LCTs available. But the RASC was determined that the Army's Navy would be represented in the Suez operation, and resorted to the time-honoured stratagem, used during the Second World War, of asking civilian personnel of the Fleet to volunteer for duties that should properly have been carried out by military personnel. There was no shortage of volunteers and three LCTs, together with a trawler as escort, were quickly provided with crews. These ships, the Mk IV LCTs *L403* and *L408* and the Mk VIII *Arromanches*, soon sailed in convoy to Malta. *L408* was crammed full of composite rations while the other two were laden down with vehicles and other stores. They then proceeded from Malta to Famagusta on Cyprus, the designated jumping-off point for the final thrust to Port Said.

On 14 October French envoys had met in secret with UK government representatives and submitted a plan that involved Israel invading Egypt across the Sinai peninsula towards the Suez Canal. Although Israel had no intention of taking the Canal this would form a pretext for the British and French to give an ultimatum to Israel and Egypt to withdraw completely from the Canal Zone. However, Israel would not go along with this plan unless Britain was party to it. The British at first were very reluctant, in view of their many links with Arab countries, to be seen as an ally of Israel, but in the end Prime Minister Eden agreed, provided that Britain's involvement with Israel would be treated as top secret.

On 29 October, Israeli troops entered Egyptian territory and after some hard fighting overcame Egyptian resistance. The Israelis then headed towards the Canal Zone, thus leading to Britain and France issuing an ultimatum to Israel and Egypt to withdraw their troops from the Canal Zone by the next day. Israel complied and halted its advance well short of the Canal Zone but Egypt refused to withdraw its forces. Britain and France then opened hostilities against Egypt on 31 October, with air strikes against air bases in Egypt, with the result that most of the Egyptian air force was destroyed on the ground. On 5 November British and French airborne troops made drops in the vicinity of Port Said, speedily overcoming resistance, while on 6 November seaborne landings took place on both sides of the canal at Port Said. The only serious resistance to the invasion forces was mounted by the so-called Port Said Militia, no more than armed civilians and some police, egged on by the Russian Consul in Port Said, who had also toured the town distributing arms to the populace. Port Said was in allied hands by 6 November with British and French troops advancing quickly south along both sides of the Canal.

The three RASC LCTs had proceeded independently to Port said and discharged their cargoes onto beaches. They then switched to ferrying vehicles and stores ashore from larger vessels unable to enter the harbour because of the large number of ships sunk there by the Egyptians. Further representation of the Army's Navy came from elements of the IWT, Royal Engineers, which was still extant after the Second World War, albeit much reduced in size. Units were at Mediterranean bases such as Tobruk and were to take part in the attack on Port Said, and also an Army Emergency Reserve Regiment had been mobilised to support regular personnel of the IWT. Vessels operated by the IWT included several ageing 'Z craft' which had to endure a high-speed tow from Tobruk to Port Said, at speeds approaching 20kts! Captured Canal Company vessels were also used, including double-decker ferries.

By 6 November it seemed that another 48 hours would suffice for the entire Canal Zone to be occupied by the allied forces, but on the evening of that day came a bolt from the blue, when Prime Minister Eden suddenly ordered a cease fire to take effect at midnight. The reason for this was that he had received a telegram from the President of the Soviet Union, Nikolai Bulganin, at the behest of Nikita Khrushchev, the General Secretary of the Russian Communist Party, stating that if the British and French did not cease hostilities against Egypt immediately, armed force, including veiled threats of missile strikes against targets in Britain and France, would be used by Russia. Russia's motives were twofold, firstly to support their protégé,

Colonel Nasser, but more importantly to distract the attention of the world at large from events in Hungary where an uprising was being brutally crushed by the Russian army. With hindsight, the Russian threat could have been ignored as the Americans immediately made it clear that such actions would lead to an instant reaction by the USA against the Soviets.

But it was American pressure that really ended the Suez operation. President Eisenhower, still smarting from what he considered being ignored by the British and French regarding military action to recover the Suez Canal, threatened dire consequences if the troops were not withdrawn. Furthermore, the UK was now on the brink of bankruptcy and appeals to the Americans for financial help were met with a flat refusal, even incurring pressure by the United States on the World Bank not to extend any monetary assistance whatsoever to Britain. Britain and France had little international support for their actions, while public opinion in Britain was sharply divided over the operation. Anthony Eden was now a sick man and on doctor's orders took a short holiday in Jamaica.

Again with hindsight, it is now believed by many experts in foreign affairs that, had Britain and France dug in their heels until the American presidential election was safely over, the Americans would have accepted the taking back of the Suez Canal as a fait accompli. This would have been especially probable as they became more and more aware that Nasser was fast becoming a leading proponent of the Soviets throughout the Arab world. However, with an ailing and absent Prime Minister, also bearing in mind the tense atmosphere at the time, Britain had little choice but to agree to the withdrawal of the British and French forces and handing over to the Suez Canal to a United National peacekeeping force.

Despite the valour and professionalism shown by the British and French forces, the Suez operation can only be called a disaster. The net results were a demoralised invasion force which had to be evacuated without attaining its objectives, the canal completely closed by block-ships sunk by the Egyptians, the loss of British and French credibility and influence in the Middle East, Prime Minister Eden being forced to resign in January 1957 and the canal, despite everything, remaining in Egyptian hands with Colonel Nasser being hailed as a hero throughout most of the Arab and non-aligned countries. Also the Soviet Union was able to complete its vicious crushing of the Hungarian revolt against communism with no intervention from the West.

During the three weeks until the final evacuation the RASC LCTs reversed their previous role, ferrying vehicles and equipment from the landing sites at Port Said to larger vessels offshore. *L408* took on a final cargo of NAAFI stores, including liquor, cigarettes and tobacco, and proceeded to Famagusta where, after discharging her load, she was employed offloading jerricans of petrol from a ship anchored off Limassol. Here it was discovered that she had lost one of her rudders. This could not be replaced in Cyprus so she sailed to Tobruk, from where she was towed to Malta by an RFA, encountering very bad weather on the way. *Arromanches* and *L403* were to remain in the Middle East until 1957, the former returning to the UK in March and the latter at Easter.

Operation 'Hardrock'

The main activities for the Army's Navy after the Suez debacle were the taking over of the ex-RN LCT Mk VIIIs, which were to be military-manned, and the establishment of the Hebrides Guided Missile Range, Operation 'Hardrock'.

Transfer of the LCT Mk VIIIs began in January 1957, and by March seven were on station at Portsmouth, a further five following slowly later, all being named after Second World War battles. Their names were *Agheila* (L4002), *Akyab* (L4037), *Abbeville* (L4041), *Audemar* (L4061), *Aachen* (L4062), *Ardennes* (L4073), *Antwerp* (L4074), *Agedabia* (L4085), *Andalsnes* (L4097), *Arezzo* (L4128) and *Arakan* (L4164). *Arromanches* (L4086) had been commissioned earlier and taken part in the Suez operation with a civilian crew. All these LCTs were administered by 76 Company RASC (LCT), which became fully operational by the end of February.

The new LCTs, larger versions of the Mk IV, were of 1017 registered tons with a length of 231ft and a beam of 38ft. Cargo capacity was 300 tons, while their cruising speed of 8kts gave a range of 4000 miles. Military manning requirements called for two commissioned officers and twenty-six other ranks, the latter inclusive of warrant and non-commissioned officers. Many problems soon emerged during the take-over from RN to RASC, one example being that the ships were required to communicate within RN radio networks. To achieve this it was necessary for the Royal Corps of Signals to provide two radio operators per ship. In addition to the shipboard operators, the squadron of LCTs had to have backup signals personnel for repair work, comprising a sergeant and a corporal, while overall supervision was carried out by a warrant officer with the title of squadron signals officer. Although the new LCTs posed some problems with more sophisticated machinery than hitherto with the Mk IVs, gradually these were overcome by the expertise of the REME workshop at HM Gunwharf, Portsmouth, while similar skills and experience were available at ST3, where there were several civil servants with appropriate nautical and marine engineering qualifications.

The reduction in men and craft of the civilian-manned element of the RASC Fleet was now beginning to bite, with a dozen high-speed target towers being paid off as surplus to requirements, following abolition of coastal artillery. This was to result in twelve masters, a similar number of chief engineers and thirty to forty ratings, becoming redundant, with more savage cuts being forecast for the future. Luckily the Suez operation, which resulted in voluntary civilian crews manning LCTs previously designated for military crews, helped to stem the tide.

Old age was also causing a reduction in the Fleet, the most noticeable being the departure in September 1957 of the coasters *Marquess of Hartington* (built in 1886) and *Sir Evelyn Wood* (built in 1896). In appropriately dank and miserable weather, both of the stalwart vintage ladies sailed from Cairnryan, lashed together in an alongside tow and bound for the shipbreakers' yard. A poignant sight indeed as a combined service of 132 years came to an end, heralded only by the long, sad note of a steam whistle.

In March 1957, Operation 'Hardrock', the establishment and maintenance of the Guided Weapons Range in the Hebrides, commenced. Although this was principally to be carried out by the new military-manned Mk VIII LCTs, some of the older civilian-manned LCTs were deployed in support. The operation began with an exploratory voyage by RASCV *Agheila* and *Abbeville* to Oban, and also to South Uist and Benbecula in the Outer Hebrides. Another location to be inspected was the uninhabited island of St Kilda, about 50 miles north-west of Benbecula. All the people living there had been evacuated by the government in 1932 because of the increasing difficulty of the islanders to eke out any kind of a living on the barren island. The proposed visit to Village Bay on St Kilda had to be postponed due to inclement weather, but on 15 April *Agheila* put an advance RAF party ashore. From then onwards the LCTs would, during the summer months, maintain a continuous service to the beach at Village Bay for RAF personnel to install electronic surveillance equipment for the Guided Weapons Range and also to construct support facilities such as accommodation and roads. The Head of Range was to be based at Benbecula. The LCTs ran from the Cairnryan Military Port to Lochboisdale, South Ford and St Kilda while the small airport at Benbecula was expanded to deal with increased traffic. Quite early in the operation it became only too clear that the beach and anchorage at Village Bay could be a dangerous location where sudden gales could erupt without warning, accompanied by heavy seas, thus rapidly placing ships in great peril. Just such conditions occurred in May of 1957 and resulted in *Abbeville* being driven hard ashore onto the rocks. She quickly became at risk of becoming a constructive total loss, but due to the excellent seamanship of Captain Tony Clark RASC and the assistance of a sister LCT, Arezzo, commanded by Captain Peter Barnard RASC, another fine seaman, the stricken vessel was saved. After three days of hard work, in bad weather, a tow line was passed by *Arezzo* to *Abbeville* and despite serious flooding of the engine room and steering flat, *Abbeville* was refloated at high water and although listing severely was successfully towed by *Arezzo* to Ayr. The commanding officers of the LCTs took to heart the lessons learned from the above incident and henceforth noted any signs of deterioration in the weather at Village Bay very seriously indeed.

Another civilian-manned RASC vessel to be deployed was the trawler RASCV *Mull*, firstly as an escort to the LCTs and then as a ferry between Benbecula and St Kilda during the winter months. The LCTs were able to operate on this run only between March and October, leaving *Mull* to carry out the service of ferrying passengers, food and mail to St Kilda. The main reason for withdrawing the LCTs in winter was that at the beach landing in Village Bay during these months, the sand was washed away by prevailing heavy seas, leaving only a hard rock beach. To overcome this, *Mull* was equipped with a work boat called *Puffin*, built to the design of a West African surfboat,

20ft in length and fitted with rollers for landing on a rocky beach. Propulsion was by water jet and she proved to be both hardwearing and successful, remaining with *Mull* until helicopters took over the service.

By 1958 the RASC Fleet had been reduced considerably, to a total of 169 vessels, including 58 in reserve of which several, including the motor barge *Katharine II* and the coaster *Malplaquet*, were due for disposal. During the latter part of the year the Fleet Repair Unit reduced its technical establishment to one lieutenant colonel, one major, one sergeant, a deputy superintendent engineer and constructor of shipping, two assistant SECSs, eight overseers and one draughtsman.

Although coastal artillery was no more, there were still several off-shore ranges, either already active or coming into service. Examples of these were Lulworth, used by the tanks of the Royal Armoured Corps, the infantry range at Hythe, experimental ranges at Shoeburyness, Pendine Sands and Eskmeals, the Castlemartin and Manorbier ranges in South Wales and of course the Hebrides Guided Weapons Range, which was finally handed over by the RAF to the Royal Artillery in the summer of 1958. All these ranges had to be patrolled by range safety craft and this duty was given to the civilian-manned vessels of the RASC Fleet, a continuation of a task carried out since the 1890s. In fact for the remainder of their existence, this was to be the *raison d'être* for the civilian element of the Fleet, despite the continuing militarisation of Army vessels.

In the summer of 1958, RASCV *Prospect*, an ex-Admiralty trawler, became yet another ship flying the Blue Ensign with Crossed Swords to carry out a rescue at sea. While on passage from Malta to Tripoli on 18 June, the Commander-in-Chief, Mediterranean, requested *Prospect* to render assistance to the Italian motor vessel *San Raimondo*, which had lost all power. The disabled ship was drifting off the Kirkennah Islands, east of Sfax in Tunisia, and, guided by US and RAF aircraft, *Prospect* found the stricken vessel and took her in tow. During the tow to Tripoli the tow line parted but was resecured, with *Prospect* delivering *San Raimondo* to Tripoli on 21 June. Salvage money was awarded to the master and crew for their excellent work.

Surprisingly, in view of severe cutbacks in numbers of civilian personnel, in 1959 a shortage of suitably qualified soldiers led to the training vessels *Yarmouth Navigator* and *Yarmouth Seaman* being transferred to civilian crewing and this was to continue until the final stand down of the civilian element of the RASC Fleet on 30 September 1988. Both these craft were converted from MFVs and in addition to training commitments carried out exercises with the RN and also undertook range safety patrols.

In April 1959 76 Company deployed four of their LCTs to load at the Joint Services Amphibious Warfare Centre near Poole. The Director of Supplies and Transport inspected the ships, after which they sailed to Benbecula. Commanded by Major Cluff the LCTs were carrying vehicles and equipment of the Guided Weapons Wing of the School of Artillery, which included `Corporal' missiles. Increasing cargoes of Royal Artillery rockets, personnel, fuel and equipment required the establishment of a new loading and discharging base for the LCTs on the Scottish mainland. Such a facility was set up at Rhu near Helensborough on Gare Loch. This mini-port featured a hard with a large apron which led to a main road, thus allowing lorries, trailers etc. direct loading or discharging across the hard through the bow doors of the beached LCTs. Blessed with good communications by road and rail, this base proved to be well-suited for the job.

The decision was taken in the same year to divide 76 Company into two flotillas, one to operate in Scotland and the other in southern England and by 1960 there were four LCTs maintaining the ever-increasing movement of freight and personnel to and from the Hebrides throughout the summer months. As for the southern flotillas, one LCT was permanently attached at Instow to the Amphibian Training Wing RASC and 18 Amphibious Squadron RASC, with commitments also to the REME Trials Branch at nearby Fremington.

On 1 April 1960, the Fleet Repair Unit became Fleet Repair Branch and in the following year moved from Kingston Barracks to Hillsea Lines, Portsmouth and in the process became purely civilian. Several ASECs continued to be appointed overseas, but with the general transition of Crown Colonies to independence, especially in the 1960s, these posts became superfluous except at Cyprus and Hong Kong. The civilian post of SECS was now brought back with the DSECS, Donald Harms, taking up the appointment, which had been a military one since 1 July 1951, held by an officer of REME.

Between the late 1950s and 1961, the RASC Fleet undertook sundry tasks in the UK and overseas. Also the RE sister fleet, the Inland Water Transport Service, was beginning to change from transport duties, with many of their vessels being formed into Port Squadrons involved with activities in support of military ports and stevedoring units.

During this period RASC vessels were taking part in exercises with the Royal Navy in various parts of the UK while in Europe undertook amphibious operations under the command of the West German Navy Amphibian Squadron. This task involved Mk VIIIs of the Southern Flotilla, now 76 Squadron RASC (LCT), in 1960 and lasted some two months. The UK LCTs attracted much praise for their expertise in beaching operations, coupled with excellent administrative and maintenance skills. RASCV *Antwerp* (later replaced by *Arezzo*) and *Aachen* were the ships involved in this NATO operation.

The Indonesian Confrontation

1960 was to be the year when the Mk VIII LCTs came into their own. As well as the Hebrides operations, they were now deployed overseas. Three Mk VIIIs were to be sent out to Singapore to replace Mk IVs which were rapidly reaching retirement age. In addition to finding crews and undergoing normal refits, extensive alterations were called for, such as extending the bridge wings to the ships' sides port and starboard, adding a boat deck on the fore deck and (mindful of the long sea passages to be undertaken with the possible risks involved) suitable lifeboats and davits fitted. All the vessels deployed were to be entirely military-manned. In January 1960 the first Mk VIII, *Ardennes*, arrived in Singapore, causing quite a stir as being entirely manned by RASC soldiers and thus a novelty to many port authorities en route. Two more LCTs, *Agedabia* and *Arromanches*, also proceeded to Singapore in September. All three were attached to 37 Company RASC (WT) at Pulau Brani. Although their primary tasks were to replace the Mk IVs, their commitments soon began to extend far beyond this, as will be shown below.

In 1961, shortly after operations recommenced in the Hebrides after winter refits, there was an urgent request from the Air Ministry that heavy radar equipment be transported to the island of Unst in the Shetlands. Although advised that conditions in the area meant it would be better to wait until June, the Ministry insisted on the urgency of the requirement, and the LCT Squadron safely landed the equipment on time at Balta Sound. The same year the Southern Flotilla was retitled 46 Squadron and among its commitments it was to be permanently at seven days' notice to be dispatched to the Mediterranean for duties with the Royal Navy. This entailed one of the LCTs being converted to a Squadron HQ. *Audemer* was chosen for this and extra housing was constructed on the flag deck to accommodate the HQ Staff.

Throughout the 1960s, Crown Colonies of the British Empire steadily became independent members of the Commonwealth, if they so desired to retain their links with the United Kingdom. Nearly all did so, regarding the Queen as Head of the Commonwealth, resulting in a final membership today of fifty-three countries, thirty-two of them republics. In spite of independence, many ex-colonies entered into agreements with Britain for military bases to be retained in their territories, a good example of this being Cyprus where British military establishments are still in existence. Ships and men of the Army's Navy have long been stationed in Cyprus as required, and also in other Commonwealth states.

North Borneo was to become part of Malaysia in 1963, but in the previous year Indonesia, which was claiming the whole of Borneo as Indonesian, commenced a confrontation against the North Borneo Territory. This involved invasion from Indonesian territory into North Borneo by guerrilla forces, who also attempted to incite the indigenous population to rebel against the forthcoming merger with Malaya. British forces in the area quickly became involved in countering the infiltration and it is interesting to note that the first elements of the Army's Navy to come up against the Indonesians were the craft and personnel of the RE IWT and throughout the confrontation until 1966 they worked in close co-operation with the RASC, later RCT, Water Transport. The RE used local craft for transport services on the coast and up rivers, later deploying their new ramped powered lighters. Previously the Singapore RE Port Squadrons had been kept busy supporting the anti-Communist terrorist campaign in Malaya, from 1948 to the mid-1950s. These Squadrons also maintained a service freighting all services ammunition from beyond the Singapore Harbour Board limits directly to ordnance depots thus avoiding arms and munitions passing through the densely populated city, where they could have been at risk from terrorist attacks.

Naturally the three RASC LCTs based at Singapore with 37 Company, Water Transport, also participated in the operations against the Indonesians and their supporters in North Borneo. The *Ardennes, Arromanches* and *Agedabia* were now manned by locally-raised crews, some of whom were Indians and Chinese from Singapore, with British officers and senior NCOs. Until then their tasks had varied from amphibious exercises on both the east and west coasts of Malaya to transporting artillery batteries to China Rock and also the setting up of a tank range in North Borneo. They also dumped at sea Japanese bombs hidden for years in the Malayan jungles and assisted in the setting up of a missile range off the Borneo coast.

The role of the LCTs in the Borneo confrontation was to secure marine communications and carriage of cargo/personnel to Brunei (which was devoid of deep water facilities and an adequate airport in 1962) from Labuan. Rioting had broken out in Brunei, instigated by Indonesian agitators, with the first LCT on the scene being *Ardennes* carrying Gurkhas tasked to act in support of the civil powers in suppressing the rioters and imposing a curfew. As the other LCTs from Singapore arrived, other duties included operating on the River Rajang to Sibu, together with voyages to Kuching and Tawau, both long passages to areas close to the border with Indonesia. These commitments led to two further vessels being deployed from Britain to boost LCT strength in Malaya and North Borneo. The newcomers to FARELF were *Antwerp* and *Arakan*, both manned by UK crews and formed into an additional squadron. All the LCTs were fitted with 20mm Oerlikon guns when operating in North Borneo, although it is believed that the Army's Navy was never called upon to open fire on either Indonesians or insurgents. What did occur however were long hours spent on lengthy sea passages.

A new type of craft was to join the British Armed Forces in 1962. This was the hovercraft, now recognised as a ship rather than an aircraft as had been the case in the very early days of these versatile machines. A tri-service unit, stationed at the Royal Naval Air Station, HMS *Aerial* at Lee-on-Solent, was tasked to investigate the possibilities of hovercraft having a military role. Officers and other ranks of the RASC were part of this Inter Service Hovercraft Trials Unit and took a leading part in the experimental trials of early civilian hovercraft as military craft.

A further advance in military hovercraft operations came about in 1964 with the forming of the Joint Service Hovercraft Unit (Far East) and its personnel included two RASC officers and two RASC soldiers trained as machine gunners. The Far East had been chosen as a suitable venue for the evaluation of military usage by hovercraft for two reasons – climatic conditions and also by 1964 a combat situation was readily available with the confrontation with Indonesia in North Borneo. Two SRN5 hovercraft were dispatched to Singapore as deck cargo in January 1965 and after a working-up period were stationed at Sabah. The terms of reference for the Joint Service Hovercraft Unit (Far East) included many diverse tasks such as support to ground forces in Malaya and seaward patrols off Singapore, together with operational trials in the areas under confrontation in North Borneo by the Indonesians. It is believed that these hovercraft, which were well equipped with radar, high, VHF and UHF radios, light armour plating and 7.62mm GPMGs, were the first craft of their type in the world to be engaged in a combat zone.

In July 1964 a unique vessel was to join the RASC Fleet. This was a prototype for a new class of general service launches, but what made her unique was that she had been designed by REME although built by J. Thornycroft. Named *Trevose*, photographs show her to have been a good-looking craft but sadly unsuitable as a GS launch and she was transferred to the training unit. No further *Trevose* class launches were built and in 1982 she was seconded to the RNR, being finally sold out of the service in January 1983. Another prototype, this time for a fast launch, entered service in March 1965. With the name of *Anglesey*, she appeared to be the only one of her type, with dimensions of 52ft x 16ft, and displaced 21 tons, drawing an after draught of 3ft 5in. She remained in Army service until the stand-down of the RASC civilian fleet in October 1988

Events in the Middle East called for a further pair of LCTs to be deployed overseas in 1965. In particular the future evacuation of British forces from Aden following independence of that colony would require support from the Army's Navy. Aden had joined the South Arabian Federation in 1963, which in turn became fully independent in 1967. Pressure had built up from nationalist insurgents, egged on by Egypt, for the British to leave Aden before the agreed date of November 1967 and the events arising from this are detailed in a later chapter The two vessels selected for the Middle East were *Arezzo* and *Agheila*, with the former stationed at Bahrain and the latter at Aden clearing stores and equipment.

In 1965, under the reorganisation of Logistic Services arising from the Macleod Report, some far-reaching changes were to affect all the vessels and personnel of the Army's Navy. A major transformation was to occur in July with the merger of the Royal Army Service Corps with transportation elements of the Royal Engineers, with the end product becoming the Royal Corps of Transport. This of course had an immediate effect on the RASC Fleet, civilian and military manned, while the amalgamation led to similar changes for the Inland Water Transport and Port Squadrons of the Royal Engineers. Full details of what the consequences of the above rebadging would mean for the two fleets will be examined in the following chapter.

Chapter 7

RCT to RLC: 1965-93

The newly-formed Royal Corps of Transport Fleet, arising from the merger of the RASC and RE fleets, was to experience many changes from its original component fleets. Once again the officers and ratings of the civilian ships of the RASC Fleet were to change their uniforms, officers removing the letters RASC from cap badges with the official ruling that they were not to be replaced by the letters RCT. In fact, as is shown in photographs, some officers did unofficially display RCT lettering below the Crown (presumably at their own expense). Ratings retained their RN round caps for some time and their cap tallies did now bear 'RCT' in gold lettering. Later the round caps were to be replaced by black berets bearing a silver crown. As regards the officers and other ranks of the RASC and RE soldier sailors, cap and tunic badges of the old Corps were replaced with RCT insignia. However, both civilians and soldiers continued to wear the Blue Ensign with Crossed Swords shoulder flashes. Also on the formation of the Royal Corps of Transport, the title of the Director of Supply and Transport (Army) was superseded by the somewhat cumbersome-sounding title of Transport Officer in Chief (Army) and this was to continue until 1977.

The Fleet Repair Branch, which had been completely civilianised in 1961, had now become responsible for the ex-RE vessels in addition to the old RASC craft. These additional vessels turned out to be a mixed bag, including as they did such diverse craft as ageing 'Z craft', tugs, barges, a cargo ship used for training stevedores and last, but not least, twelve ramped powered lighters (RPLs). All craft of the RCT Fleet were now to be designated RCTVs, although again a further significant change in titling was to come about in the following year.

Perhaps the most interesting of the ex-RE craft to become part of the RCT fleet was the previously-mentioned cargo ship used for training the stevedoring personnel of the Royal Engineers Port units. The ship, although kept in good repair, was not to undertake any voyages, but served as a static training vessel. Called *Empire Stevedore*, the ship was to remain at Marchwood Military Port, formerly the responsibility of the Royal Engineers but now to be a part of the Royal Corps of Transport. She had been at Marchwood for some time before the rebadging of 1965 and had a somewhat colourful background. Originally a German ship, she had been involved in conveying weapons and munitions to General Franco's Nationalist forces during the Spanish Civil War of 1936–9. She could in fact be described as a gun-runner because under international law it was forbidden for weapons to be delivered to either side during the Civil War. Unfortunately the author has been unable to discover her original German name. The ship fell into British hands in 1945 and eventually became part of the RE Fleet. She replaced another stevedore training ship with an 'Empire' prefix, but the author was unable to discover her full name. Names of the twelve ramped powered lighters taken into the RCT Fleet from the RE Fleet were as follows (year of building in brackets): *Avon* (1960), *Bude, Clyde, Dart, Eden, Forth, Glen, Humber* and *Itchen* (all in 1962), and *Kennet, Lodden* and *Medway* (all in 1967).

In 1965 another RN LCT, HMS *Rampart*, joined the Army's Navy and was renamed *Akyab*. Her silhouette was quite different from the existing Army Mk VIIIs, having a raised forecastle and an elevated bridge to afford clear vision ahead over it. These alterations were to accommodate a ramp large enough to handle the new, larger tanks.

In that same year, a ship of the Army's Navy was chosen to carry out a remarkable operation, which would entail two voyages behind the Iron Curtain to Finland, to deliver two large pressure vessels to the Helsinki power station on behalf of the British firm of boiler specialists, Babcock and Wilcox, who had been unable to find any merchant ships to do the job. The vessel chosen was the LCT *Abbeville*, commanded by Major Tony Pheby, and the first voyage was to take place in the late spring, the second in the summer. As the RASC Fleet became the RCT in July 1965, she would probably have been designated RASCV on her first voyage and RCTV on her second. The pressure vessels, loaded on bogies, were both loaded at Stobcross Quay, Glasgow, and were secured with great care on the vehicle deck by shore riggers. The deck had had to be strengthened not only because of the heavy weight of the load but also because both passages would be made north about. On the first trip, to take advantage of sheltered waters, they entered the Baltic via Limfjorden rather than the Skaggerak, but on the second voyage Abbeville traversed the Skaggerak and Kattegat. On both occasions when in the Baltic they were closely shadowed by Warsaw Pact warships. Indeed, on the first voyage one Russian ship passed so close astern that she cut *Abbeville*'s logline streamed from her stern. Although Major Pheby attempted to obtain recompense from the Russians for this, he was unsuccessful. *Abbeville* received a civic reception at Helsinki, with the British Ambassador and senior Finnish and Russian officers attending. A Russian Major-General, Y.Y. Malakhov, was photographed on the ship's flag deck with her coxswain WOII Taggart. The Finns had set up a landing beach near the power station but problems arose because the water was very shallow, but by ballasting the after tanks to raise the bows and with as much speed as was safe, on both trips the pressure vessels were discharged on their bogies through the bow doors and down the ramp. At the end of the operation, Babcock and Wilcox expressed their delight at a job well done.

In October 1966 the publication of a Royal Warrant resulted in another important change for the Army's Navy. The Warrant read:

'Her Majesty the Queen has graciously permitted operational vessels of the Army flying the Army Ensign commanded by Army officers and manned by military personnel in uniform to be titled "Her Majesty's Army Vessels" and to fly the Union Flag at the fore when moored or dressed overall under way.'

Of course, when the above warrant was issued there was no such thing as an Army ensign, the only flag flown by Army vessels being the Blue Ensign with Crossed Swords, which had been the flag for RASC craft and now was flown by all RCT vessels, military or civilian manned. The RE Fleet, on its merging into the new RCT Fleet, had to abandon its own Blue Ensign defaced by a Winged Thunderbolt held in a Clenched Fist.

It therefore became necessary for a new Army ensign to be designed for RCT ships which would meet the requirements of the Royal Warrant. Neither of the two Blue Ensigns described above would suffice as these were Corps flags, even though the only Army ships now in existence were operated by the RCT. The task of designing it fell to HQ Maritime Group RCT, Portsmouth, commanded by Brigadier P. Henson OBE, while it would be manufactured by the Flag Loft, HM Dockyard, Portsmouth. The Army Ensign's design was finalised as Blue Ensign defaced by Crossed Swords, which were in turn superimposed with a Lion and Crown. This did not mean of course that at that time, or in the future, only vessels of the RCT would be entitled to fly the Army Ensign and be titled HMAV. For example, in the highly unlikely event that the Brigade of Guards were ever to operate a ship, commanded by an officer of the Brigade and manned by guardsmen in their uniforms, then that vessel would be entitled to fly the Army Ensign. Although in 1966 it appeared inconceivable that any ships would ever fly the Army Ensign except those of the RCT Fleet, events were to overtake this in 1993 when the Royal Corps of Transport was amalgamated with other Corps to form the Royal Logistic Corps, which led to vessels of the new RLC Fleet which complied with the conditions of the Royal Warrant being permitted to fly it. The first occasion on which the new Army Ensign was flown was by RCT LCTs during an exercise named 'Waggon Trail' in the Solent at Stokes Bay on 17 May 1967. Observing the new Ensign afloat and later inspecting one ashore, was Sir Alan Jolly QMG, Admiral Sir Desmond Drayer, G.W. Reynolds Esq MP, Parliamentary Under-Secretary of State for Defence (Army) and Major-General E.H.G. Lonsdale, Transport Officer-in-Chief (Army).

In April 1966, the Joint Services Hovercraft Unit (Far East) was disbanded after completing a successful programme of trials and evaluations. Other trials of hovercraft had taken place in the UK (temperate conditions), Africa (desert conditions) and in the Canadian Northwest (arctic conditions). Later that year 200 Squadron RCT was formed as an operational military hovercraft trials squadron, consisting of four SRN6 Mk 2s, each with a capability to carry thirty men. The Hovercraft Squadron was divided into two Troops, each with their own workshop and tasked to undertake trials and evaluations of hovercraft in military operations. Under the direction of the Squadron Headquarters, the next few years would see the Army's hovercraft being deployed to many areas in the UK and overseas in order to examine the usefulness of these uniquely adaptable craft in a wide range of environments.

Following the formation of the RCT, the former RE Port Training Regiment ceased to have only a training role and became 17 Port Regiment RCT. Similarly the Water Transport Companies RASC had a change of name, *eg* 20 LCT Support Regiment RCT. Thus, as regarded the UK, RCT water transport units were divided between seagoing military- or civilian-manned craft and those, with mainly military crews, engaged in port/stevedoring operations. Both these groups came under the command of Q (Movements) 1 with their major task being the movement of stores and equipment between the UK and Northwest Europe within the framework of NATO.

Aden 1967

Most of the handovers of former Crown Colonies to their new independent governments in the 1960s were peaceful, accompanied by a dignified ceremony with great goodwill on both sides. But there was to be a notable exception in Aden, where the handover was due in November 1967. For some time prior to this there had been serious fighting between nationalist insurgents and the security forces, and a district of Aden, known as Crater, had become a no-go area for the police and army, having been taken over by very well-armed rebels. This presented the serious risk that the British withdrawal might take place under fire, putting not only the garrison but also the civilian population in serious danger. Therefore, the removal of military stores and equipment, and personnel including civilian British subjects, began some months before the formal handover. Playing an important part in this sealift was the LCT *Agheila*, which had been on station at Aden since 1965, along with Merchant Navy LSTs on charter to the Army. *Agheila* in fact left Aden before the final evacuation, returning to Portsmouth some months beforehand. She was the only overseas-based LCT to do this, the rest being disposed of locally. Before that, she carried out a long voyage to Durban with a special cargo for the South African armed forces, thus becoming the first Army-crewed LCT to cross the equator. At this time *Agheila* was commanded by Captain C.E. Rawlinson RCT who, after pre-sea training in the officers' training ship HMS *Worcester* (the author had also gone to this establishment, albeit many years earlier), had served in the Canadian Pacific shipping company as a cadet and navigating officer. While undergoing RNR training he was offered a direct commission in the Army and joined the RCT Fleet. He later moved into the mainstream of the Royal Corps of Transport, holding a number of command and staff appointments until leaving the Army in 1990. Having gained an MBA, he subsequently graduated from Edinburgh University with a PhD in military logistics management. At the time of writing this book, he was serving as an officer in the Royal Army of Oman, being in charge of the Sultan's Armed Forces School of Transport. This is a rare privilege as he is the only non-Omani officer in their Army to hold such a senior post.

In the event the withdrawal from Aden was accomplished without too many problems, thanks largely to Lieutenant-Colonel 'Mad Mitch' Mitchell leading his Argyll and Sutherland Highlanders into the Crater on 4 July and remaining there until the very last moment of the final day in November. Although `Mad Mitch' and his `Jocks' were criticised by some, including his Commanding General, for their somewhat heavy-handed treatment towards the inhabitants of the Crater, it is now recognised that this action certainly saved lives.

Malta

Elsewhere Britain was retaining bases in countries that had gained independence but remained in the Commonwealth. British forces were to remain for some time in Malta following independence in 1964 and included were launches of the Army's Navy. In particular three RASC/RCT craft were to carry on doing a task which for many years in several British colonies had been a speciality for Army vessels, that is providing maritime transport for colonial governors. Malta was served at different times in this respect by three craft, firstly conveying by water the Governor and then, with change of the national status, the UK High Commissioner. The three launches involved were the 50ft launch *Scrooge* ('Dickens' class), which was military manned, the 44½ft fast launch *Eden* ('British Rivers' class) and the 48ft target tower *Call Boy* ('Derby Winner' class), these latter two crewed by local civilians. In the later days of her service, *Scrooge* was employed for recreational purposes and renamed *RB II*. In this role she was used by all the British forces stationed on the island for beach parties etc. She was sold locally out of service in 1972, renamed *St Mary* and used for taking tourists on cruises. *Call Boy* and *Eden* were both sold to commercial interests in 1973, the former, renamed *Hornblower II* and still used for tourist cruises from St Pauls Bay while the latter, at the time of writing, was working as a fishing boat.

The UK and Norway

In 1967 the UK-based LCTs began to take part in NATO exercises in Europe, notably in Norway. *Andalsnes* was to pioneer this task by sailing first to Zeebrugge, followed by a passage to the Norwegian port of Tromso. She carried troops and vehicles under winter conditions and was the first of the Army LCTs to operate well above the Arctic Circle. She then went on to make two more voyages to Norway, on the first one carrying hovercraft of 200 Hovercraft Squadron RCT, to take part in an evacuation exercise. The second visit to Norway was to the southern town of Andalsnes to pay an official visit to the town after which the vessel was named. The town lies several miles from the sea at the head of Romsdalsfjord and during the Second World War saw heavy fighting for the town while the evacuation of British troops was taking place in 1940. The visit to the town was considered a great success by both sides with the townsfolk offering much hospitality to the crew of *Andalsnes*. In 1968 Mr Harms, Superintending Engineer and Constructor of Shipping, retired after seven years in the post and was superseded by Mr A.S. Blight CEng, MIMechE. Alan Blight was to hold this appointment until the date of his retirement in 1989, having witnessed the demise of the civilian-manned craft of the RCT Fleet on 30 September 1988.

Hong Kong and the Far East

In 1968 the military hovercraft unit, 200 Squadron RCT, was deployed to Singapore and undertook trials throughout the Far East and Australia. Other commitments of the RCT Fleet included a presence in Hong Kong which was to continue until the year before the colony was handed back to China in 1997.

An outstanding feature of the RCT fleet in Hong Kong was a beautifully maintained 'British Rivers' class fast launch called *Humber*. This vessel was mainly employed to convey Army VIPs, in particular the Commander British Forces (CBF), a post usually held by a lieutenant-general. The author, then serving as a senior marine officer in the HK Government Marine Department, often noted the extremely smart appearance of *Humber* and her well-turned-out crew. Her hull was painted an unusual shade of blue, while her always clean upperworks and woodwork, enhanced by shining brass fittings, fully justified a noteworthy place among other VIP launches, such as HE The Governor's ceremonial barge, manned by Marine Department seamen and the Commodore-in-Charge Hong Kong's barge with Royal Navy personnel. *Humber* was crewed by locally enlisted personnel of the Hong Kong Military Service Corps, while the coxswain would be a British NCO of the RASC, later RCT.

A further embellishment to the launch for many years was provided by a coxswain who commanded her for a considerable time during the 1960s. This was Staff Sergeant 'Pop' Tye BEM, RASC/RCT, a splendid representative of the Army's Navy, always immaculately turned out and, above all, the proud possessor of a magnificent handlebar moustache, clearly visible from behind as well as in front. It was widely believed that his hirsute adornment was the finest in Hong Kong, possibly throughout the Far East, while the author can certainly testify that his appearance on formal occasions always gave just that extra edge to any ceremonial activities involving *Humber*. Staff Sergeant Tye, on completion of his Army service, chose to take his discharge in Hong Kong and settled into civilian life there. He obtained the post of Inspector on the Star Ferries, where his equally smart bearing in his Inspector's uniform, coupled with the bristling moustache, soon made him a familiar figure to the thousands of passengers daily crossing the harbour by ferry. It was during his time with the ferries that the 'Cultural Revolution', instigated in 1966 throughout China by Chairman Mao Tse-tung, spilled over into Hong Kong, leading to riots and widespread disruption of daily life by Communist elements in the colony. This soon developed into a campaign lasting several months involving bomb attacks on government buildings and leading commercial enterprises in failed attempts to bring Hong Kong to a standstill. A prime target of the terrorists was the Star Ferry Company, providing as it did an important lifeline for the many commuters travelling daily between Victoria and Kowloon. With his military background it was natural for 'Pop' Tye to be involved in security precautions as part of his duties as an Inspector on the Star Ferries. It was at the height of the bombing campaign that 'Pop' was to be thrust into the public gaze with a courageous act. While on duty at the Hong Kong side ferry terminal he became aware of a suspicious object that had been left on one of the passenger embarkation decks. Immediately clearing the area of passengers, he then took the object, consisting of a carrier bag, in his hands and made his way towards one of the embarkation deck windows, with the intention of depositing the bag into the waters of the harbour. Unfortunately the bag, which contained an incendiary device, exploded before he could do so, with the result that 'Pop' suffered severe burns. The Hong Kong press gave considerable coverage to this incident and by the time he returned to duty following treatment for his injuries, his reputation with the public had been greatly enhanced. However, history does not reveal whether his valuable moustache suffered any irreparable damage in the fire!

Throughout the post-war years when the Army's Navy maintained a presence in the colony, their craft were often to be engaged in many tasks peculiar to Hong Kong. Apart from the obvious commitments to provide water transport for the various military units of the garrison to and from Hong Kong Island or Kowloon to the outlying islands or remote areas in the New Territories, many of the latter completely devoid of roads or rail links, the RASC/RCT craft were often deployed on somewhat unusual tasks. During the summer months the colony was invariably subjected to typhoons passing near to Hong Kong or, less frequently, suffering considerable damage and loss of life caused by the centre of a mature typhoon passing directly over the colony resulting in winds of hurricane force. This in turn leads to very rough seas and flooding, sometimes accompanied by serious landslides, throughout urban and rural districts. Naturally these conditions also cause much damage to shipping throughout Hong Kong waters, with vessels being driven ashore or colliding with other ships and in extreme cases being sunk with loss of life. Following the passage of a typhoon, calls for assistance would come from many isolated villages in the New Territories, with the affected locations often impossible to reach by land. The Armed Forces would always deploy men and equipment to render aid, such as medical assistance, evacuating people from areas of devastation, supplying temporary accommodation and restoring damaged bridges and roads. The vessels of the RASC/RCT Fleet would play a full part in such operations by providing water transport and lines of communication to and from remote areas following the passage of typhoons. In many cases sea transport was the only means of getting aid to the offlying islands and those villages in the New Territories unapproachable by land, even in good weather.

Within the Hong Kong garrison there existed a unique unit, in fact the sole surviving such unit in the British Army, 414 Animal Pack Transport Troop, consisting of mules trained to carry heavy loads while their handlers were Gurkhas drawn from these soldiers from Nepal who for many years formed an integral part of the British Army serving in the colony. The splendid animals of 414 Troop always 'brought the house down' at the annual Queen's Birthday Parade, beautifully cleaned, polished and well behaved while wearing ceremonial saddle cloths and gleaming brass accoutrements. Also the mules, belying an undeserved reputation for evil temper, were often seen at fetes and charity fairs giving rides to children and never once misbehaving while carrying out this task. But of course their *raison d'être* was to provide transport in harsh terrain where only tracks existed. It followed therefore that the mules, with their handlers, were frequently carried as unusual cargo in Army LCTs to 'jumping off' locations in the New Territories, from where they could proceed along tracks denied to vehicles up into mountainous regions. The author is not aware whether, when seaborne, the mules suffered from *mal de mer*!

An important role for the British Armed Forces in Hong Kong was that in times of unrest, such as the 'Cultural Revolution', provision was made for military aid to the civil community. Close co-operation between land forces and the Royal Hong Kong Police was maintained at all times. This was symbolised by the acronym POLMIL. Even in peaceful times, at least once a year for an entire day the Army could be seen taking over from the Police certain tasks, such as traffic control for instance. Naturally the RASC/RCT vessels were involved in support of the RHKP at such times by providing water transport as necessary. Although it never happened, in the event of, say, the ferry crews obeying a call for strike action, the Army vessels would also be called upon to provide cross-harbour services. RASC/RCT craft were based at Sham Shui Po and also used Gordon's Hard on Lantao Island, which the Army's sailing club also utilised.

Elsewhere in the Far East the Port and Maritime Squadrons of 33 Maritime Regiment RCT were being kept busy and covering a large area. Based at Singapore, their sphere of operations covered Malaysian waters, including Borneo, while following rebadging, as in the UK, 33 Maritime Regiment now found itself operating different types of craft from RASC days. In addition to the already existing RASC Fleet vessels, *eg* 'British Rivers' and 'Derby Winners' class fast launches, harbour launches and general service launches, previous RE craft were incorporated into the new RCT 33 Maritime Regiment. These additional craft included ramped powered lighters, barges, tugs and 'Z craft', all previously manned and operated by the port elements of the Royal Engineers.

RCT vessels and men had important commitments in Borneo, where the confrontation with the Indonesians was not to end until 1966. In this location 37 Maritime Squadron deployed a general service launch and three harbour launches, while 10 Port Squadron provided a Uniflote for supplying the bases at Wallace Bay and Kalabakan. An additional task was to crew the Brunei government vessel *Nakhoda Manis* until she was transferred to the Royal Brunei Malay Regiment.

When Singapore seceded from Malaysia in 1965 and the Borneo campaign with Indonesia ended in 1966, it was only a matter of time before a the British forces in Singapore became surplus to requirements. As the various units of the British Army left the city state, or were disbanded, much of their equipment was offered to the

161

Singapore government for their forces or sold locally to commercial interests. The first Mk VIII LCT to be deployed to Singapore in 1960, *Ardennes*, was acquired by the government, in whose service she was to remain as the Singapore naval vessel *Cairn Hill* until 1975. With Aden finally evacuated in 1967, there now remained only Hong Kong, Cyprus and Malta as British overseas bases with significant representation from the Army's Navy.

There was, however, a small military presence in British Honduras, the only British possession in Central America, necessary to combat bandits infiltrating from neighbouring Guatemala, a country that had long laid claim to the colony. Included in the garrison were several RCT launches, usually commanded by NCOs and kept busy as in the mainly jungle terrain communications with the interior and border regions were dependent on usage of the rivers and creeks. Although operations against bandits in border regions and on the coast were involving RCT launches in certain areas of British Honduras, as in other colonies throughout the Empire a launch was provided for the use of the Governor.

Marchwood Military Port

The previous Royal Engineers port and stevedoring elements which had been transferred to the Royal Corps of Transport were now consolidated at Marchwood Military Port. With the title of 17 Port Regiment RCT, there were four troops within the regimental structure. Ramped powered lighters and towed flexible barges or dracones, together with attendant tugs and workboats, were the responsibility of 471 and 473 Troops. The remaining two Troops, 472 and 474, had the task of operating and manning Mexeflotes, large pontoons powered by two harbourmaster outboard engines. Designed to fulfil several functions, they could be used as static piers, even with T head extensions, also as large lighters moving cargoes from ship to shore or vice versa, from ship to ship or between different shore locations. A further feature was their capability to be attached to Royal Fleet Auxiliary LSLs, either dismantled aboard the LSL for long ocean passages, or secured outboard to the sides of the ship in a vertical position. Upon arrival at an anchorage or berth, they could be lowered down to the water and loaded *in situ* by the ship's gear. Alternatively, they could be released from the ship's side, moved round to the bows and loaded through the bow doors and ramp. Lashed firmly across the bows, they could also be utilised as a hard landing for the LSL's ramp. The LSLs could, in suitable weather conditions, make passages with the Mexeflotes secured to the ship's sides, which avoiding having to dismantle and stow them. These powered pontoons were to be deployed in many places at home and overseas, while although responsible to Port Operations in whichever port they were working, the Mexeflotes, manned by soldier sailors of the RCT, were often based aboard the LSLs, especially in remote locations or under combat conditions. The ubiquitous Mexeflotes were to come into their own when providing valuable service during the Falklands campaign of 1982.

The carriage of military cargoes from UK to Belgian ports was badly affected by a seamen's strike in 1966. Marchwood Military Port took up the strain while the RCT landing craft undertook the freighting of the cargoes. In 1968 another strike led to a repeat performance by Marchwood and the LCTs, with the latter by now having been found to possess the capability to carry up to thirty-two standard-sized containers. This commitment to carry military cargoes between Marchwood and the Continent was to continue for many years to come. Three large dolphins were constructed off Marchwood Hard in 1967 to provide more secure berthing for LCTs and also larger vessels in the future, such as the chartered Ministry of Transport LST *Empire Gull* (ex-HMS *Trouncer*), which was later to become an RFA. In 1970 a new class of RFAs, landing ships (logistic), were also to operate from Marchwood Military and although officially under Ministry of Defence (Navy), have always been tasked by the Army.

The reason for these berthing additions was the massive programme of replacing the now obsolete Centurion tanks, the standard tank of the British Army in Germany under NATO command, by the new and larger Chieftain main battle tank. Substantial numbers of Chieftains were loaded at Marchwood and discharged at Antwerp, while similar numbers of Centurions were to make the return voyage to Marchwood and this activity was to continue until 1970. Afterwards a new programme was to be instigated, with Chieftain tanks sold to Iran being loaded into LCTs at Marchwood and ferried out to a heavy lift ship at anchor in Cowes Roads for delivery to Iran.

The year 1969 was marred by a serious accident involving HMAV *Abbeville*, which on 10 October was in collision with the Dutch coaster *Phoenix*. At the time *Abbeville* was in company with three other LCTs, *Aachen*, *Agheila* and *Andalsnes*, all of them bound for Gothenburg, having departed Portsmouth early that morning. By evening the four LCTs were passing through the Straits of Dover, sailing independently but at the time in line ahead, with *Abbeville* leading. Although weather conditions were excellent with calm seas, visibility due to fog patches was at times down to 50 yards. Shortly after 21.30 hours, *Abbeville* transmitted a radio signal to the effect that she had collided with another vessel. She then made a further signal reporting that the vessel she had struck (later identified as the *Phoenix*) had foundered within five minutes. One crew member of the *Phoenix* had died but all the crew of *Abbeville* were safe. However, the LCT had sustained severe damage to her bow doors and had to put into Dover the following day, while the other three Army ships continued their voyage to Sweden.

Empire Stevedore, the static ship used for training the stevedores of the RCT Port Squadrons at Marchwood was replaced in 1969. Her replacement, *Marchwood Freighter*, previously named *Woodlark*, although kept in a seaworthy condition, was likewise never destined to make any voyages under the Blue Ensign with Crossed Swords. Instead she remained alongside at Marchwood as a static training vessel for the Army's stevedores until she was disposed of in 1974.

By the late 1960s, it was becoming evident that the existing range safety and control craft were coming to the end of their active lives. Supervision of seaward firing ranges was being carried out mainly by the 'Derby Winners' class of target towers and 50ft 'Dickens' class launches. The slow speed of the 'Dickens' launches was also proving a handicap when dealing with modern coastal traffic that would, if straying into danger areas, show a clean pair of heels to these launches. By 1968 this problem had been noted and in 1969 a new class of command and control launches (CCLs) was ordered, consisting of six twin screw, 41ft fibreglass launches, all bearing names of seabirds. Possibly due to acceptance of the lowest bid being the sole criterion for awarding the tender to build these launches, various shortcomings soon came to light, leading to unreliability with a high record of breakdowns. The first in service of the 'Seabirds' was *Petrel* (1970) and she almost immediately had to be returned to the builders for the rectification of serious faults. The remainder of the class were named *Fulmar* (1970), *Tern, Skua, Shelduck* and *Shearwater* (all in 1971). Despite faults and breakdowns, their much higher speeds and reputations as good sea-boats, made for an improvement upon the elderly launches now beyond their 'sell-by dates'.

The military hovercraft trials squadron, 200 Squadron RCT, had returned to their UK base from the Far East by Christmas 1969. The Squadron then undertook trials for NATO, especially in Norway, but also in southern Europe. With the success of the Squadron in tackling all tasks given to them, one would have thought that the future of military hovercraft in the British Army would be secure. One example of this in Norway called for four SRN6 Mk 2 hovercraft to land over a hundred Norwegian soldiers, together with their weaponry, clothing and equipment, including skis and sleds. The simultaneous landing of the four hovercraft upon a presumed lightly-defended beach resulted in the troops and equipment being offloaded in less than 30 seconds, with not a single man getting his feet wet. Rapid withdrawal of the craft then met a time-limit of less than 2 minutes from touchdown. This landing could not have been accomplished by regular landing craft due to shallow water studded with rocks offshore and the operation amply demonstrated how hovercraft could cross dangerous waters to deposit men and equipment ashore well above high water marks, thus avoiding personnel, weapons and stores becoming saturated by water. Sadly, despite these successful trials, the need to cut costs meant that in 1974 the Ministry of Defence announced that the military hover-craft project was to be abandoned, so while many other countries took up this concept with enthusiasm, Britain, the inventor of hover-craft, was to be left bereft of military hovercraft.

The 1970s

With the advent of the 1970s, the RCT Fleet was now fully committed to several specific roles, namely servicing the military outposts in the Outer Hebrides, and the carriage of military vehicles, equipment and stores from Marchwood to ports on the Continent (both these tasks carried out by the Mk VIII LCTs with military crews), while range safety and control was maintained in the UK by the civilian-manned command and control launches. Both these types of craft were mostly based at HM Gunwharf, Portsmouth, together with the vessels used for training purposes.

Overall administration of the Fleet, as far as the military-manned craft were concerned, was invested in 20 Maritime Regiment RCT stationed at St George Barracks, Gosport. The civilian-crewed vessels were incorporated into 18 Maritime Squadron RCT, which was part of 20 Maritime but with its administration located at the Gunwharf. The previous title of 20 Maritime had been 20 LCT Support Regiment and during their tenure at St George Barracks additional responsibilities had fallen upon them. This came about due to the discontinuance of an Army Headquarters at Portsmouth. Until then the Senior Army Officer (Portsmouth) would have been stationed at Headquarters but now the senior ranking Army officer at Portsmouth had to be found elsewhere. Among other duties, for hundreds of years the Senior Army Officer in the Portsmouth district held the hereditary title of Military Governor of the Ancient Fortress of Portsmouth, together with being the Keeper of the Keys of the City. Ceremonial duties included the presentation of the Keys of Portsmouth to HM The Queen whenever the Monarch made an official visit to the City, a purely symbolic gesture as of course Portsmouth has no city gates. The powers that be now decreed that in future the Commanding Officer of the St George Barracks, namely the CO of 20 LCT Support Regiment RCT (reformed in 1971 as Maritime Regiment RCT), should take on these ceremonial duties and also be appointed Station Commander, Portsmouth/Gosport. This situation was to continue until 1989 when all maritime activities at St George Barracks were transferred to Marchwood Military Port and the Keys of Portsmouth were handed over to the RE Diving Establishment at HM Gunwharf. It should be noted that the actual keys were lodged at the Portsmouth Guildhall as had always been the case.

In 1972 the Army's Navy received another feather in its cap when the Royal Aircraft Establishment sought assistance in the manning of a research vessel. Previously crewed by RAF Marine Branch personnel, the rundown of the RAF Fleet coupled with a shortage of officers and airmen with marine qualifications, meant that the RCT civilian element was requested to take over the operation and manning of the craft, an ex-RN inshore minesweeper of the 'Ham' class, which had been converted to carry out sea trials of RAF scientific equipment. The vessel was commissioned with an RCT civilian crew and renamed RCTV *Richard George Masters VC*. Commanded by the late Captain Bourne, who was later to become the last RCT Fleet Master Superintendent, the ship was to gain the distinction of making the last foreign-going passage by a civilian-manned vessel of the RCT Fleet, this being a return voyage to Gibraltar. She was later replaced by *Colonel Templer*, an ex-trawler also modified by the RAE for research work and this ship was to remain with the RCT until the stand-down of the civilian element in 1988.

Further acknowledgement of the skills and expertise of the Army's Navy came in 1974. The then Government of Iran, already buying substantial numbers of British tanks, was also taking delivery of two landing ships, *Larak* and *Henga*, built by Swan Hunter. No officers in the Iranian navy had any experience in commanding this type of ship and specifically lacked the skills involved in beaching them. The RCT was approached by the Iranians for assistance in training its captains designate in all aspects of command relative to this class of ship. Arrangements were therefore made for Major Simon Birch MBE RCT to join *Larak* and instruct the Iranian captain. Major Birch was to spend two weeks on this task in the Solent and the Channel and at the end of this time the Iranian captain `passed out' successfully by discharging tanks on to the beach of a bay in Dorset, with the exercise being watched by a number of senior Iranian officers. A similar training schedule was carried out some weeks later, this time in Iran, for the new captain of the other landing ship, *Henga*, and on this occasion Major Murray Jones RCT acted as his mentor.

Also during this year, as examples of the versatility of Army LCTs, clearance of projectiles by these craft from the Maplin Sands was being carried out, while HMAV *Abbeville*, commanded by Captain Roy Potts RCT, proceeded to Tromso and brought back the remains of a Halifax bomber shot down while attacking the German battleship *Tirpitz* during the war. The wreckage was discharged at Felixstowe for onward transportation to the RAF Museum at Hendon. Also in 1974 a similar aircraft recovery exercise was carried out by HMAV *Audemer*, commanded by Major Birch. Having embarked a Royal Navy diving team, *Audemer* proceeded to Norway and loaded a Skua dive bomber following its retrieval from a lake into which it had crashed. Audemer brought the fuselage back to Britain and discharged it on the hard at Lee-on-the-Solent, from where it was taken to the Fleet Air Arm Museum, Yeovilton.

Two years later, four of the Mk VIII LCTs, despite their age, were still in commission in the UK as HMAVs, these being *Audemer, Abbeville, Antwerp* and *Agheila*. However, their days were numbered, although *Audemer* was to soldier on until 1978 while *Agheila*, with an RCT civilian crew from 18 Maritime Squadron, was to be employed in ferrying duties from Marchwood until being disposed of in 1979.

In 1976 an ex-RAF 43ft rescue launch, numbered 1667, was transferred to the RCT Fleet and renamed *Minoru*, a name previously held by a 'Derby Winner' class high-speed target tower. The latter *Minoru* was sold out of RCT service to commercial interests in March 1981, renamed and at the time of writing this book was believed to be in use by the Irish Air Corps. The reason for this transfer from the RAF to the RCT was part of the continuing rundown of the RAF Marine Branch, which also included the transfer of eleven seagoing vessels and one harbour craft from RAF manning to civilian crews supplied by a commercial ship managing company. This involved retitling the

craft from HMAFVs to AFVs while the final closedown of the RAF's
Navy occurred at midnight on 31 March 1986. This signalled the
demise of a fleet with a fine and distinguished record, especially in the
field of air-sea rescue during the Second World War, and which had
been in existence since the inception of the Royal Air Force in 1918.

During 1976, as part of the Army's Navy's modernisation programme, a new class of vessel was to come into service, designated
landing craft logistic (LCL). Only two of these were to be built and
their function was to eventually replace the remaining Mk VIII LCTs.
It had been apparent for some years that there needed to be a new
type of ship to replace the Mk VIIIs, some of which had been in Army
service since 1956 and of course before that they had been RN vessels
for many years. In view of this, the then Transport Officer in Chief
(Army) had directed in 1969 that a start be made on research into
what kind of craft would be appropriate. Terms of reference would,
inter alia, ascertain what should be the correct road to take, an
updated but larger version of the Mk VIII or starting from scratch
with an entirely new design. There were schools of thought supporting
both the options, and both courses of action had pros and cons to
offer. The Mk VIIIs had in their favour a long record of reliability,
together with being adaptable for either deep-sea or coastal voyages.
Simple to build and operate, and able to carry a variety of cargoes, Mk
VIIIs also had excellent handling properties. Their principal drawback
was that their maximum speed was 8kts. Because it was essential that
a greater speed be achieved, it now became a choice of hull design, in
essence either a blunt bow, such as the Mk VIII design but incorpo-
rating updates, or a completely innovative design with a pointed and
streamlined bows section which was thought by some would help to
increase speed. While these arguments were still unresolved, an incident
occurred in October 1974 which was to provide the casting vote on
the final design.

This involved HMAV *Abbeville*, a Mk VIII LCT commanded by
Captain Simon Birch RCT, which was on passage from Harwich to
Tromso. Although on departure weather conditions were normal,
when half-way across the North Sea the vessel encountered a sudden
gale. Speed was reduced but as conditions worsened Captain Birch
decided to seek shelter at Den Helder, the principal Dutch naval base.
This entailed turning the ship with a consequent risk of broaching and
the manoeuvre was rendered even more perilous as the gale had now
reached storm force. Carefully timing the turn to take advantage of a
less powerful wave onslaught (the average wave height by now was

168

Illustrations for Chapters 7 and 8

Army hovercraft, 1966. In the
foreground is a SRN 6 Mk. II.
(HMSO/Crown copyright)

Launch of the Landing Craft Logistic HMAV *Arakan* at Brooke Marine Ltd, Lowestoft, on 23 May 1977.

HMAV *Aachen* landing Army vehicles in Schleswig-Holstein in West Germany in the 1970s. She was the only Army LST with twin funnels, a modification to keep exhaust fumes out of the accommodation. (HMSO/Crown copyright)

HMAV *Audemer* taking the disabled Danish coaster *Sine Boye* in tow, early April 1976, in the Irish Sea, continuing the Army's Navy tradition of rescues at sea. (Painting by Major Bill Wynn-Werninck)

Range safety launch RCTV *Alfred Herring VC* at sea between St Kilda and the Outer Hebrides in the late 1970s. (Painting by Major Bill Wynn-Werninck)

Range safety craft of the RCT Fleet exercising in the Solent in the 1980s. In the foreground is RCTV *Sir John Potter*. (HMSO/Crown Copyright)

Ramped powered lighters of the RCT Fleet at American Corner in Belize, 10 miles up the Rio Grande. (Author's collection)

The Falklands War: an RCL
being loaded aboard the
P&O ship *Strathewe* for
passage to the Falklands
in 1982.
(HMSO/Crown Copyright)

The RCL *Arromanches* at
Port Stanley, Falkland Islands,
in 1982. The 'tiger-stripe'
camouflage did not last long.

The *Arromanches* transferring
Argentinean prisoners to the
British ro-ro ferry *St Edmund*
for repatriation after the
British victory in the Falklands.

HMAV *St George* secured at 10 Port Squadron RCT, Akrotiri, Cyprus in 1983. Alongside her is RCTV *Hyperion*.

A mexeflote with an RCT work boat in attendance transporting a Sandringham flying boat from Lee-on-Solent to its permanent home at the City Aircraft Collection at Southampton in 1983.

HMAV *Arakan* landing the last surviving conning tower of a Great War U-Boat, recovered from the Baltic.

In an example of the Army's Navy maintaining naval traditions, a senior officer is 'piped over the side' of HMAV *Ardennes* in the 1980s. (HMSO/Crown Copyright)

At a Royal Review at Spithead on 27 July 1990 commemorating the 150th anniversary of the founding of the Cunard Line, HMAV *Ardennes* (foreground) represented the Army's Navy. HMY *Britannia* is shown passing between *Ardennes* and the *QE2*, while Concorde flys past. (Painting by Major Bill Wynn-Werninck)

An aging RPL in Belize. When the British garrison withdrew in 1994, the last three RPLs in the Army's Navy were sold to commercial interests in Belize. (Author's collection)

some 40ft) Captain Birch got onto a new southerly course without damage and made a safe arrival at Den Helder. Reporting on the voyage, Captain Birch emphasised how the bluff bows had weathered the heavy seas most satisfactorily with no great amounts of water entering the tank deck, which could have imperilled *Abbeville* through free surface effect. In fact the only water shipped was little more than spray, easily dispersed through her freeing ports. The outcome of this was the adopting of the bluff bows concept as the design for the new landing craft logistic, a contract for which had already been placed by the Director General (Ships) with the shipbuilders Brooke Marine Ltd of Lowestoft.

Work on the first LCL now commenced with the design and construction of a prototype LCL which was to be eventually named *Ardennes*. Proof that the blunt bow design was the correct one was confirmed by the tank-testing of a model by the Admiralty Experimental Establishment. It was also decided that an officer of the RCT with LCT experience should be appointed as Army Project Liaison Officer and be part of the design team. The officer chosen was Major Tony Pheby, who had much experience in commanding Mk VIII LCTs. Readers will recall his successful voyages to Helsinki with pressure vessels for a power station, at the time he was commanding the LCT *Abbeville*. At first working out of Portsmouth, Major Pheby soon based himself at Lowestoft in order to maintain closer links with Brooke Marine, Royal Navy and other Army departments in dealing with any design or construction problems. He was also to be in due course the first CO of the prototype LCL. More tank tests were continuing at the Admiralty Experimental Establishment, which resulted in raising the height of the poop deck slightly to improve sea-keeping properties. Also in order to achieve the best design for bows, bow doors and ramp, a full-scale mock-up of the bow doors was built at Brooke Marine's yard. It is interesting to note that despite the early arguments about the speed being affected by choosing either blunt or sharp bows, tank tests revealed that in fact the final factor governing speed was not the bow shape, but the fixed requirement for a shallow draught hull, necessary for beaching. In the event the maximum speed of the LCL was only 10kts, not a great advance on the Mk VIII. The length of the LCL was to be 237ft and power was to be supplied by two Mirrlees Blackstone ESL 8 MGR diesel engines giving a cruising range of 4000 miles. The Mk VIIIs obtained their power from four Paxman engines, two to each shaft and 1840bhp.

Innovations in the LCL included a soundproofed control compartment situated at the after end of the engine room which dispensed with engine room personnel having to wear ear protectors, while engines could also be controlled from the bridge. After some time in service a theory was advanced that another factor leading to the low speed of the LCLs was due to the small size of their propellers. Larger-sized ones were therefore fitted to replace the originals, but unfortunately the result was only a very small increase in speed to about 10½kts. The wheelhouse was equipped with the most advanced navigational aids, while her mast and funnel profiles were pleasing to the eye.

Perhaps the most important improvement, certainly as far as the crews were concerned, was the shift towards Merchant Navy standards of accommodation, rather than the more spartan RN style in the Mk VIIIs. Catering facilities were contained in a modern galley fitted with updated cooking and food preparation equipment and this was complemented by a spacious dining area for the troops. Also good cabin accommodation for all crew members was installed while extra berths were fitted for passengers. All this was vastly superior to the more utilitarian accommodation in the Mk VIIIs. Not for nothing were the soldier crews of that class of LCTs entitled to `hard lying money'.

To facilitate beaching operations a heavy-duty winch was fitted at the stern for the paying-out and weighing of the large kedge anchor. Maximum cargo capacity was 350 tons and LCLs were able to discharge and load on beaches with up to 250 tons of cargo aboard. They would be capable of operating in rough seas, *eg* off the Hebrides and other UK waters, Norway in support of northern NATO forces, the North Sea and also be able to undertake long voyages to and from the Mediterranean.

On 29 July 1976, HMAV *Ardennes* was launched with due ceremony by Her Royal Highness, Princess Alice, Duchess of Gloucester. Major Pheby duly commissioned *Ardennes* at Portsmouth on 2 December 1977, the Commissioning Order being given by Major General P.H. Benson CBE, Director General of Transportation. This somewhat American-sounding title had replaced that of Transport Officer in Chief (Army) in 1977. Tony Pheby's appointment as Army Project Liaison Officer had been taken over by Major David Nicholas RCT and his task was to supervise the construction by Brooke Marine of the second, and last, LCL, HMAV *Arakan*. Like his predecessor, he in turn was also to become the first CO of a new LCL, but sadly *Arakan* was destined to be the last of the class.

Of the Mk VIIIs still in service, HMAV *Audemer* was to go out in style, with the years 1976–9 proving to be her glory years during which period she displayed the high standards expected of ships belonging to the Army's Navy. Among these were of course longevity, saving life at sea and representing the Army's Navy at Royal Fleet Reviews. In early April 1976 *Audemer*, commanded by Major Peter Robyns RCT, was in the Irish Sea bound for the Clyde. Having received advice from HM Coastguard that a Mayday message had been sent by a vessel requesting assistance having run out of fuel, Major Robyns proceeded to the position of the helpless ship. The distressed vessel turned out to be the Danish coaster *Sine Boye*, which was completely dead in the water, including being without lighting or auxiliary power in addition to lacking main engines. She was rolling heavily in a moderate swell and fair sea, but a line was successfully passed to her from the LCT. *Audemer* then took the Danish vessel in tow and brought her safely to port at Milford Haven. Ultimately Major Robyns and his crew received salvage money for their staunch efforts.

At the 1977 Silver Jubilee Fleet Review, HMAV *Audemer* represented the Army's Navy and performed this task magnificently. The Review by HM The Queen aboard HMY *Britannia* took place at Spithead on 28 June, with some 180 vessels took part. This was the first time that one of Her Majesty's Army Vessels had participated in a Royal Fleet Review and the Commanding Officer and crew were recipients of congratulations from all concerned on the smart appearance of ship and men, especially as pressure of work dictated that *Audemer* had only five days to prepare for the Review. The Royal Navy was of the opinion that she was the best turned-out vessel at the Review, praise indeed as apparently most naval ships would have had six months to prepare. A further feather in *Audemer*'s cap was that she was the oldest ship present, just taking this title from HMS *Reclaim*, the deep diving and submarine rescue ship. *Reclaim* was launched on 12 March 1948 and was the only RN vessel present that had also been at the 1953 Coronation Review. On the day of the Review *Audemer* was host to several VIPs who, mustered on the flag deck, were able to pay homage to the Queen as she passed in Britannia. This gathering of dignitaries, including Lt General Sir Anthony Farrar-Hockley, GOC Southeast District, has been captured in a painting by Major B.V. Wynn-Werninck RASC Retd.

Audemer had one last task to perform before her long service with the Army was to come to an end. This occurred on 24 April 1979 and was almost the finale to her long and distinguished career as an Mk VIII LCT with both the RASC and RCT. Now commanded by Captain Roy Potts RCT, she on passage through the Solent when she picked up a Mayday message from the sail training ship *Sir Winston Churchill*, to the effect that she had dragged her anchor off Cowes in a violent northerly gale. She had subsequently grounded on a mud flat near the entrance to Cowes Harbour and quite close to the break-water. The mishap had occurred just before the tide started to ebb and so it was essential to refloat her before she became hard aground. If this happened, in all probability as the tide fell there would have been a grave risk of the sailing ship heeling over with severe damage being caused, perhaps even becoming a total loss. Being the nearest ship, *Audemer* immediately accepted the call for help and proceeded to Cowes in poor weather conditions, including the strong gale resulting in heavy and confused seas and with pitch darkness adding to the difficulties of the rescue operation. *Sir Winston Churchill* had a crew of fifty-five at the time, forty-seven of whom were teenage girls and an attempt by them to pass a line to *Audemer* with an inflatable dinghy was a failure due to the fierce wind and powerful seas. Luckily the Cowes Harbour Master managed to pass a line by using his more suitable duty launch and once the line had been received aboard *Audemer*, the sailing ship was winched off and towed to safety, with the operation being illuminated by *Audemer*'s searchlight. For excellent seamanship and tenacity of purpose, Captain Potts and his crew were to receive a Certificate of Commendation from the GOC Southeast District, General Farrar-Hockley. Incidentally Major Wynn-Werninck later made an excellent painting of this rescue and also another of *Audemer*'s previous rescue of the Danish ship *Sine Boye*.

Although the 'Seabird' command and control launches were still managing to fulfil their tasks at the various firing ranges, they were subject to failings such as excessive noise, poor accommodation and recurring difficulties with fuel. It was therefore decided that a 15m class of launches, based on the commercial Talisman 49 hull and to be designated as range safety launches, was to enter service between 1977 and 1986, eventually to replace the GSLs, CCLs and *Anglesey*. Usually known as the 'Honours' class because all were named after winners of the Victoria Cross or George Cross, or alternatively bearing the names of those distinguished RASC officers who had attained the rank of general. Thirteen of this class were built. The first to enter service was *Samuel Morley VC* (December 1977), followed by *Richard Masters VC* (April 1980), *Joseph Hughes GC* (November 1980), *James Dalton VC* (March 1981), *Sir Cecil Smith* (July 1982), *Sir John Potter* (August 1982), *Sir Paul Travers* (October 1982), *Sir William Roe* (January 1983), *Sir Reginald Kerr* (March 1983), *Sir*

Humphrey Gale (April 1983), *Geoffrey Rackham* GC (December 1985), *Walter Cleall GC* (May 1986) and *Sir Evan Gibb* (August 1986). Readers will recall that there were previous vessels with the names of *Reginald Kerr*, *Humphrey Gale* and *Evan Gibb*, all of them LSTs taken over from the Royal Navy in 1946.

Two additional craft were built for the RCT Fleet in the late 1970s and early 1980s for service in the Atlantic and the Outer Hebrides. These were 24m RAF-designed RTTL Mk 3 air-sea rescue launches, but fitted out somewhat differently for Army service. Classified as RCTVs, their names were *Alfred Herring VC* (1978) and *Michael Murphy VC* (1983). Both these fine craft were to remain in the Army's Navy until 1 October 1988 when, with the other civilian-manned launches, they were transferred to the Royal Maritime Auxiliary Service.

In 1977 the RCT Maritime Regiment based at St George Barracks, Gosport, was granted the Honorary Freedom of the Borough of Gosport and this was marked by the usual ceremonial commemoration of the event, while in 1979 the regiment became the 20 Maritime Regiment RCT. Another ceremonial occasion was carried out by 20 Maritime when their commanding officer presented the Keys of Portsmouth to the nearly installed Lord Mayor.

The LCL *Ardennes* (commanded by Major Guy Yeoman RCT) was now fully operational, having completed her initial tasks in Scotland, followed by NATO exercises at Antwerp, also Denmark in conjunction with the Danish Navy. Later she was to carry the Lieutenant Governor and Commander-in-Chief from Jersey to the UK upon his retirement. Meanwhile the other LCL, *Arakan*, commanded by Major David Nicholas, was settling down to carrying NATO cargoes from Marchwood to Antwerp.

Among overseas commitments Belize was still proving to be a trouble spot with a requirement for a presence by British forces. The first RPL had arrived there in 1977 aboard the landing ship dock HMS *Fearless* and others were to follow in commercial heavy lift ships. In December of that year the then Quartermaster General personally persuaded the Belize Sugar Corporation to permit the RPLs to dock for refits at their slipway in Corozol, North Belize. RPLs were to continue service in Belize for many years to come, even after Belize had become an independent Commonwealth country in 1981. Of course, discerning readers will have appreciated that when events were taking place in 1977, Belize was still called British Honduras. However, the author decided to use the post-colonial name of the country as not only is it now a more familiar title, but the inhabitants frequently used the name Belize before independence. With the Naval Dockyard in Malta closing in 1977, this effectively brought to an end a very long history of the British Armed Forces being stationed on the George Cross Island, which had provided the Maltese people with employment and a thriving economy in the provision of supplies and services to the Navy, Army and Air Force. So now, apart from Belize, the only other overseas locations where craft of the RCT Fleet could be found were the Crown Colony of Hong Kong and the British base at Akrotiri in Cyprus. Another base, this time in the UK, to be lost in the latter part of the 1970s was the Hard at Rhu, situated between Helensburgh and Garelochhead. After many years service with the Army's Navy, it was now to be relinquished to the Royal Navy and is believed to be still in use by the RN as a storage facility. In 1978 the short-lived title of Director General of Transportation was replaced by Director General of Transport and Movements, which was to survive until 1993.

The Falklands War, 1982

A new ship was to join the RCT Fleet in 1981. This was the ammunition carrier *St George*, which replaced the elderly Royal Fleet Auxiliary *Empire Gull*, a veteran of many years on the BAOR supply run from Marchwood to Antwerp. *St George* was built at Bideford by Appledore Shipbuilders and on 1 October 1981 she was commissioned at a ceremony officiated by the Chaplain General in the presence of the GOC Southeast District, General Sir Paul Travers KCB. It could be said that she, commanded by Major A.M. Paterson RCT, was probably the finest-looking ship in the Army's Navy since the pre-war *Sir Hastings Anderson*, which readers will recall being lost in the Japanese attack on Singapore in 1942. With her very comfortable crew accommodation, *St George* proved to be a popular ship with the soldier-sailors. An added attraction was that she made several ocean voyages in addition to her regular runs between Marchwood and the Continent. Among her long-haul passages were visits to Cyprus, Gibraltar, Canada and the United States. Her range of modern navigation systems included an autopilot, believed to be the first to be installed in an Army ship. Sadly, unlike most Army craft, she was not to achieve longevity of service. Seven years to the day after commissioning on 1 October 1981, *St George*, together with her civilian-manned sisters from 18 Maritime Squadron RCT, was transferred to the Royal Maritime Auxiliary Service on 1 October 1988.

When Belize became an independent Commonwealth country in 1981, an uneasy calm was to follow. The British government was hoping it would now be able to withdraw British forces, the newly independent Belizean government being advised that they should no longer assume some 2000 British soldiers plus RAF Harriers would continue to be stationed there. Despite long, drawn-out attempts to mediate with the Guatemalan military dictatorship, the threat of an invasion of Belize by their bellicose neighbours persisted and so throughout the 1980s there was still a need for British military support. As far as the RCT Fleet was concerned that meant the RPLs were to remain on station. These workhorses were, however, ageing rapidly and it was decided that a new class of vessel would be needed to replace them.

The new class of vessels were to be designated as ramped craft logistic (RCL) and classified as RCTVs, coming into service between 1982 and 1985. Nine were built and all took names from the old Mk VIII LCTs, except for the names *Ardennes* and *Arakan* which of course had been given to the two LCLs. The following names and pennant numbers, shown in brackets after names, were allocated to the RCLs. Two prototype were named *Arromanches* (L105) and *Antwerp* (L106) and completed in 1982, while the remainder were called *Andalsnes* (L107), *Abbeville* (L108), *Akyab* (L109), *Aachen* (L110), *Arezzo* (L111), *Agheila* (L112) and *Audemer* (L113). They were somewhat larger than the RPLs but still small enough to be carried on the upper decks of commercial heavy-lift ships, a capability that was shortly to be tested during operations in the South Atlantic to recapture South Georgia and the Falkland Islands from the Argentinean aggressors.

1982 was to see the invasion of the Falkland Islands and their dependencies by Argentina, a country held in thrall by a military dictatorship. This occurred on 2 April, followed the next day by the invasion of South Georgia. The small parties of Royal Marines, at both Port Stanley and Grytviken, South Georgia, put up a stout resistance, inflicting casualties on the invaders and even damaging the Argentine warship *Guerico*. However, the overwhelming numbers of the Argentine forces was to prevail and eventually the two groups had to surrender. The reaction of the British government and people, under the strong leadership of Prime Minister Margaret Thatcher, was immediate and positive, resulting in a Task Force, titled `Operation Corporate', of more than a hundred ships and 28,000 men being assembled and despatched to the South Atlantic, a voyage of 8000 miles. South Georgia was recaptured on 25 April and all Argentine forces in the Falkland Islands finally surrendered on 14 June. This campaign, the fiercest since the Korean War, was a triumph for British sailors, soldiers and airmen, despite being outnumbered by enemy air and ground forces.

No ships of the RCT Fleet were to participate in the Falklands until after the cessation of hostilities, but elements of the Port Squadrons were seconded to the RFA Landing Ships Logistic to operate the Mexeflotes attached to these ships and of course were to face the same perils of air attacks as the RFA crews. However, the two prototype RCLs, *Arromanches* and *Antwerp*, were sent to the Falklands following the reoccupation of the islands, both travelling as deck cargo aboard heavy lift commercial ships. The two RCLs had first to be overpainted with black `tiger' stripes, a form of camouflage recommended by the Royal Marines as being suitable for the South Atlantic. Sadly, within a short period of time the stripes had washed off, resulting in the two vessels reverting to their naval grey. A new unit, 73 Squadron RCT, had been formed at Port Stanley and the RCLs found themselves very busy with a range of tasks as the islands began to recover from enemy occupation and war damage. Among their varied duties was the transporting of large numbers of Argentine prisoners of war from their holding areas to the ships waiting at Port Stanley harbour to repatriate the POWs back to Argentina.

The remaining RCLs were to come into service gradually until 1985 and this year marked the final new building of sizeable craft for the RCT Fleet, with the exception of the last two 'Honours' class of RSLs, *Walter Cleall GC* and *Sir Evan Gibb*, which entered service in 1986. From then on only small numbers of craft, such as work boats for port operations or Rigid Raiders for evaluation, were to be added to the Fleet, while the trend would be to whittle down the strength of the Army's Navy, whether civilian or military manned. Neither were any more transfers from the RN nor the RAF to occur and thus the only changes to the RCT Fleet were a programme of gradual disposal, at least until 1988, of vessels wearing the Blue Ensign with Crossed Swords.

The not-very-successful 'Seabird' or *Petrel* class of command and control launches had already started to be struck off the list of RCT craft. In 1979 *Shearwater* had been written off as a loss, while *Tern* was transferred to the Marchwood shipwrights in 1983, with *Petrel* going to the RN the following year to be stationed at HMS *Vernon*. The Sea Cadet Corps was to benefit by receiving *Shelduck* in 1986, the RMAS gained *Fulmar* in October 1988 and *Skua* was taken over by the RNR, also in October 1988. The last two of course had fallen victim to the closing down of the entire civilian-manned element of the Fleet, together with HMAV *St George*.

Although the reason for the building of the RCLs was to replace the RPLs, many RPLs were to continue in service, especially overseas, for some time after the early RCLs had started to come into service. Nowhere was this more evident than in Belize, where the British Army was to maintain a presence until 1994. One reason for this was an incident in 1986 when a party of Guatemalan tourists built a makeshift lavatory on the Belizean island of Hunting Cay. Naturally this set alarm bells ringing with memories of the party of Argentine scrap metal merchants setting up a base in South Georgia, which had sparked the Falklands campaign. No time was lost therefore in dealing with the situation. A party of Royal Engineers went into action and swiftly dismantled the offending structure. After erecting a more elegant edifice, in order to emphasise that Belize, although an independent country, was part of the Commonwealth and moreover enjoyed the protection of the British Army, a large Union Flag was raised over the new building. This and other incidents confirmed the need to retain British forces in Belize and, as far as maritime supply craft were concerned, this meant RPLs. These vessels were ideal for negotiating the creeks and rivers so they continued to remain on station until the British garrison had been scaled down to a small training establishment.

With the forming of the RCT, the crews of military-manned vessels saw some changes in items of uniform. As mentioned at the beginning of this chapter, the civilian crews had changed their uniforms accordingly but the soldier-sailors had begun to wear some naval-type clothing items prior to 1965. An example in the post-war period was that Army personnel in the RASC Fleet had been issued with white polo-neck sweaters, similar to those worn by submariners of the RN, and also blue working trousers. With woollen pullovers becoming standard issue in all three services (the RN resisting this item until 1974), each service retained their service colours for these new uniform items. The civilian members of the RCT Fleet were the first to have navy blue 'woolly pullies' following the lead of the Royal Navy but wearing the shoulder flash of Blue Ensign with Crossed Swords. They also took up the Action Working Dress (AWD) of the RN consisting of light blue shirt with dungaree trousers. It was soon realised that the blue woollen pullovers and blue trousers, together with AWDs, were also more suitable for the military mariners than khaki and this rig soon became standard for soldier-seamen, coupled with black berets bearing the Corps badge and not forgetting the time-honoured shoulder flash. It thus transpired that the men of the maritime element of the RCT were to become the only soldiers in the British Army to wear naval uniform, albeit slightly modified, issued by the stores department of the Royal Navy. At the time of writing this book, the position remains the same with 17 Port and Maritime Regiment, Royal Logistic Corps. Also over the years, certain new Army trades had come into being, examples of which were Marine Engineer, Navigator/Ocean Watchkeeper and Diver, Shallow Water.

The year 1988 proved to be devastating for the Army's Navy. Almost at a stroke, 20 Maritime Regiment RCT, situated at St George Barracks, Gosport, suffered not only the loss of the entire civilian-manned 18 Maritime Squadron but also HMAV *St George*, flagship and pride of the military fleet. Details of the farewell Fleet Review on 30 September are given in the Preface. All the 'Honours' class of RSLs, except *Sir William Roe* which was retained for service in Cyprus with a military crew, the last two CCLs, *Anglesey*, *Yarmouth Navigator*, *Alfred Herring VC*, *Michael Murphy VC* and two harbour launches, *05* and *08*, together with the civilian crews headed by their Master Superintendent, were transferred en bloc to the Royal Maritime Auxiliary Service. HM Gunwharf was also taken over by MOD (Navy) and became part of the shore establishment HMS *Nelson*. Sadly the transfer was not to last very long. On 3 June 1991 a contract was given to Messrs James Fisher of Barrow-in-Furness to man and operate the former Army craft. This led to all the ex-civilian Fleet crews, now RMAS, being made redundant. So, regrettably, the long history of the civilian-manned Fleet of the Army's Navy, together with their seemingly eternal home, HM Gunwharf, finally came to an end. With the disbanding of the civilian Fleet, together with the transfer of HM Gunwharf to the Royal Navy, there was no longer a requirement for the maritime part of the RCT to remain at St George Barracks in Gosport.

As had been planned for some time, 1989 saw the transfer of the soldier-sailors to Marchwood Military Port near Southampton. A merger had taken place between 20 Maritime and 17 Port Regiments to become 17 Port and Maritime Regiment RCT and from then on all RCT marine activities, including the training of ships' crews and stevedores, would be centralised at Marchwood.

The Gulf War and Yugoslavia

In 1990 a ship of the RCT Fleet was to represent the Army's Navy at a Royal Review at Spithead on 27 July, in commemoration of the 150th anniversary of the founding of the Cunard Line in 1840.

Chosen as representative of the Army at the Review was the LCL HMAV *Ardennes* and a painting by Major Bill Wynn-Werninck Retd shows her cheering ship while HMY *Britannia*, with The Queen embarked, passes between *Ardennes* and *QE2*. Other ships in the painting include HMS *Broadsword*, with the Cunarders *Vistafjord* and *Atlantic Conveyor*.

The following month, in fact within a few days, Iraq invaded Kuwait and Marchwood Military Port was galvanised into high-speed activity as a multi-national operation began to be mounted with the objective of firstly preventing Saddam Hussein from carrying out his threat to make further advances, this time into Saudi Arabia, and secondly expelling all Iraqi invaders from Kuwait. Although many months were to elapse before military action commenced, with intense diplomatic overtures being made to reach a peaceful outcome, time was not being wasted by the coalition of several countries, led by the United States, dedicated to accomplishing the liberation of Kuwait. Vast numbers of men, ships and aircraft were to be deployed into Saudi Arabia, neighbouring countries and adjacent waters by the coalition, which eventually consisted of forty nations. The British contribution amounted to 43,000 men, six destroyers, four frigates, three minesweepers, five support ships, 168 tanks and 300 armoured vehicles, together with seventy Tornado and Jaguar frontline aircraft.

The Gulf War actually commenced on 17 January 1991, with allied air forces mounting air strikes against selected targets in Baghdad and elsewhere in Iraq. Although ground combat flared up on 29 January when Iraqi forces captured the Saudi frontier town of Khafji, with the Saudis recapturing the town on 31 January, the real attacks on Iraqi occupation forces did not commence until 24 February. Hostilities ended on 27 February when Iraq had no option but to surrender and a permanent cease-fire was agreed between Allied and Iraqi commanders on 3 March. Although no seagoing craft of the RCT Fleet were involved in the Gulf War, elements of the Port and Stevedoring Squadrons played a considerable part in the build-up to military action. Some of these men were to spend several months at the Saudi port of Jubail during the period of operations.

In 1991 there were further overseas commitments for British Forces, this time in the former Yugoslavia, where fighting was to break out between the different ethnic communities, particularly in such places as Croatia, Bosnia and Herzegovina, with Serbia attempting to retain control over these breakaway republics. This state of affairs led to the United Nations or NATO setting up either peacekeeping or relief operations and the British Army, with troops of other nations, would take part in these actions. The first British troops were deployed under the charter of the United Nations to the former Yugoslavia in late November 1991 and a British presence there was to continue at various times and places up to the present day. The port of entry for these operations was the Croatian port of Split and this was to continue regardless of wherever the troops were to operate. As with the Gulf War, no seagoing RCT vessels were normally sent to Split. However, the author has been informed that the two LCLs, *Ardennes* and *Arakan* did visit the port in 1997, but no further details are to hand. However, again as in the Gulf War, elements of Port and Stevedoring Squadrons were involved at various times. Marchwood Military Port has been kept very busy though, as being the main loading and unloading facility for British Army equipment being sent to, or received from, the theatre of operations. In particular the RFA LSLs were being loaded and discharged in regards to the operations in the former Yugoslavia, also commercial ships on charter to the Ministry of Defence were attended to at Marchwood.

1993 was to be the year when once again, hopefully for the last time, a further merger of various Corps in the British Army took place. It was on 5 April that the amalgamation of the Royal Corps of Transport with several other Corps, some with long histories, came to fruition with the new title of Royal Logistic Corps. This resulted in many diverse support activities in the British Army unifying with one badge and details of this will be reviewed in the next chapter.

Chapter 8

The Royal Logistic Corps: 1993 to the Present

On 5 April 1993, the Royal Logistic Corps was created, embracing the former Royal Corps of Transport, Royal Army Ordnance Corps, Royal Pioneer Corps and Army Catering Corps, together with the Postal and Courier elements of the Royal Engineers. As far as the Army's Navy was concerned, its ships now would be designated Royal Logistics Corps Vessels (RLCVs), except those commanded by commissioned officers, which would remain HMAVs. The Blue Ensign defaced by Crossed Swords would continue to be the ensign worn by RLC vessels under the command of NCOs, while HMAVs carried on flying the Blue Ensign with Crossed Swords beneath a Lion and Crown. The only change in uniforms was a rebadging of caps, collars etc, while the shoulder flash of the Blue Ensign with Crossed Swords continued to be worn by the soldier-sailors. The title of Director General of Transport and Movements was replaced by Director General of Logistic Support (Army).

In 1994, with the threat from Guatemala now greatly diminished, the British Army finally withdrew from Belize, leaving behind only a small training presence. The last three RPLs, which were still in service and had been based in Belize for some time, were disposed of in that country. Their names, it is believed, were *Avon*, *Bude* and *Medway*.

June of that year saw the 50th anniversary of the D-Day landings in Normandy on 6 June 1944 and various events were to take place in Britain and France to commemorate the invasion. The first event at which vessels of the Army's Navy participated was the D-Day Commemoration Review of warships and merchant ships, many with veterans embarked, which took place at Spithead on Sunday 5 June. This Review was the biggest since the Coronation Review of 1953, with the Royal Navy, Royal Fleet Auxiliary Service and Merchant Navy ships participating, together with warships and merchant ships from Belgium, Canada, France, Greece, the Netherlands, Norway, Poland and the United States. The Army's Navy was represented by the Landing Craft Logistic HMAV *Ardennes*, commanded by Major Robinson RLC, while two RCLs were present at Spithead in support. Quite good pictures were shown of *Ardennes* in the BBC coverage of the Review, especially while HMY *Britannia* was passing her. *Britannia* had not only HM The Queen embarked, but also several Heads of State, including President Clinton. Few will ever forget the stirring sight of thousands of British and Commonwealth veterans of the Normandy Landings proudly marching in review before the Queen on the somewhat wet beach at Arromanches on 6 June, the actual date of the 50th Anniversary of D-Day.

Again TV coverage by the BBC was in the main superb and without doubt the final *pièce de résistance* was the backdrop provided by the three ships of the Army's Navy beached on the Arromanches sands, thus providing the symbolic presence in memory of the hundreds of landing craft which were there fifty years ago. The LCL HMAV *Arakan*, with Major Fiddler RLC in command, took centre stage and was flanked on either side by two RCLs, RLCV *Arromanches* commanded by Staff Sergeant Parr RLC and RLCV *Arezzo*, under the command of Staff Sergeant Boyes RLC. All three were beached with perfect stationing in line abreast. Commentary on BBC TV was spot-on, with an accurate description of *Arakan* and her role as an Army ship. But unfortunately, while the commentator was giving his spiel, the camera was fixed firmly throughout on one of the RCLs! Sadly, the D-Day commemorations were probably the last occasions of that kind at which ships of the Army's Navy would play a significant role.

The years following 1994 were to see sizeable reductions in the RLC Fleet for several reasons. The ending of the Cold War had brought about great reductions in British forces stationed in Germany and other European countries and this led to subsequent cutbacks in sea transport of military cargoes between the United Kingdom and ports on the Continent. Another reason for Fleet reductions was the forthcoming handover of Hong Kong to China, which would occur at midnight on 30 June 1997. The threat of privatisation on the grounds of saving money for the Treasury was ever-present and, due to sweeping changes in MOD thinking, newly-titled bodies had started to emerge. Classed as `agencies', these were based on commercial practices and were perhaps somewhat biased towards the privatisation of the support elements of the armed forces.

As regards the Royal Logistic Corps Fleet, as the ships and military crews remain under the Quartermaster General's Department at the time of writing this book and as part of the HQ Army (Land), the 17th Port and Maritime Regiment it appears that for the time being the status quo will remain. However, the task of training officers and other ranks at Marchwood in nautical skills were to come under one such agency, the Army Individual Training Organisation. This led to the General in command now being titled Chief Executive, with the way ahead becoming a 'business plan' to replace what used to be known as a clear aim. Although not widely known at the time, two of the RCLs were to change names, actually by the simple expedient of exchanging their name boards. This was *Arromanches* taking the name of *Agheila* and vice versa. The thinking behind this, especially as it occurred prior to the 50th Anniversary Commemorations of the D-Day landings, was to ensure that any Army's Navy presence should include a ship bearing a name synonymous with D-Day. RCL *Arromanches* would eminently fulfil this requirement, the bulk of the British troops involved having landed on the beach at Arromanches on D-Day Unfortunately *Arromanches* was stationed many thousands of miles away at Hong Kong, but a straight swap of names with another RCL in home waters would solve the problem.

After 1994 the Royal Logistic Corps Fleet was now to suffer a run-down in craft, due especially to the forthcoming handover of Hong Kong to China in 1997. The intention was to ensure that all Army craft in Hong Kong were to be taken out of service and sold locally well before the handover at midnight on 30 June 1997. Among the Army vessels serving in Hong Kong were three RCLs and one of these was RLCV *Abbeville*, which was duly disposed of locally and in good time before the handover date. However, because they failed to achieve a realistic sale price, *Agheila* (ex-*Arromanches*) and *Antwerp*, the two prototype RCLs, were transferred to Cyprus and there listed for sale 1995/97. The remaining Army craft at Hong Kong reached their selling price and also met their target date for disposal. The handover of Hong Kong to China more or less signalled the end of the British Empire as such and the event, with Great Britain represented by the Prince of Wales, was carried out with dignity on both sides and marred only by heavy rain, although some Chinese schools of thought would argue that such rainfall was a good omen for the future. Following the lowering and raising of the two flags, accompanied by the playing of the National Anthems of both countries, Prince Charles and the last Governor, Chris Patten, aboard the Royal Yacht *Britannia*, took their departure from what was now the Hong Kong

Special Administrative Region of China. Although technically the ceremony of transfer of power had brought to an end the association of Britain with Hong Kong which had lasted since 1839, the fact that Britain is a co-signatory of the Sino-British Declaration of 1984 would indicate that such an association would continue for some time yet. Sadly this would not mean that the British Army would have a role in the ex-colony and thus an association between Hong Kong and British Army vessels, stretching back to before the turn of the century, had come to an end.

The following year of 1998 was to see further setbacks to the Royal Logistic Corps Fleet and raise further conjectures as to the future of the Army's Navy. In April of this year it was announced that the Army was to end the military presence on St Kilda after forty-one years of soldiers manning a camp and radar base on this otherwise deserted island. During these years the Army's Navy had played a significant role in supplying this small outpost and guarding the South Uist missile range. The soldiers were now to be replaced by civilians who will carry out the tracking of the guided missiles but unlike the soldiers whose tours of duty lasted six months, their civilian substitutes would spend only two weeks at a time on the island. Although for some time supplies were being delivered by helicopter once a fortnight from Benbecula, while a weekly mail drop was carried out by light aircraft, Army vessels were still carrying out certain support functions to the St Kilda outstation. Furthermore, it was surmised that, despite the civilianisation of the operations at the island, there would probably still be a call for some involvement by the RLC Fleet.

However, an even more severe blow to the Army's Navy was to occur with the Defence Review being promulgated only a short time after the change of personnel on St Kilda. Contained within the Review was the startling revelation that the two landing craft logistic, *Ardennes* and *Arakan*, were to be disposed of, *Ardennes* with immediate effect and *Arakan* by April 1999. These ships, the biggest and most sophisticated vessels in the RLC Fleet, now had go. Notwithstanding that both craft were getting on in years, *Ardennes* built in 1976, *Arakan* in 1978, they apparently still had some mileage left in them and it was hoped in 1997 that it might be approved for them to undertake a Ships' Life Extension Programme (SLEP), which would also increase their length to 92m. Needless to say, following the shock news emanating from the Defence Review, these tentative proposals were out of the question. The demise of the two LCLs also spelled the end of Army ships making voyages to St Kilda. Built to replace the

Mk VIII LCTs, *Ardennes* and *Arakan* were the only vessels of the Fleet to regularly visit this remote, sea-girt and lonely outpost of the British Army. In any event, they could operate there only during the summer months and actually the last visit paid to St Kilda occurred in August of this year.

So now the Army's fleet of ships has dwindled to almost certainly the lowest levels in all the years since the first records of vessels actually owned by the Board of Ordnance. Records in early days are far from being complete, but certainly from the estimates for 1839-40, when twelve sizeable (between 45 and 80 tons) vessels were on the strength, all in home waters, while several unlisted small craft would have been stationed at various establishments, the Army's Navy had never been at such a low ebb as in the autumn of 1998. The present strength of craft amounts to fourteen, taking into account the two LCLs awaiting disposal by April 1999 and therefore these have not been included. There are six RCLs, the youngest of which would have come into service in 1985, *Arromanches* (ex-*Agheila*), *Aachen*, *Arezzo* and *Audemer*, all based in the UK. Two more, *Akyab* and *Andalsnes*, have Cyprus as their base. Additionally, there are four workboats, three named *Bream*, *Roach* and *Perch*, built in the 1960s and 1970s. The fourth is named *Millreef*, built in 1987. Finally the Fleet has four LCVPs, none named, only numbered. These are quite small landing craft, usually found at Marchwood but sometimes elsewhere, *eg* one is presently in the Falklands.

A knock-on effect of the disposal of the LCLs has been the reduction of RLC officers being trained in maritime skills such as navigation and seamanship. This has of course arisen as there will no longer be HMAVs commanded by commissioned officers. The six RCLs will continue to be commanded by senior NCOs and titled RLCVs, while the reduced programme for officers attaining maritime skills will be for watchkeeping only. At Marchwood Military Port the Training Wing will continue to train non-commissioned personnel in maritime subjects, while port operating trades will carry on being trained in stevedoring and allied techniques suitable for port operations. Officers will receive an element of port and maritime training. The port itself continues to be kept busy with the loading and discharging of RFA LSLs and commercial ships engaged in support activities in such places as the former Yugoslavia and the Gulf.

Overseas presence of the Army's Navy in Cyprus and the Falklands continues while another centre of activity exists at the port of Split in Croatia, which serves as an entry port for British forces involved with

NATO or UN operations in the former Yugoslavia. All in all, however, the situation regarding the Army's Navy, in particular the ships and men of the Royal Logistic Corps Fleet, is now in a very fluid state indeed and could change very rapidly with little warning.

The Future?

Sadly, in the author's opinion, it has now become all-too-apparent that the future of the Army's Navy cannot be anything other than bleak. In the wake of the various body blows that have befallen the ships and men of the Royal Logistic Corps Fleet, things have gone only from bad to worse. Vessels have been disposed of piecemeal, with no signs of any replacements whatsoever. Mostly they went because of the reductions in overseas commitments, although other reasons, some perhaps not so evident, such as pressure from the Treasury on grounds of economy, could have contributed.

To recap, 1994 saw the last of the RPLs being sold out of service following the withdrawal of British Forces from Belize, in 1997 all the craft stationed in Hong Kong prior to the handover to China went and in 1998 the replacing of military personnel on the island of St Kilda by civilians to carry out the tracking of the guided missiles using the South Uist missile range. However, the most savage blow dealt to the Army's Navy was to occur with the Defence Review published in the summer of 1998.

Contained within the Review, although not receiving as much publicity as some cuts, was the devastating news of the two Landing Craft Logistic becoming redundant. *Ardennes* was taken out of service immediately and *Arakan* had to comply by April 1999, however events have overtaken this programme as *Arakan* recently suffered damage during an exercise and no funds are available to repair her. As far as the RCLs are concerned, although there might be many years service for them, as they become older so maintenance costs will increase, while eventually a decision would have to be made whether or not an expensive SLEP would be justified or the vessels be made surplus to requirements. Their future, however, might be under another threat, which could be abruptly applied, on the grounds of cost-cutting. This threat, a very real one, would be to sell all the RCLs out of the service and offer commercial organisations the chance to tender for the tasks and roles presently carried out by Army craft. In this event, those tendering may very well be interested in also buying the RCLs and transferring them to the Red Ensign with manning by Merchant Navy crews.

The ultimate danger, of course, would be if the Army itself would decide that there was no longer any necessity for an Army's Navy, in view of the end of the Cold War and loss of the Empire. As an example, would there be a requirement for the base at Akrotiri at Cyprus in the foreseeable future? The author believes that senior officers of the Royal Logistic Corps are divided on what should be the way ahead or indeed whether there should be Army craft manned by soldiers at all. Probably Marchwood Military Port will survive as one can visualise the need for a facility dedicated to the handling of military cargoes while British forces remain involved with overseas commitments in the Gulf and the former Yugoslavia, also in carrying aid to developing countries suffering natural disasters such as recently happened in Central America. Here again, though, it might be considered an option to replace soldier stevedores by civilian labour at Marchwood, for example. It is probable that the use of Mexeflotes, especially when used in conjunction with the RSA LSLs, would be a factor in any future conflicts involving amphibious landings, such as was the case in the Falklands campaign.

The greatest effect that the 1998 Defence Review will probably have in any future reduction in the RLC Fleet would be the inevitable loss of those officers, NCOs and other ranks with maritime skills and experience. Already the training in marine disciplines for officers has been reduced and for those already trained and serving afloat there is bound to be an exodus of ambitious young officers who will see no future in what remains of the Army's Navy. The result, probably sooner than later, will see officers transferring to the mainstream activities of the Royal Logistic Corps as a career move for a better future. Depending on whichever option is taken regarding the RCLs, a similar position will arise with the trained and experienced NCOs and soldier sailors, though perhaps not quite so soon. These men will inevitably seek a greater fulfilment in a career with better prospects than soldiering on with an ever-diminishing organisation fraught with serious threats to the very existence of an Army fleet.

However, perhaps there does exist a faint light at the end of the tunnel. For some time there have been occasional suggestions that rather than having three separate supply organisations for the Navy, Army and Air Force, there could be a single multi-service body to cater for all three services in the field of logistics. To date, the author is unaware of any firm proposals how such a radical approach could come about, *ie* which of the three services could undertake such a task. Plans do exist for new types of landing craft to come into service with the two new amphibious warfare ships now building for the Royal Navy as replacements for the ageing assault ships *Fearless* and *Intrepid*. Both of these new ships will have flooding-down capabilities for deployment of their landing craft. Although such craft will be designed for assault tasks and probably manned by Royal Marines, there could be occasions when they might be utilised for supply purposes following the initial landings. In which case there might be a role for Army personnel to become involved with these new RN ships, to be named *Albion* and *Bulwark* with the designation of LPDs.

It is noteworthy that throughout the nineteenth and twentieth centuries, many determined attempts to do away with the Army's Navy have been thwarted and there might yet be a reprieve for the present RLC Fleet. To be realistic, however, bearing in mind that in this day and age there is little or no room to take into account such ethos as long and distinguished service, great achievements in war and peace, together with the proud traditions of probably the only military Fleet in the world with such a continuous existence dating back to the reign of Henry VIII, it is this author's opinion that in all probability it is only a matter of time before there will no longer be an Army's Navy.

Sadly the only values at the present time are those of economy and if possible making a profit, while sentimental considerations play no part whatsoever in planning for the future. Despite modern thinking that nostalgia must not impede progress, nonetheless the prospect that the sight of the Blue Ensign with Crossed Swords flying proudly from a vessel of the British Army will have gone for ever, can only invoke melancholy in the hearts of present or past soldier sailors of the Army's Navy.

Appendix I

Board of Ordnance Fleet taken from Estimates of 1839/40

Name	Tons	Year Built	Where Stationed	Numbers of Crew				Total Crew	Service Employed on
				Masters	Mates	Seamen	Boys		
Sir James Kempt	80	1832	Woolwich	1	1	3	1	6	See note 1
Somerset	80	1830	Woolwich	1	1	3	1	6	See note 1
Ebenezer	70	1805	Woolwich	1	1	3	-	5	See note 1
The Queen	82	1839	Woolwich	1	1	3	2	7	See note 1
Richard	55	1808	Purfleet	1	-	2	-	3	See note 2
Marlborough	60		Portsmouth	1	-	3	-	4	See note 3
Joanna	60	1804	Portsmouth	1	-	3	-	4	See note 3
Earl of Chatham	50	1809	Portsmouth	1	-	2	1	4	See note 4
Hussey	68	c1836	Portsmouth	1	-	2	1	4	See note 5
			Portsmouth						
Wellington	45	1824	Portsmouth	1	1	2	-	4	See note 5
Beresford	45	1824	Devonport	1	-	2	1	4	See note 6
Gosport	68	1812	Devonport	1	-	2	-	3	See note 6
			TOTAL	12	5	30	7	54	

Notes:

1. Conveying stores to and from the various stations in Great Britain and Ireland.
2. Conveying powder from Purfleet, Faversham, Powder Works, Bow Creek, etc.
3. Arming and disarming Her Majesty's Ships at Chatham and Sheerness: also as Powder Vessels, and occasionally going to Woolwich for stores.
4. Conveying powder to and from Her Majesty's Ships at Spithead.
5. Arming and disarming Her Majesty's Ships at Portsmouth.
6. Arming and disarming Her Majesty's Ships at Plymouth etc. The *Beresford* is also employed as a Powder Vessel in conveying powder, etc., to Her Majesty's Ships in Plymouth Sound.

Appendix II

War Department Fleet List 1911

Name	Nature of Vessel	Built	Length	Beam	Draught	Disp.	I.H.P.	W'k'g'sp d	Station
			ft	ft	ft	tons		kts	
Abercorn	Sc	1903	85	17.2	9	145	250	9.6	Lough Swilly
Alice	B	1900	70	17.5	6	140	-	-	Woolwich
Arctic	B	1900	70	18	6.5	-	-	-	Shoeburyness
Australia	B	1906	84	22	7.7	-	-	-	Gibraltar
Cambridge	Sc	1892	75	17	8.5	130	110	8.5	Cork
Carrigaline	Sc	1892	48	12	6.7	35	60	8	Falmouth
Clyde	S	-	46.2	13	7.6	40	-	-	Bermuda
Courier	Sc	1889	52	11	5.7	33	75	10	Devonport
Crystal	Sc	1902	50	13	6.1	42	83	8.5	Isle of Wight
Darenth	B	1880	65	16	5	50	-	-	Woolwich
Dorothy	B	1907	60	17	6.5	108	-	-	Cork
Dorothy	S	1887	52.5	11.7	5.7	-	-	-	Jamaica
Drake	Sc	1891	87	16	8	100	150	9	Pembroke Dk.
Eagle	Sc	1895	60	13.5	7	65	80	8	Devonport
Emerald	Sc	1899	50	13	5.7	40	70	8	Woolwich
Empress	B	1892	61	11	5	-	-	-	Singapore
Endeavour	Sc	1899	52	11	5.7	83	75	9	Woolwich
Forth	B	1893	62.5	16.5	5.8	-	-	-	Shoeburyness
Fusee	Sc	1902	69.5	13	6.9	62	80	8	Weymouth
Gog	B	1886	105	30	7.2	400	-	-	Woolwich
Gordon	Sc	1907	71	15.5	7	106	200	9.5	Sheerness
Haldane	Sc	1907	78.5	16.7	9.2	125	220	9.5	Portsmouth
Haslar	Sc	1903	97.7	18.2	10.3	175	320	10.2	Pembroke Dk.
Havelock	S	-	39.6	12	7.1	50	-	-	Bermuda
Henry	S	1872	77.7	19.3	6	140	-	-	Chatham
Hercules	Sc	1893	85	17.1	10.2	170	350	10	Hong Kong
Hurst	Sc	1904	68	12	6.5	39	250	12	Portsmouth
Ida	Sc	1887	57.5	10	4.7	30	60	8	Devonport
Jasper	Sc	1902	60	13	5.7	38	80	8.5	Malta
John Adye	S	1888	80	20	6.9	185	-	-	Portsmouth
Joule	Sc	1890	48	11.2	5.7	35	60	9	Devonport
Jubilee	Sc	1887	65	12	6	60	75	10	Hong Kong
Katharine	Sc	1882	116	20	7.9	260	200	8.2	Woolwich
Ladysmith	Sc	1902	68.5	12.5	6.9	62	90	9	Cork
Langdon	Sc	1902	81	16.5	8.7	127	250	9.5	Dover
Lansdowne	Sc	1890	120	20	11.6	350	600	10	Portsmouth
Lighter (unnamed)	B	1903	75	25	6.5	130	-	-	Hong Kong
Lord Kitchener	Sc	1899	60	9.5	5.7	20	65	9	Bermuda
Lord Vivian	B	1802	71.4	18	8.6	140	-	-	Woolwich
Lord Wolesley	Sc	1896	117	22	11.7	500	375	8.5	Woolwich

Appendix II

Name	Nature of Vessel	Built	Length ft	Beam ft	Draught ft	Disp. tons	I.H.P.	W'k'g'sp'd kts	Station
Louise	Sc	1901	87	17.5	9.7	145	300	9.5	Bermuda
Mafeking	Sc	1902	58.5	12.5	6.9	52	90	9	Portsmouth
Magog	B	1900	90	30	7	260	-	-	Woolwich
Marquess of Hartington	Sc	1886	140	24	13.5	670	280	9	Woolwich
May	Sc	1902	81	16.5	8.7	125	25	9.5	Gibraltar
Meteor	Sc	1894	75	15	8.2	78	160	10	Jamaica
Moonstone	Sc	1904	87	17.5	9.7	145	280	9.5	Singapore
Moore	Sc	1904	97	18.7	10.2	185	370	10	Portsmouth
Omphale	Sc	1905	87	17.5	9.7	140	230	9.5	Hong Kong
Onyx	Sc	1902	50	13	5.7	38	80	8.5	Mauritius
Osprey	Sc	1895	110	20	11.5	288	500	10	Devonport
Othello	B	1892	61.5	13.5	5	60	-	-	Devonport
Palliser	Sc	1899	68	15	7	65	150	9.5	Shoeburyness
Playfair	Sc	1901	97	18.7	10.2	185	350	10	Leith
Quadroon	Sc	1898	57	13	5.7	35	60	9	Gibraltar
Rodney	Sc	1902	50	10.2	5	25	60	9	Jamaica
Russell	Sc	1902	75	16.5	8.5	112	200	9.5	Isle of Wight
Satellite	Sc	1894	65	14.5	7.7	88	140	9.5	Harwich
Sapphire	S	1910	50	12	5.5	-	-	-	Singapore
Scow	B	1896	48.5	26	4	-	-	-	Lough Swilly
Seagull II	S	1901	43	13	5	45	-	-	Pembroke Dk.
Shamrock	B	1897	60	17	6	105	-	-	Cork
Sir E. Markham	Sc	1898	85	17.1	10.2	170	350	10	Malta
Sir E. Wood	Sc	1896	160	24	14	850	450	9	Woolwich
Sir F. Walker	Sc	1903	93.5	18.7	10	175	320	10	Devonport
Sir G. Murray	B	1900	70	17.5	6	140	-	-	Portsmouth
Sir G. White	Sc	1900	57	13	5.7	35	70	9	Portsmouth
Sir H. Alderson	Sc	1898	90	18	8	157	350	10	Sheerness
Sir P. Buller	Sc	1895	130	23	12.5	570	400	9.5	Woolwich
Sir R. Hay	Sc	1896	100	20	10	280	200	7.5	Portsmouth
Sir S. Northcote	S	1889	86	20	6.9	175	-	-	Portsmouth
Sir W. Nicholson	B	1907	60	17	6.5	118	-	-	Portsmouth
Somers	Sc	1904	87	17.5	9.7	150	270	9.5	Jamaica
Stowart	Sc	1902	75	16.5	8.5	112	200	9.5	Weymouth
Swale	Sc	1891	48	12	6.7	35	70	8	Sheerness
Thalia	H	-	212	40	-	-	-	-	Woolwich
Tommy Atkins	Sc	1898	75	15	8	78	120	10	Hong Kong
White Rose	Sc	1902	41	8.5	5.1	12	30	8	Woolwich
Wyndham	Sc	1903	80	17	8.5	140	200	9	Cork
Oil Motor Launch	Sc	1902	30	7	3.2	3	-	6	Shoeburyness

And 11 other Lighters (unnamed) and 3 Tow barges, Tongkang I, II, and III.

Particulars supplied by the courtesy of the Secretary for War, 1911
NOTE: In 2nd col, B = tow barge, H = hoy, S = sailing, Sc = screw steamer)

Appendix III

War Department Vessels 1898-1914

An extract from The Naval Pocket Book

Name	Nature of Vessel	Year	Tons	Length & Beam
Abercorn	STR	1903	95gt	85ft x 17ft 2in
Admiral	SMV	1891	24	48ft x 12ft
Advance	STR	1884	100	70ft x 17ft
Albert	S/Vessel	-	-	-
Alexandra	STR	1883	57	65ft x 12ft
Alfreda	STR	1903	-	93ft x 18ft 7in
Algoa	STR	-	-	-
Alice	Tow Barge	1900	70	70ft x 17ft 5in
Ampere	SMV	1890	24	48ft x 11ft 2in
Arctic	Tow Barge	1900	70	70ft x 18ft
Armstrong	SMV	1901	96gt	85ft x 18ft
Australia	Tow Barge	1906	-	84ft x 22ft
Beryl	SMV	1902	-	50ft x 13ft
Burgoyne	SMV	1886	125	95ft x 17ft 5in
Cambridge	STR	1892	100	75ft x 17ft
Carrigaline	SMV	1892	24	48ft x 12ft
Cecil	S/Vessel	1878	30	42ft x 12ft
Clyde	S/Vessel	-	40	46ft x 13ft
Collingwood Dickson	STR	1889	60	69ft 5in x 13ft
Courier	SMV	1889	33	52ft x 11ft
Creole	-	1890	-	70ft x 10ft
Crystal	SMV	1902	30	50ft x 13ft
Darenth	Tow Barge	1880	80	65ft x 16ft
Dodo	SMV	1893	24	50ft x 12ft
Dorothy	S/Vessel	1887	-	52ft 5in x 11ft 7in
Dorothy	Tow Barge	1907	118	60ft x 17ft
Dragon	SMV	1892	24	48ft x 12ft
*Drake**	STR	1891	165	87ft x 16ft
Dundas	SMV	1887	125	98ft x 17ft 5in
Eagle	STR	1895	85	60ft x 13ft 5in
Edgewater	STR	1892	-	90ft x 25ft
Elf	STR	PURCHASED BY RN 1911	-	-
Emily	Hoy	1867	-	42ft x 12ft
Empress	Screw Str	1885	100	77ft x 15ft 5in
Endeavour	SMV	1889	50	52ft x 11ft
Enterprise	-	-	16	44ft x 9ft
Erg	SMV	1892	25	48ft x 11ft
Falcon	Paddle Str	1874	130	80ft x 16ft 5in

Name	Nature of Vessel	Year	Tons	Length & Beam
Farad	SMV	1890	25	48ft x 11ft
Forth	Tow Barge	1893	-	62ft x 16ft 5in
Fusee	STR	1902	62	65ft x 13ft
General Elliot	STR	1889	110	80ft x 17ft
General Lee	STR	1891	24	48ft x 12ft
General Skinner	STR	1891	144	80ft x 18ft
General Stotherd	STR	1902	220	90ft x 19ft
Georgina	S/Vessel	1889	165	82ft x 18ft 7in
Gog	Tow Barge	1886	400	105ft x 30ft
Gordon	SMV	1885	125	95ft x 19ft 5in
Gordon	STR	1907	38	71ft 6in x 15ft
Grand Duchess	-	1874	50	52ft x 13ft
Haldane	STR	1907	125	18ft x 16ft 7in
Haslar	SMV	1903	175	70ft x 18ft
Havelock	S/Vessel	1885	30	39ft 6in x 12ft
Henry	S/Vessel	1887	160	77ft x 19ft
Hercules	STR	1898	370	85ft x 17ft 2in
Hoptown	SMV	1891	27	48ft x 11ft
Hurst	STR	1904	39	68ft x 12ft
Ida	STR	1887	70	57ft x 10ft
Jasper	SMV	1902	38	50ft x 13ft
John Adye	S/Vessel	1888	175	86ft x 20ft
Joule	SMV	1890	27	48ft x 11ft 2in
Jubilee	STR	1887	57	65ft x 12ft
Katharine	STR	1882	360	116ft x 20ft
Ladysmith	STR	1902	50	58ft x 12ft 5in
Langdon	STR	1902	125	81ft x 16ft 5in
Lansdowne	STR	1896	320	120ft x 20ft
Lighter	Tow Barge	1903	130	60ft x 20ft
Lily	STR	1878	50	67ft x 16ft 5in
Lizard	STR	1882	-	62ft x 9ft 1in
Little Violet	-	-	-	-
Lord Heathfield	SMV	1886	125	100ft x 19ft
Lord Kitchener	STR	1899	20	50ft x 9ft 5in
Lord Napier	STR	-	20	70ft x 11ft
Lord Panmure	STR	1859	620	150ft x 21ft
Lord Vivian	Hoy	1862	140	71ft x 18ft
Lord Wolesley	STR	1896	500	117ft x 22ft
Louise	STR	1903	145	87ft x 17ft
Mafeking	STR	1902	50	58ft x 12ft 5in
Magog	Tow Barge	1900	105	90ft x 30ft
Maroon	SMV	1895	24	50ft x 12ft
*Marquess of Hartington***	STR	1886	630	140ft x 24ft
May	STR	1902	125	81ft x 16ft 5in
Meteor	STR	1894	90	75ft x 15ft
Miner No 1	SMV	1887	80	60ft x 15ft 5in
Miner No 2	SMV	1887	80	60ft x 15ft 5in
Miner No 3	SMV	1887	80	60ft x 15ft 5in
Miner No 4	SMV	1878	80	60ft x 15ft 5in
Miner No 5	SMV	1878	80	60ft x 15ft 5in

Name	Nature of Vessel	Year	Tons	Length & Beam
Miner No 6	SMV	1878	80	60ft x 15ft 5in
Miner No 7	SMV	1878	80	60ft x 15ft 5in
Miner No 8	SMV	1879	80	60ft x 15ft 5in
Miner No 9	SMV	1880	80	60ft x 15ft 5in
Miner No 10	SMV	1879	80	60ft x 15ft 5in
Miner No 11	SMV	1880	80	60ft x 15ft 5in
Miner No 12	SMV	1880	80	60ft x 15ft 5in
Miner No 13	SMV	1880	80	65ft x 75ft
Miner No 14	SMV	1880	80	65ft x 75ft
Miner No 15	SMV	1881	80	65ft x 75ft
Miner No 16	SMV	1886	80	65ft x 75ft
Miner No 17	SMV	1904	230	50ft x 13ft
Moonstone	STR	1903	145	87ft x 17ft 5in
Moore	STR	1907	185	97ft x 18ft 7in
Musquash	SMV	1895	27	50ft x 12ft
Napier of Magdala	SMV	1891	177	80ft x 18ft
Nellie	SMV	1891	-	54ft x 13ft
Ohm	SMV	1890	25	48ft x 11ft 1in
Omphale	STR	1905	170	87ft x 17ft 5in
Onward	STR	1892	35	76ft x 10ft 5in
Onyx	SMV	1902	38	50ft x 13ft
Osprey	STR	1895	225	110ft x 20ft
Othello	Tow Barge	1892	60	68ft x 15ft
Pearle	SMV	1896	17	50ft x 13ft
Pembroke	SMV	1891	24	48ft x 9ft
Pennar	SMV	1902	230	85ft x 18ft
Playfair	STR	1904	185	97ft x 18ft
Plymouth	St Cutter	-	-	30ft x 7ft 2in
Primrose	SMV	-	15	56ft x 9ft
Quadroon	STR	1898	35	57ft x 13ft
Queen	STR	1887	55	65ft x 11ft 7in
Rodney	STR	1902	25	50ft x 10ft 2in
Ruby	SMV	1900	25	50ft x 13ft
Russell	STR	1902	100	75ft x 16ft
Sapphire	STR	1910	100	50ft x 12ft
Satellite	STR	1894	70	65ft x 19ft
Scow	Tow Barge	1896	-	48ft x 25ft
Seagull II	S/Vessel	1891	45	43ft x 13ft
Sebastapol	Hoy	1857	-	64ft x 18ft 2in
Shamrock	Tow Barge	1897	100	60ft x 17ft
Sir Charles	SMV	1891	24	48ft x 12ft
Sir Charles Pasley	SMV	1893	120	93ft x 18ft
Sir Donald	SMV	1891	27	48ft x 12ft
Sir Edwin Markham	STR	1893	120	85ft x 17ft 2in
*Sir Evelyn Wood***	STR	1896	850	160ft x 24ft
Sir Francis Head	SMV	1889	120	80ft x 17ft
Sir Frederick Chapman	SMV	1895	110	80ft x 18ft
Sir George Murray	Tow Barge	1900	70	70ft x 17ft 5in
Sir Frederick Walker	STR	1903	175	93ft x 18ft 7in
Sir George White	STR	1900	50	57ft x 13ft

Name	Nature of Vessel	Year	Tons	Length & Beam
Sir Hastings Anderson	STR	1898	150	90ft x 18ft
Sir Henry Harness	SMV	1897	30	80ft x 18ft
Sir Howard Elphinstone	STR	1886	102	117ft x 22ft
Sir James	SMV	1891	29	48ft x 12ft
Sir John Jones	SMV	1886	100	83ft x 15ft 9in
Sir Lintern Simmonds	STR	1890	27	57ft x 10ft 3in
Sir Lothan Nicholson	SMV	1897	27	80ft x 18ft
*Sir Redvers Buller***	STR	1895	790	130ft x 23ft
Sir Richard Fletcher	SMV	1886	100	77ft x 15ft 5in
Sir Robert Hay	STR	1896	270	100ft x 20ft
Sir William Green	SMV	1889	110	80ft x 17ft
Sir William Jarvis	SMV	1900	120	90ft x 18ft
Sir William Nicholson	Barge	1907	90	60ft x 17ft
Sir William Reid	SMV	1889	110	80ft x 17ft
Sir Stafford Northcote	S/Vessel	1889	175	20ft x 6ft 5in
Solent	SMV	1885	125	100ft x 17ft
Somers	STR	1904	150	87ft x 17ft 5in
Stanhope	STR	1890	80	88ft x 17ft
Steam Launch No 4	-	-	80	88ft x 17ft
Steam Launch No 5	-	-	20	42ft x 11ft
Steam Launch No 69	-	1877	20	42ft x 12ft
Steam Launch No 70	-	1877	20	42ft x 11ft 7in
Steam Launch No 85	-	1877	20	42ft x 11ft
Stewart	STR	1902	100	75ft x 16ft
Swale	SMV	1891	27	48ft x 12ft
Sybil	STR	1902	112	80ft x 16ft
Tyler	Hoy	-	-	212ft x 40ft
Tommy Atkins	STR	1883	57	65ft x 12ft
Tongkang I	-	LTR	-	-
Tongkang II	-	LTR	-	-
Tongkang III	-	LTR	-	-
Topaz	SMV	1902	-	50ft x 15ft
Tortoise	STR	1894	57	50ft x 12ft
Tremayne	SMV	1894	57	48ft x 12ft
Victor	SMV	1886	125	95ft x 17ft
Violet	SMV	1886	16	45ft x 8ft 5in
Volta	SMV	1889	27	50ft x 11ft
Watt	SMV	1890	27	48ft x 11ft
White Rose	STR	1902	12	41ft x 8ft
Witch	Tow Barge	1903	-	16ft x 13ft
Wyndham	STR	1903	125	30ft x 17ft

Abbreviations:

SMV	Submarine mining vessel
STR	Steamer
*	Built at Devonport
**	Note heaviest tonnage

Appendix IV

Vessels Constructed 1920-39

Name	Type	Year	Gross Tonnage	Duties employed on
General McHardy	Steam Target Tower	-	-	Passenger T/T
Sir Desmond O'Callaghan	Steam Target Tower	1927	-	Passenger T/T
Sir Noel Birch	Steam Target Tower	1926	-	Passenger T/T
Lord Plumer	Steam Target Tower	1927	250	Passenger
Victoria	Steam Vessel	-	-	Passenger (B)
Oudenarde	Motor Vessel	-	-	Passenger (B)
Sir Robert Whigham	Motor Target Tower	1930	-	Passenger T/T
Sir Hastings Anderson	Motor Vessel	1934	-	Passenger (B)
Crystal II	Motor Vessel	1934	-	Passenger (C)
Sir Walter Campbell	Steam Coaster	1928	525	Passenger T/T
Malplaquet	Motor Coaster	1939	528	Cargo & Pass
Vawdrey	Motor Coaster/Barge	1934	98	Cargo & Pass (A)
John Adams	Motor Coaster/Barge	1934	90	Cargo & Pass (A)
Blenheim	Motor Coaster/Barge	1937	-	Cargo & Pass
Katharine II	Motor Coaster/Barge	1930	-	Cargo & Pass
Geoffrey Stanley	Motor Coaster/Barge	1929	-	Cargo & Pass
Henry Cadell	Motor Coaster/Barge	1930	100	Cargo & Pass
Fusee II	Motor Pass Vessel	1935	-	Passenger
Sir Cecil Romer	Motor Pass Vessel	1929	-	Passenger
Wuzzar	Motor Launch Vessel	1930	-	Passenger (A)
Jackdaw	Motor Launch Vessel	1935	-	Passenger (A)
Raven	Motor Launch Vessel	1931	-	Passenger (A)
'General' class: 10 built	High Speed T/T	1936-7	-	High Speed T/T
'Bird' class: 10 built	High Speed Range Vessel	1937	-	Range Clearance

(A) - Transferred to Irish Government 1938.
(B) - Lost to enemy action Far East 1941.
(C) - Being reconstructed by enthusiasts, Medway 1986.

Appendix V

Responsibilities Regarding Waterborne Craft

(Directive issued by War Office, June 1944)

1.   Introduction

It is necessary, as a wartime measure, to lay down a dividing line between the functions of the Directorate of Transportation and the Directorate of Supplies and Transport as regards the provision, manning, operation and maintenance of waterborne craft. This differentiation provides a guide as to whether any special unit formed to meet military requirements should be manned by RE or RASC, as an indication of the division of responsibility for operational theatres in the future. In all theatres, the closest co-operation will be maintained between the two services, in order that the maximum value may be obtained from all the craft, personnel, repair and maintenance facilities available.

2.   General Responsibilities

The general principles on which the organisation and responsibilities of the Directorates of Transportation and of Supplies and Transport should be based are as follows:

(a)   Directorate of Transportation – for the provision, manning, and operation of craft forming an integral part of bulk movement on the L. of C. of the Army, including such craft as are necessary for the construction, working and repair of ports of loading and discharge.

(b)   Directorate of Supplies and Transport – for the provision, manning, and operation of such waterborne craft as are required for, and whose normal use is intercommunication, distributive movement of personnel and material, such as the daily maintenance of a formation.

205

Conditions peculiar to a particular theatre, or considerations leading a theatre commander to vary application of these principles, may arise, but they will, when practicable, be applied.

3. Provision, Manning and Operation

To fulfil the general responsibilities set out in paragraph 2 above, the responsibility for provision, manning, and operation, of all craft will be as follows:

(a)　The Directorate of Transportation will be responsible for:
   (i)　Tugs.
   (ii)　Dumb and self-propelled barges and lighters, except special craft for the carriage of bulk petroleum.
   (iii)　Pontoons and special ferries, *eg* the Rhine Ferry.
   (iv)　Floating cranes and other floating equipment used for port operation.
   (v)　Craft required in connection with construction and repair of ports and inland waterways.
   (vi)　Coastal craft when used for bulk delivery on Army lines of communication.

(b)　The Directorate of Supplies and Transport will be responsible for the RASC Static Water Transport Services, and in addition:
   (i)　Launches, including target towing launches.
   (ii)　Cabin cruisers.
   (iii)　Pull boats.
   (iv)　Drifters, MFVs, schooners and small coasters.
   (v)　Radio-controlled targets.
   (vi)　Fire boats and targets.
   (vii)　Dumb and self-propelled barges or lighters, and small tankers for the carriage of bulk petroleum products.
   (viii)　Small coasters when used for distribution purposes.

(c)　RASC craft operating in ports or inland waterways will come under the co-ordinating control of Transportation or other authority responsible in those areas.

(d)　In cases where Transportation or S. and T. units require, as part of their unit equipment, ancillary craft of types which are normally the responsibility of the other service, the latter service will be responsible for provision of craft and supply of spare parts, but not for manning or operation. Where Transportation or S. and T. units temporarily require craft which are the responsibility of the other service, such craft will be issued on loan to the unit requiring them.

(e)　Amphibious vehicles, though they may be used for ship discharge as lighters, will be provided, manned and operated under arrangements made by the Directorate of S. and T., though they will, when so employed, be under the co-ordinating control of the authority responsible for the work of the beach or port.

4.　Maintenance and Supply of Spare Parts and Stores

Responsibility for the maintenance of craft of both services, and supply of ships' stores and spare parts, will be as follows:

(A)　Maintenance.
    (a)　Transportation and S. and T. units are responsible for the maintenance and repair of their own vessels, but where repair facilities are limited it will be necessary to pool all resources of both services: sometimes in conjunction with the Royal Navy and Ministry of War Transport.
    (b)　It will be the responsibility of REME to repair petrol and high-speed diesel engines of Transportation and S. and T. units, when these can be removed from vessels to REME workshops.

(B)　Supply of spare parts and marine boat stores.
    (a)　The Directorate of Transportation will be responsible for making provision for:
    (i) Spare parts listed in the Vocabulary of Transportation stores.
    (ii) Spare parts for craft provided by Services and by Departments other than the War Office for IWT RE use, from sources agreed from the appropriate Services and Departments.
    (iii) Spare parts for craft and for marine engines not included in the Vocabulary of Transportation stores, but which have been provided through Transportation stores channels, whether operated by Transportation or S. and T. personnel.

(b)   The Directorate of Supplies and Transport will be responsible for making provision for:

(i) Marine stores, paints, and other stores listed in the Vocabulary of RASC Marine Stores, for all Army Services. These will be issued through the various S. and T. Boat Stores Depots at home and overseas.

(ii) All machinery and spare parts required by S. and T. vessels, whether operated by S. and T. or IWT personnel.

(iii) Fuels and lubricants for all Services as laid down.

Appendix VI

Control of Water Transport Services, Post-War Policy

When the policy regarding the control of water transport services in the Army was reviewed after the war, the questions requiring decision were as follows:

1. Should all water transport be under one service?
2. If so, should this service be the Transportation Service or the RASC?
3. If not, how were the functions to be redefined?
4. In either case, should REME undertake the third and fourth line overhaul and repair of all components of Port, IWT, and water transport engines and equipment, which could be moved to a REME workshop?
5. In either case, should Transportation units, such as Port Operating Companies, have their own launches for domestic use and inter-communication, as part of their war equipment?

The RASC Case

In presenting the RASC side of the story, it was submitted that the RASC Fleet had been in existence for 60 years, while the IWT, RE only started, as an adjunct to the railway system, in the war of 1914–18, and so was put under the Director-General of Transportation. The RASC is, by its charter, the transport branch of the Army, and the exception to this rule (railways), is a technical quasi-civilian branch of engineering and operation.

The amphibians presented a further link between land and water, taking the place of tug and lighter in certain cases.

The RASC moves stores in bulk by road and air to areas of distribution to augment the railway, and where railways so not exist or are broken. The same principle could be applied to movement of stores in bulk by inland waterways.

The RASC would provide craft as required by Transportation for port working, as it did already for beach working by the provision of amphibians in the same way as it supplies lorries and tippers for the Works Service, and bridging lorries for Field RE. It could be argued that those responsible for the operation of a port must have their own craft: but in civil practice this is not so, as the Port Authorities call on tug and lighter companies.

As a major user service, the RASC could take on the provision of craft, marine engines and spares required by the RE for river-crossing operations.

Specialist vessels for port construction, repair, and maintenance, such as dredgers and floating cranes, could remain with Transportation, and be manned by their personnel, or they could belong to Transportation, and be manned by the RASC.

Finally, the RASC Fleet and Water Transport Service were still very much in being, operating and maintaining some 1500 craft, and had taken over most of the IWT functions of the Transportation Service in all theatres, while IWT (Tn.) had virtually ceased to exist at home and overseas owing to releases.

The Transportation Service Case

The Transportation Service claimed its historical background from the 1914–1918 war, including a cross-channel barge service which had conveyed over 1½ million tons to France.

It quoted Field Service Regulations, Vol. I, as stating that `Transport between the terminal points is provided normally by railways or inland waterways, the executive control of which is the responsibility of the transportation service' and as going on to describe road transport as a supplement to inland water transport, and not *vice versa*.

The Transportation Service must continue to be responsible for port operating, and IWT was intimately connected with port lighterage and the discharge of ships. The latter could often be discharged direct into IWT craft.

Provision of all craft, marine engines, spares and stores would be undertaken by the Directorate of Engineer Stores for all RE requirements, both Field and Transportation. This should be simple, and should help standardisation to a greater degree than by the RASC undertaking this as the major user service.

It had been decided that transportation stores were to be the responsibility of the DES, and that the former Transportation constructional units were to come under the Chief Engineer of a theatre, and it was therefore argued that the Transportation Service could now easily take on the operation of all water transport, whereas the RASC had acquired new or increased commitments, *i.e.* amphibians, supply and maintenance by air, complicated provision and distribution of POL, and the Army Fire Service.

Finally, the Transportation Service had very close contact with Q (Movements) Staff on all movement matters, other than movement by air.

Comments

It will be seen that it was a delicate question of decision between tradition, proved service, and the unity of transport control, one the one hand, and a more even spread of the maintenance load between the two services and the centralisation of everything to do with boats within the Corps of Royal Engineers, on the other.

It was not in any case easy to define responsibilities by functions, and not practicable to do so by types of craft.

REME had carried out some repairs for RASC water transport units, obtaining the necessary spares from the boat stores depot.

The Decisions

The following decisions were made, on the grounds stated.

If one service took over all water transport, it must be Transportation as that service must continue to operate the main L. of C., and must retain its own vessels and craft for port working.

Although, if this were done, there might be some saving in manpower and a little to gain over provision and repair, on balance more would be lost than gained. The considerable number of trained personnel in the RASC, and their experience, would be wasted. Transportation would have to take on all sorts of tasks, such as towing artillery targets, running launches, etc., which were not its functions: that service must concentrate on its primary function of operating the main L. of C.

By using both the RASC and Transportation, the Army stood to gain flexibility, a wider knowledge of water transport throughout the Army, and the ability of one service to help the other.

The former ruling would therefore be adhered to as the principle for the division of functions, though the wording required revision. The RASC in Italy, for instance, had really exceeded their functions as laid down (see Chapter 4).

The question of the standardisation of craft, marine engines and stores, and provision, was to be examined with a view to making one service responsible for all Army provision.

As a general guide, repairs were to be carried out on the major user principle.

The operation, maintenance, and repair, of craft hired or requisitioned by the Principal Sea Transport Officer in an overseas port would have to be considered by the Joint Planning Staff, as being an inter-Service and inter-departmental matter.

Transportation units were to have launches for their domestic and inter-communication use as part of their war equipment.

Appendix VII

Particulars of RASC Craft 1939-45

Fast Launches

(a) 40ft – Enclosed wheelhouse and cabin, open welldeck aft. Cruising speed about 20kts, maximum speed 23kts. Twin Perkins Diesel engines.

(b) 45ft – Enclosed wheelhouse and cabin (four berths). Cruising speed about 16kts, maximum speed 20kts. Triple Power Meadows Petrol engines.

(c) 48ft – Large enclosed wheelhouse and cabin accommodation. Cruising speed 18kts, maximum speed 21kts. Triple Perkins Diesel engines.

Harbour Launch

36ft – An open launch fitted with canvas dodgers giving limited protection from weather. Capacity 50 men or 5 tons of stores. Speed 8-10kts. Engines either Kelvin or Vosper. An outstandingly good seaboat for its size; a company of these craft crossed the English Channel in a Force 6-7 wind shortly after D-Day. Used in every theatre with great success. Their capacity made them invaluable for harbour and estuary work.

General Service Launches

45ft and 50ft – Designed to cater for the needs of small garrisons supplied by sea. Capable of carrying passengers and cargo, the former in a passenger cabin, and the latter in a small hold complete with derrick. Good seaboats and handled well.

Ambulance Launches

112ft – Converted Fairmile Type `B' Naval motor launch. Fitted to carry 20 lying or 40 sitting cases, with accommodation for the medical staff. Good fast seaboats with beautiful lines.

The conversions involved the following modifications:

(a)   Flush deck over crews' accommodation and engine room.

(b)   Erection of two ambulance wards, 7-8ft high, with maximum width of 12ft on deck: the fore ward was about 24ft long, and the after ward about 29ft long.

(c)   Stretchers were arranged in three tiers along the sides of the wards.

(d)   Wheelhouse and bridge cabins for master and mate were erected on top of the fore ward, the proper officers' quarters being used for three or four medical orderlies, medical stores, etc.

(e)   A W.C. in each ward, and a surgery at the after end of the after ward. Combined drying room and storage for blankets and linen. Refrigerating outfit and ice store.

(f)   Comfortable mattresses for the stretchers.

Motor Fishing Vessels

61½ft, 75ft, and 90ft – These were, as their name implies, built on the lines of a fishing vessel, and were stoutly built good seaboats. Essentially small cargo carriers, and could only carry passengers in fine weather, *ie* on deck or seated in the hold. Used as coastal carriers of cargo, as `mother' ships to small craft, and as fire-fighting vessels. The 61½ft type had a large hold forward, capable of carrying 20 tons, a speed of 10kts, and Kelvin, Widdops, or Lister engines, the larger types were in proportion.

Target Towers

68ft and 69ft. High speed towers designed to meet the needs of coastal artillery training. Their machinery was rather complex, and required very skilled engineers to ensure correct maintenance and running. Good seaboats, and carried small cargoes in the open sea in an emergency.

Military Oil Barges

80ft and 104ft. These vessels were designed for the carriage of petroleum ship to shore, in estuaries, or coastwise in fair weather. Capable of discharging into shore installations, or direct into jerricans, eight at a time. The older, 80ft type were converted dumb barges, and difficult to handle. The later 104ft type was a better seaboat, and more manoeuvreable. The 80ft type had a freeboard of only 2ft when loaded to capacity, and a speed of 6-8kts. The crew's quarters left much to be desired; no heating was possible, and no cooking except when empty; yet crews lived aboard for 14 months.

T.I.D Steam Tug

A very useful tug, but not sufficiently powerful to tow a barge in bad weather.

Minca Barges

Dumb pre-fabricated wooden barges made in Canada.

Landing Craft, Tank (L.C.T.)

These vessels were similar in arrangement to an oil tanker, the bridge, engines, accommodation for crew, stores, etc., all being at the after end. The rest of the hull, which was rectangular, formed the hold; and a ramp at the forward end could be let down to allow vehicles to pass in or out.

These craft were extremely useful for ferry work with M.T. They were used by the RASC mainly for dumping unserviceable ammunition at sea, their low flat deck making them invaluable for the purpose.

The LCT Mark IIIs, which were converted into the LCT (E)s, *ie* emergency repair, and fitted for tropical service, were selected for use as floating workshops for repair of amphibians in the Far Eastern theatre. Particulars of the Mark III were as follows:

Length: 192ft; beam: 31ft; gross tonnage: 305 tons
Maximum loads:
      Cargo, homogenous, 300 tons;
      Cargo, vehicles in tons, 260 tons;
      Cargo, vehicles, 3-ton lorries, numbers, 10.
Cruising range: 1460 miles.
Crew complement:
      Normal, two officers, ten ratings;
      Tropical, three officers, 14 ratings.

When converted for use as workshops, the hold was completely plated over to accommodate personnel, workshop machinery space, generator room, battery charging room (40 batteries), etc. The workshop machinery included 6½in lathe, 4½in lathe, 26in drilling machine, grinders, woodworking machine, portable forge, electrical and oxy-acetylene welding sets, and electrical workshop equipment.

`J' Class Launches

American craft. Length, 27½ft; draught, 2ft 3in; speed, 10–12kts; crew, 2; passengers, 14.

Swamp Glider

Brownback Sea Sled – A flat-bottomed craft with an air propeller at the stern to supply the motive power. At full speed, the craft planed, *ie* lifted a great part of its length out of the water. Length, 17ft; beam, 6ft; depth, 8–9in; draught, light, 7in; loaded, 11in; maximum load, including crew, 1200lbs; speed, with five men aboard, 21½kts at 2900 revolutions a minute; motor, 75hp, 4-cylinder, air-cooled.

The glider could be used to advantage in shallow waterways fouled by weeds, and in swamp, for such duties as despatch work, rescue work, ferry work, delivering small quantities of stores, rations, etc. It was therefore properly a RASC craft. It was, however, quite unsuitable for use in very narrow creeks with overhanging vegetation or high reeds.

Appendix VIII

Military Crew Complements of RASC Vessels 1939-1945

Ranks	LCT and Amb. Launch	MFV 45ft	MFV 61½/75ft	MFV 90ft	Target Towers		Fast Launches 44½/45/48ft	GS 50ft	Harbour 36ft
					68/72ft	57ft			
Captain	1	0	0	0	1	0	0	0	0
Subaltern	1	0	0	1	0	1	0	0	0
WO II Navigator	0	0	1	0	0	0	0	0	0
WO II Marine Engineer	1	0	0	0	0	0	0	0	0
S/Sgt Navigator	1	0	0	0	0	0	0	1	0
S/Sgt Marine Engineer	0	0	0	0	1	1	0	0	0
Sgt Navigator	0	1	0	1	1	1	1	0	0
Sgt Marine Engineer	1	0	0	1	1	0	0	0	0
Corporal Navigator	1	0	1	0	0	0	1	1	1
Corporal Marine Engineer	0	1	1	1	0	1	1	1	0
L/Cpl Navigator	0	1	0	0	0	0	0	0	0
L/Cpl Waterman	1	0	1	0	0	1	0	0	0
Private Waterman	3	1	2	2	1	1	1	1	1
Private Marine Engineers	1	1	1	0	1	0	0	0	1
Private Electrician	1	0	0	0	0	0	0	0	0

Note: The 90ft MFVs were Fire Boats, and the complement shown above applied only when the vessel was 'on station'. For long voyages, the crew was as for LCT or Ambulance Launch.

Appendix IX

Organisation of IWT, Persia and Iraq, 31 December 1942

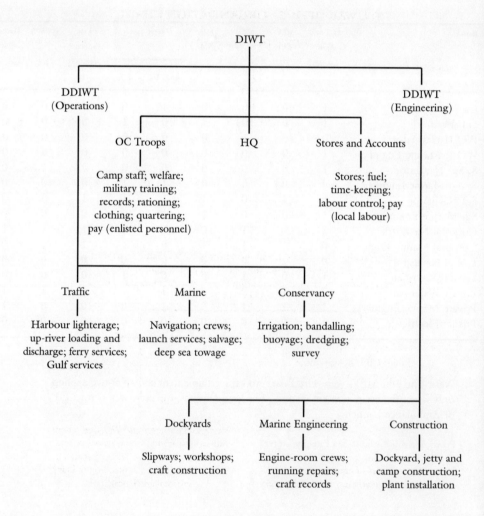

DIWT

DDIWT (Operations)

DDIWT (Engineering)

OC Troops

HQ

Stores and Accounts

Camp staff; welfare;
military training;
records; rationing;
clothing; quartering;
pay (enlisted personnel)

Stores; fuel;
time-keeping;
labour control; pay
(local labour)

Traffic

Marine

Conservancy

Harbour lighterage;
up-river loading and
discharge; ferry services;
Gulf services

Navigation; crews;
launch services; salvage;
deep sea towage

Irrigation; bandalling;
buoyage; dredging;
survey

Dockyards

Marine Engineering

Construction

Slipways; workshops;
craft construction

Engine-room crews;
running repairs;
craft records

Dockyard, jetty and
camp construction;
plant installation

Appendix X

Organisation Chart of the RASC Fleet
as at 1 September 1945

STI, WAR OFFICE - ORGANISATION CHART

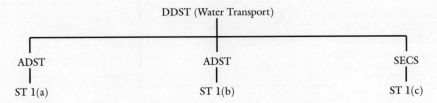

DDST (Water Transport)

ADST	ADST	SECS
ST 1(a)	ST 1(b)	ST 1(c)

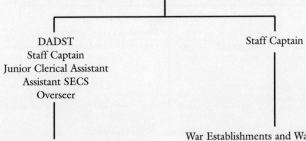

ADST

Policy, planning, organisation, and operation of RASC Water Transport
Services at home, overseas, and in the field. Policy, provision, and issue, of
RASC marine stores of all units of the army. Fire Boats. Ammunition dumping.

DADST
Staff Captain
Junior Clerical Assistant
Assistant SECS
Overseer

Staff Captain

Policy, provision, and issue of marine stores. Control and administration of Home Boat Stores Depot. Scales of equipment for RASC vessels. Workshops machinery for RASC vessels.

War Establishments and War Equipment tables. Preparation of units for overseas. Personnel questions. Training matters. Supervising Officer, controlling military and civilian clerical staff.

Appendix X

ST 1(b). Provision and Maintenance

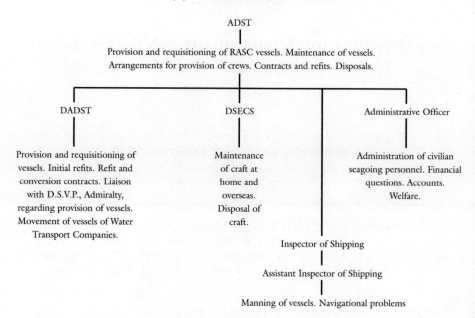

ADST

Provision and requisitioning of RASC vessels. Maintenance of vessels.
Arrangements for provision of crews. Contracts and refits. Disposals.

DADST

Provision and requisitioning of
vessels. Initial refits. Refit and
conversion contracts. Liaison
with D.S.V.P., Admiralty,
regarding provision of vessels.
Movement of vessels of Water
Transport Companies.

DSECS

Maintenance
of craft at
home and
overseas.
Disposal of
craft.

Administrative Officer

Administration of civilian
seagoing personnel. Financial
questions. Accounts.
Welfare.

Inspector of Shipping

Assistant Inspector of Shipping

Manning of vessels. Navigational problems

S.T. 1(c). New Construction and Conversion

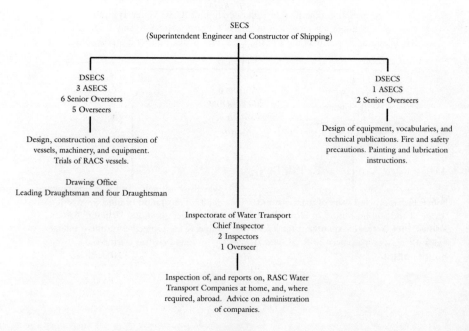

SECS
(Superintendent Engineer and Constructor of Shipping)

DSECS
3 ASECS
6 Senior Overseers
5 Overseers

Design, construction and conversion of
vessels, machinery, and equipment.
Trials of RACS vessels.

Drawing Office
Leading Draughtsman and four Draughtsman

DSECS
1 ASECS
2 Senior Overseers

Design of equipment, vocabularies, and
technical publications. Fire and safety
precautions. Painting and lubrication
instructions.

Inspectorate of Water Transport
Chief Inspector
2 Inspectors
1 Overseer

Inspection of, and reports on, RASC Water
Transport Companies at home, and, where
required, abroad. Advice on administration
of companies.

220

Appendix XI

Marine Craft – RASC Vessels 1952

General

1. This regulation refers to the RASC vessels in use; lists the builders and dates of completion of the standard craft and also gives the displacement, length, cargo and type of engine of miscellaneous craft.

36ft harbour launches (Builders - various)

203, 206, 225, 227, 232, 234, 238, 257, 260, 271, 274, 280, 282, 289, 298, 300, 308, 309, 330, 331, 344, 363, 364, 393, 396, 401, 402, 406, 408, 418–421, 426, 427, 429–431, 435–440, 442, 444, 446, 448, 451, 452, 453, 455, 457–460, 463, 466, 467–469, 471–476, 478, 480, 484, 486, 488, 490–493, 495–501, 503, 506 and 507.

40ft general service launches ('Barracks' and 'Barrack Lines')

Builder	Vessel	Date of completion
C.C. Underwood Ltd,	*Buller*	26.2.44
South Benfleet,	*Connaught*	26.2.44
Essex	*Victoria*	11.4.44
Ranalagh Yacht Yard Ltd,	*Alma*	11.3.46
Wootten Creek,	*Gibraltar*	20.3.46
Isle of Wight	*Malta*	1.5.46
	Mandora	23.5.46
	Salamanca	18.7.46
	Talavera	28.3.46
	Corunna	18.7.46

44ft 6in fast launches ('British Rivers')

Builder	Vessel	Date of completion
British Power Boat Co Ltd,	*Avon*	29.6.45
Hythe,	*Almond*	30.6.45
Southampton	*Alness*	10.7.45
	Adur	17.7.45
	Arun	19.7.45
	Axe	24.7.45
	Blackwater	1.8.45

221

Builder	Vessel	Date of completion
	Blythe	14.8.45
	Bure	28.8.45
	Beaulieu	5.9.45
	Burry	1.9.45
	Brora	8.9.45
	Beam	19.9.45
	Butley	24.9.45
	Carron	16.10.45
	Crouch	12.10.45
	Conway	28.9.45
	Clyde	30.9.45
	Colne	18.10.45
	Coquet	27.10.45
	Char	5.11.45
	Dee	9.11.45
	Derwent	31.10.45
	Dart	9.11.45
	Dovey	12.11.45
	Esk	15.11.45
	Eden	12.3.46
	Erme	20.11.45
	Forsa	23.11.45
	Fowey	28.11.45
	Frome	30.11.45
	Foyle	20.12.45
	Glaven	20.12.45
	Garth	4.1.46
	Humber	1.11.46
	Hull	4.1.46
	Hamble	16.1.46
	Holford	30.5.46
	Hayle	26.9.46

45ft fast launches ('Bird')

Builder	Vessel	Date of completion
British Power Boat Co Ltd, Hythe, Southampton	*Woodcock*	4.2.38

45ft general service launches ('Shakespearean Female')

Builder	Vessel	Date of completion
Groves & Guttridge Ltd, East Cowes, Isle of Wight	*Bianca*	10.4.44
	Cleopatra	17.1.45
	Desdemona	22.2.45

Builder	Vessel	Date of completion
	Hermia	21.3.45
	Jessica	2.5.45
	Juliet	4.6.45
	Lucetta	31.8.45
	Miranda	5.9.45
	Nerissa	24.11.45
	Cordelia	20.12.45
	Cressida	8.2.46
	Octavia	14.3.46
	Celia	3.6.46
Phillips Anderson & Co Ltd,	*Olivia*	8.12.44
Granton,	*Ophelia*	14.2.45
Edinburgh	*Paulina*	12.4.45
	Perdita	31.1.45
	Portia	31.8.45
	Rosalind	28..9.45
	Sylphia	24.11.45
	Titania	5.4.46
	Ursula	14.5.46
	Viola	12.7.46

48ft fast launches (home service) ('Derby Winners')

Builder	Vessel	Date of completion
Groves & Guttridge Ltd,	*Bahram*	11.7.41
East Cowes,	*Blue Peter*	11.9.41
Isle of Wight	*Captain Cuttle*	25.3.42
	Call Boy	24.11.43
	Manna	25.8.44
	Felstead	13.12.44
	Flying Fox	15.3.45
J.S. White & Co Ltd,	*Coronach*	25.9.41
Isle of Wight	*Isinglass*	20.1.42
	Grand Parade	29.11.41
	Humorist	29.1.43
	Hyperion	6.2.43
	Minoru	25.8.43

50ft general service launches ('Dickens')

First Series

Builder	Vessel	Date of completion
Wm. Weatherhead & Sons,	*Barkis*	24.11.43
Cockenzie	*Bumble*	31.12.43

Builder	Vessel	Date of completion
	Buzfuz	5.5.44
R.A. Newman & Sons,	*Dodger*	3.4.44
Poole,	*Dombey*	12.12.43
Dorset	*Dorrit*	18.5.44
	Peggotty	11.8.44
	Pickwick (*Scroti*)	11.1.45
	Pinch	30.4.45
	Podsnap	3.10.45
	Prodgit	15.12.45
F. Curtis Ltd,	*Chasband*	1.1.44
Looe	*Chuzzlewit*	25.2.44
	Copperfield	30.3.44
	Cratchit	7.9.44
	Fagin	28.10.44
	Gamp	6.1.45
	Gummidge	10.3.45
	Marley	29.5.45
	Micawber	7.9.45
	Nickleby	13.11.45
	Quilp	19.2.46
Second Series		
Groves & Guttridge Ltd,	*Scrooge*	12.2.45
Isle of Wight	*Sikes*	19.7.46
	Snodgrass	17.9.46
	Squeers	4.11.46
	Stiggins	18.12.46
W. Weatherhead & Sons,	*Brownlow*	26.2.46
Cockenzie	*Cherryble*	28.3.46
	Smike	27.5.46
	Traddles (fitted F.W. Tanks)	12.8.46
	Weller	4.10.46
	Winkle	13.12.46
British Power Boat Co Ltd,	*Barnaby Rudge*	29.4.46
Hythe,	*Benjamin Allen*	7.5.46
Southampton	*Bob Sawyer*	16.5.46
	Bowler	7.6.46
	Jackson	18.6.46
	Linkinwater (fitted F.W. Tanks)	25.6.46
	Lowton	11.7.46
	Mac Stinger	24.9.46
	Martin	11.7.46
	Mr Toots	23.7.46
British Power Boat Co Ltd,	*Newman Noggs*	29.7.46
Poole,	*Oliver Twist*	4.10.46
Dorset	*Raddle*	25.9.46
	Rose Maglie	29.5.46
	Sergeant Snubbins	18.10.46
	Sidney Carton	13.11.46

Builder	Vessel	Date of completion
	Tracy Truman	25.11.46
	Uriah Heep	13.12.46
	Wardle	6.2.47

68ft target towing launches ('Battles' K, L, S and Z)

Builder	Vessel	Date of completion
British Power Boat Co. Ltd,	*Langemark*	18.5.44
Poole,	*Laventie*	27.5.44
Dorset	*Le Cateau*	27.5.44
	St Julien	16.6.44
	Salonika	10.7.44
	Sambre	9.8.44
	Scarpe	30.9.44
	Scheldt	2.11.44
	Shaiba	2.11.44
	Sharon	2.11.44
	Suvla	28.12.44
	Zeebrugge	25.1.45

69ft target towering launches ('Battles' A, B and C)

Builder	Vessel	Date of completion
J.I. Thornycroft & Co Ltd,	*Aisne*	26.10.43
Woolston Works,	*Albert*	1.2.44
Southampton	*Amiens*	24.3.44
	Antwerp	24.4.44
	Arleux	23.5.44
	Armentieres	13.6.44
	Arras	26.7.44
	Bapaume	12.12.44
	Bazentin	15.1.45
	Bethune	7.3.45
	Bullecourt	20.6.45
	Cambrai	17.7.45
	Ctesiphon	11.10.45

Type	Displacement Tons (light)	Length (ft)	Cargo	Engines
Powered cutters *PC 2, 3, 7, 9*	2	20	Personnel	Stuart Turner Petrol 2 cyl.
Motor launches *Fusee 2* (steel hull) *Crystal 2* (steel hull)	- -	68½ 56	Personnel and luggage	Diesel Allas 4 cyl. Type M43E. Diesel Widdop 3 cyl. Type ZF3.
Dumb barges *Arctic 2* *Aquabelle* *Chestnut* *Gog* *Elm*	36 (approx) - 7½ 186 7½	62½ - 36 105 36	Accommodation barge - 10 tons 200 tons 10 tons	- - - - -
Military oil barges *MOB7-13*	144	104	125 tons	Compound steam, oil-fired
Ramped cargo lighters (RCLs) Nos *977, 1018, 3001, 3003–3007, 3009–3011, 3016, 3018, 3023–3025*	-	54½	24 tons	Twin Chrysler 6 cyl. 90hp each. Petrol.
Slow tenders *T6, 8, 9 10*	2	20	Personnel	Coventry Victor Cub diesel, 2cyl.
Tugs *TID 100*	70	70	-	Triple expansion oil-fired
Motor barges *Blenheim* *Katharine 2* *Geoffrey Stanley* *Henry Caddell* *Vawdrey*	115 195 92 104 78	95 119½ 95 93½ 92	100 (5600 cu ft) 100 (7200 cu ft) 100 (5280 cu ft) 100 (6160 cu ft) 100 (5280 cu ft)	Diesel Mirlees 7 cyl. Type GR7 Twin diesel Widdop 3 cyl. Type ZH3 Diesel Widdup 4 cyl. Type EMX4 Twin diesel Ruston 5 cyl. 5 VPHM Diesel Ruston 5 cyl. 5 VPHM.
Motor fishing vessels *MV 51* *MV 160, 210, 221* *MV 1502*	25 53 220	40 64½ 97	20 20 35	Diesel Atlantic type 6 BE Diesel Widdop 4 cyl. EMX4 Diesel crossly 4 cyl. Type HRL4

Appendix XI

Type	Displacement Tons (light)	Length (ft)	Cargo	Engines
Admiralty trawlers				
Copinsay	531	164	600 cu ft refrigeration cargo space – 75 tons (measurement) general cargo.	Steam triple expansion. Oil-fired.
Mull	531	164	500 cu ft refrigeration cargo space – 160 tons (measurement) general cargo.	Steam triple expansion. Oil-fired.
Oxna	531	164	600 cu ft refrigeration cargo space – 75 tons (measurement) general cargo.	Steam triple expansion. Coal-fired.
Prospect	515	164	4100 cu ft refrigeration cargo space. Passenger room for 10.	Steam triple expansion. Oil-fired.
Old type target towers				
Lord Plumer	212	101	-	Steam triple expansion. Oil-fired.
Russell	106	80	-	Steam compound coal-fired.
Sir D. O'Callaghan	114	79½	-	Two steam triple expansion. Coal-fired.
Sir N. Birch	191	101½	-	Triple expansion. Coal-fired.
Sir R. Whigham	152	89½	-	Diesel Widdop 5 cyl. Type ZH5.
Coasters				
Malplaquet	416	157	450 tons (capacity 20,000 cu ft)	Diesel Mirless 8 cyl. Type ER8.
Marquis of Hartington	422	145½	200 tons (capacity 19,000 cu ft)	Steam compound coal-fired.
Sir Walter Campbell	525	148	200 tons (capacity 17320 cu ft)	Steam triple expansion. Coal-fired.
Sir E. Wood	545	167	375 tons (capacity 21760 cu ft)	Steam compound oil-fired.
Ammunition dumping craft (LCTs) Mk III; *442, 475, 565, 742*	327	192	150	Two Paxton Ricardo Diesels 12 cyl. Type 12TPM.
Mk IV; *1060, 1111, 1204*	200	185½	150	Two Paxton Ricardo Diesels 12 cyl. Type 12TPM.
Landing ships tank *Charles Macleod Evan Gibb Frederick Clover Humphrey Gale Maxwell Brander Reginald Kerr Snowdon Smith*	2310	346	2000 tons	Two triple expansion. Oil-fired.

227

Appendix XII

Brief Record of the Names of the LCT MK VIIIs Operated by RASC/RCT Crews

No	CS	Name	Origin of Name
L4002	MJBK	*Agheila*	1942. Western Desert battle involving XXX Corps and 2 (NZ) Division in Cyrenacia, west of Benghazi.
L4041	MJCP	*Abbeville*	1940. Battle in northern France involving rearguard of BEF.
L4061	MJCZ	*Audemer*	June/July 1944. Breakout battle from Normandy Bridgehead across the River Divres at Pont D'Audemer.
L4062	MJDB	*Aachen*	1944/45. Rhineland battles.
L4073	MJDJ	*Ardennes*	1944/45. Last German armoured offensive against the Americans through the forests of the Ardennes.
L4074	MJDM	*Antwerp*	1944. Battle to open up Antwerp and the Scheldt.
L4086	GRKP	*Arromanches*	June 1944. 'Overlord' landings.
L4085	MJDN	*Agedabia*	1942. Western Desert battle south of Benghazi in pursuit of Rommel.
L4097	MJFJ	*Andalsnes*	Norway 1940. Battle for the town of Andalsnes during evacuation of British forces.
L4128	MJFL	*Arezzo*	1944. Amphibious battle in Italy south of Florence involving DUKWs and LVTs.
L4164	MJCF	*Arakan*	1944/45. Amphibious landings along the Arakan coastline of Burma.
L4037	-	*Akyab*	(Ex HMS *Rampart*) 1944/45 amphibious landing on the Island of Akyab during the Arakan operations in Burma.

Appendix XIII

RASC Fleet List 1964

Department of Agriculture and Fisheries for Scotland

Name of Vessel	Signal Letters
Brenda	MCWC
Clupea	GOAJ
Explorer	MLBG
Fidra II	MKQQ
Longa	GPZN
Mara	GXMW
Minna	GKPS
Norna	MBUP
Rona	GKGZ
Scotia	GPYM
Ulva	GXSR
Vigilant	MNWB

War Department RASC Fleet

Name of Vessel (all RASCV)	Signal Letters	Type of Vessel
Aachen	MJDB	LCT VIII
Abbeville	MJCP	LCT VIII
Agedabia	MJDN	LCT VIII
Agheila	MJBK	LCT VIII
Almond	GCMQ	Launch
Alness	GCMV	Launch
Andalsnes	MJFJ	LCT VIII
Antwerp	MJDM	LCT VIII
Arakan	MJCF	LCT VIII
Arctic II	GNPX	Barge
Ardennes	MJDJ	LCT VIII
Arezzo	MJFL	LCT VIII
Arromanches	GRKP	LCT VIII
Arun	GCNJ	-
Audemer	MJCZ	LCT VIII
Barham	MFDJ	Launch
Barnaby Rudge	MQVF	Launch
Beaulieu	MGCPY	Launch
Blue Peter	MFDM	Launch
Bob Sawyer	MQSL	Launch
Butley	GCVN	Launch

Name of Vessel (all RASCV)	Signal Letters	Type of Vessel
Call Boy	MFFT	Launch
Captain Cuttle	MFJQ	Launch
Coquet	GDBF	Launch
Coronach	MFLL	Launch
Derwent	GDCS	Launch
Eden	GDDZ	Launch
Erme	GDFN	Launch
Forsa	GDFX	Launch
Fowey	GDFY	Launch
Foyle	GDGR	Launch
Frome	GDJB	Launch
Humber	GDLY	Launch
Humorist	MFMM	Launch
Hyperion	MFNQ	Launch
Isinglass	MFMR	Launch
Jackson	GNQR	Launch
LCM 7102	MNQQ	-
LCM 7211	MNRF	-
LCM 7212	MNRF	-
LCM 7213	MNRN	-
Linkinwater	MSZD	-
MV 50	GNQG	-
Martin	MSZB	Launch
Minoru	MPFN	Launch
Mull	GSQK	Trawler
Newman Noggs	MQRL	Launch
Oliver Twist	MSYX	Launch
Peggoty	MFQP	-
RCL 977	MNRV	-
RCL 3001	MNRW	-
RCL 3003	MNRZ	-
RCL 3005	MNSL	-
RCL 3006	MNSZ	-
RCL 3009	MNTV	-
RCL 3011	MNVB	-
RCL 3016	MNVJ	-
Raddle	MSYY	Launch
Rose Maglie	MSYZ	Launch
Scrooge	MGMX	Launch
Sergeant Snubbins	MQRD	Launch
Smike	MQRG	Launch
Snodgrass	MGNX	Launch
Uriah Heep	GNQN	Launch
Yarmouth Navigator	MJLT	MVF
Yarmouth Seaman	MLJZ	MVF

Note: Registered ships are also shown in Parts I and II

Appendix XIV

Commissioning Order of HMAV Ardennes, 1977

By Major General P.H. Benson
Commander of the Most Excellent
Order of the British Empire
Director General of Transportation

HMAV *ARDENNES* – COMMISSIONING ORDER

HM Army Vessel ARDENNES is to be commissioned at Portsmouth on 2 December 1977. You are to proceed forthwith to commission her for Sea Service.

On commissioning you will be under my full command. You are to bring to my immediate notice, and to the notice of the appropriate local authority, anything which gives you cause for dissatisfaction with the ship or any part of her and any other matters of importance, in particular those relating to the Ship's Company.

May GOD's blessing be upon the ship and Company hereby entrusted to your command and may your joint endeavours to uphold the high traditions of the Army in the service of Her Majesty the Queen be crowned with success and happiness.

Given under my hand this second day of December nineteen hundred and seventy seven.

MAJOR GENERAL

To: Major A.W. Pheby Royal Corps of Transport

Copy to: The Deputy Under Secretary of State (Army)
              The Quarter Master General
              The Flag Officer Portsmouth
              Commander 3 Transport Group (RCT (L of C)

Appendix XV

Army Fleet Review
30 September 1988

HER MAJESTY'S ARMY VESSEL ST GEORGE

When the dedicated Military Line of Communication to BAOR was established in the mid-seventies, ammunition and explosives were being shipped across the English Channel by the RFA vessel EMPIRE GULL. This vessel was an old Second World War LST and as such was eventually taken out of service towards the end of that decade. To replace it HMAV ST GEORGE was ordered by the RCT and was built, in conjunction with an identical order by DMS(N); the ships were built in 1980/81 by APPLEDORE SHIPBUILDERS. HMAV ST GEORGE was commissioned into service in October 1981 and since that date has maintained a regular sailing service from UK to continental ports. In addition she has taken cargo, including ammunition and explosives to Cyprus, Gibraltar, the United States of America and Canada.

ARMY FLEET REVIEW
TO MARK THE FORTHCOMING TRANSFER
OF
THE ARMY DEPARTMENT FLEET –
18 MARITIME SQUADRON RCT
&
HMAV ST GEORGE
TO
THE DIRECTOR OF MARINE SERVICES (NAVAL)

18 MARITIME SQUADRON RCT

The Army Department Civilian fleet is celebrating its 470th Anniversary this year taking into account that it is directly descended from the time when wharves were first constructed to allow ships to be furnished with cannon, each known as 'The Gunwharf', with that at Woolwich first being built about 1518 and at Portsmouth in 1662. Subsequently the Office of Ordnance was established in the Tower of London in 1597, which led to the Board of Ordnance and eventually to the formation of the War Department Fleet in 1855. During this time it has expanded and contracted reaching a high point at the end of the Second World War, when it was responsible for something in excess of 1000 vessels large and small. There are now some 17 vessels and 80 personnel to be transferred to DMS(N).

In 1978 the AD Fleet was formed into 18 Maritime Squadron RCT as part of 20 Maritime Regiment RCT. In recent years its vessels have been deployed around the coast of the United Kingdom providing Range Safety cover for the 7 major seaward

232

firing ranges operated on behalf of the Ministry of Defence. In addition its training vessels have provided the requisite facilities for the seamanship, navigation and engineering training of generations of soldiers of the RASC and RCT since the end of the Second World War.

CURRENT VESSELS OF 18 MARITIME SQUADRON RCT

24 METRE RANGE SAFETY CRAFT
Alfred Herring VC
Michael Murphy VC

15 METRE RANGE SAFETY CRAFT
Samuel Morley VC
Richard Masters VC
Joseph Hughes VC
James Dalton VC
Sir Paul Travers
Sir Cecil Smith
Sir Reginald Kerr
Sir Humphrey Gale
Geoffrey Rackham GC
Walter Cleall GC
Sir Evan Gibb

52 FOOT FAST LAUNCH
RCTV Anglesey

TRAINING VESSELS
RCTV Yarmouth Navigator
Harbour Launch 05
Harbour Launch 08
 REVIEWING OFFICER
Major General C E G Carrington CBE
Director General of Transport and Movements

COMMANDINAG OFFICER 20 MARITIME REGIMENT RCT
Lieutenant Colonel G J Yeoman MBE RCT

OFFICER COMMANDING HMAV ST GEORGE
Major P C Oliver RCT

MASTER SUPERINTENDENT 18 MARITIME SQUADRON RCT
R F Bourne Esq

SENIOR GUESTS
Rear Admiral K J Eaton
Brigadier J F Rickett OBE
Colonel M W H Branch OBE
Lieutenant Colonel J F B Collins RCT
Commander (Retd) D Nairne RN
W D Shepherd Esq

ARMY FLEET REVIEW 1988
PROGRAMME OF EVENTS

TIME	LOCATION	EVENT
10:30–11:00	HM Gunwharf	Reviewing officer and guests arrive HM Gunwharf and tour vessels of 18 Maritime Squadron RCT before embarking in HMAV ST GEORGE.
11:00	HM Gunwharf	Reviewing officer and guests embark in HMAV ST GEORGE.
11:15	HM Gunwharf	HMAV ST GEORGE sails to Spithead anchorage.
12:00	Spithead	HMAV ST GEORGE anchors. Reviewing officer and guests muster on flag deck.
12:15	Spithead	Fleet sail past HMAV ST GEORGE Reviewing officer takes the Salute.
12:30	Spithead	Luncheon.
14:15	Spithead	HMAV ST GEORGE weighs anchor and returns to HM Gunwharf.
15:00	GM Gunwharf	Guests depart.

Bibliography

Blight, `Fleet repairs through the ages', *REME Journal* (April 1976).

Boileau, Colonel D.W. (compiler), *The Second World War 1939–1945, Army, Supplies and Transport, Volumes 1 and 2*, The War Office (London 1954).

The British Empire 1497–1997, Telegraph Group (London 1997).

Cooley, Reg, *The Unknown Fleet* (Stroud 1993).

`The Corps of Royal Engineers 1066–1996, *Regiment* (April/May 1996).

Crew, Graeme, *The Royal Army Service Corps* (London 1970).

Critchley, Mike, *British Warships and Auxiliaries* (Liskeard, various dates).

The Falklands War (London 1983).

Hammerton, Sir John (ed.), *World War, 1914–1918, Volumes 1 and 2* (London 1934).

Harris, John, *The Sea Shall Not Have Them* (1971).

Institution of the RASC, *The Story of the RASC 1939–1945*

Institution of the RASC/RCT, *The story of the RASC and RCT 1945–1982* (London 1983).

James, Tony, *The Royal Fleet Auxiliary: The Vital Link* (Liskeard 1985).

Jane's Fighting Ships (various editions).

The Morning Calm (magazine of the British Korean Veterans Association, various articles).

Palmer, Ralph, *A Shopkeeper at Sea* (St Peter Port, Guernsey 1985).

Plummer, R., *The Ships that Saved an Army* (1990).

Sigwart, Captain E.E., *Royal Fleet Auxiliary* (London 1969).

Soldier Magazine.

Toft, Jack, *The Making of a Service Corps Seaman* (Ewell 1994).

The War in Pictures, Volumes 1–6, 1939–1945.

Abbreviations

AB	Able Seaman	GPMG	General Purpose Machine Gun
ADC	ammunition dumping craft	GS	general service
ADMT	Assistant Director of Military Transport	GSL	general service launch
AFV	Air Force Vessel	HL	harbour launch
AL	ambulance launch	HMAFV	Her Majesty's Air Force Vessel
ALF	Allied Land Forces	HMAV	Her Majesty's Army Vessel
ARAMCO	Arabian American Oil Company	HMS	His/Her Majesty's Ship
ASC	Army Service Corps	HMY	Her Majesty's Yacht
ASECS	Assistant Superintendent Engineer and	HQ	headquarters
	Constructor of Shipping	IRA	Irish Republican Army
BEF	British Expeditionary Force	IWT	Inland Water Transport
BEM	British Empire Medal	KCB	Knight Commander of the Most Honourable
BKVA	British Korean Veterans Association		Order of the Bath
BMC	beach mine clearance	LBV	loading barge vehicle
BOAC	British Overseas Airways Corporation	LCL	landing craft logistic
CBE	Commander of the Order of the British	LCPV	landing craft personnel and vehicle
	Empire	LCT	landing craft tank
CBF	Commander of British Forces	LCV	landing craft vehicle
CCL	command and control launch	L of C	lines of communication
CEng	Chief Engineer	LPD	landing platform dock
C-in-C	Commander-in-Chief	LSD	landing ship dock
CO	Commanding Officer	LSL	landing ship logistic
CRASC	Commander, Royal Army Service Corps	LST	landing ship tank
DBR	dumb barge ramped	MBA	Master of Business Administration
DDST	Deputy Director of Supplies and Transport	MBC	Motor Boat Company
DEMS	defensively equipped merchant ships	MBE	Member of the Order of the British Empire
DIWT	Director of Inland Water Transport	MC	Military Cross
DMS	Director of Marine Services (Naval)	MELF	Middle East Land Forces
DSECS	Deputy Superintendent Engineer and	MFV	motor fishing vessel
	Constructor of Shipping	MGB	motor gun boat
DSO	Distinguished Service Order	MIMECHE	Member of the Institute of Mechanical
DST	Director of Supplies and Transport		Engineers
DSTO	Divisional Sea Transport Officer	ML	motor launch
DUKW	amphibious vehicle	MN	Merchant Navy
EAASC	East African Army Service Corps	MOB	military oil barge
ELAS	Greek Communist Guerrilla Force	MOWT	Ministry of War Transport
ETA	Estimated Time of Arrival	MP	Member of Parliament *or* Military Policeman
FARELF	Far East Land Forces	MT	motor transport
FRU	fleet repair unit	MTB	motor torpedo boat
GHQ	general headquarters	NATO	North Atlantic Treaty Organisation
GOC	General Officer Commanding	NCO	non-commissioned officer

Abbreviations

OBE	Officer of the Order of the British Empire	ST *or* S&T	supplies and transport
OC	officer commanding	ST1, ST3	branches of the Directorate of Supplies and
OCTU	Officer Cadet Training Unit		Transport
PAC	parachute and cable (rocket)	STO	Sea Transport Officer
PBR	powered barge ramped	TID	towing in dock
PhD	Doctor of Philosophy	TF	train ferry
PLUTO	Pipeline Under The Ocean	TOIC	Transport Officer-in-Chief (Army)
POLMIL	Organisation for Co-operation between Army	UN	United Nations
	and Police in Hong Kong	VC	Victoria Cross
POW	prisoner of war	VE Day	Victory in Europe Day
Q	Quarter-Master-General's Staff	VIP	Very Important Person
QM	Quarter-Master	VJ Day	Victory over Japan Day
QMG	Quarter-Master-General	WAASC	West African Army Service Corps
Q(MOV)(M)	Movements branch of Quarter-Master-	WD	War Department
	General's Staff	WDV	War Department vessel
RAE	Royal Aircraft Establishment	WT	water transport or wireless telegraphy
RAF	Royal Air Force		
RASC	Royal Army Service Corps		
RASCV	Royal Army Service Corps Vessel		
RCL	ramped craft logistic		
RCT	Royal Corps of Transport		
RCTV	Royal Corps of Transport Vessel		
RE	Royal Engineers		
REME	Royal Corps of Electrical and Mechanical		
	Engineers		
RFA	Royal Fleet Auxiliary		
RHKP	Royal Hong Kong Police		
RIASC	Royal Indian Army Service Corps		
RLC	Royal Logistic Corps		
RLCV	Royal Logistic Corps Vessel		
RMAS	Royal Maritime Auxiliary Service		
RN	Royal Navy		
RNR	Royal Navy Reserve		
RPL	ramped powered lighter		
RSL	range safety launch		
SEAC	South-East Asia Command		
SECS	Superintending or Superintendent Engineer		
	and Constructor of Shipping		
SLEP	Ships Life Extension Programme		
SMS	Submarine Mining Service		
SMSV	Submarine Mining Service vessel		

Index

Page references in *italics* refer to illustrations.

Aachen (i) 142, 163, *170*
Aachen (ii) 183, 193
Abbeville (i) 142-4, 153-4, 163-4, 167-8, 177
Abbeville (ii) 11, 183, 191
Abercorn 31
Abingdon 83
Aden 61-2, 108, 128, 150-1, 156-7, 162
Aerial, HMS 149
Agedabia 142, 147, 149
Agheila (i) 142-4, 151, 156, 163, 167
Agheila (ii) 183
Agheila (iii) (ex-*Arromanches*) 191
Akayah 135
Akyab (i) (ex-*Rampart*) 142, 153
Akyab (ii) 183, 193
Albert Canal 101
Albion 196
Alert 30
Alexandria 59, 62, 90
Alfred Herring VC 171, 181, 186
Algiers 51, 53, 58
Allenby 32
Allied Schooner Control Committee 55
Amara 92, 95
Ambulance Launch Company (395 Company) 71, 83-4, 89, 107-9, 128
Ammunition Dumping Craft 82, 108, 110-12, *115*, 121, 134-5, 138
Amphibian Companies 60
Andalsnes 158
Andalsnes (i) 142, 157-8, 163
Andalsnes (ii) 183, 193
Anglesey 150, 180, 186
Anglo-Iranian Oil Company 91-2
Antwerp 70, 72, 81, 101, 163, 181-2
Antwerp (i) 142, 147, 149, 167
Antwerp (ii) 183-4, 191
Appledore 134, 182
Arakan (i) *120*, 135
Arakan (ii) 142, *149*, *170*, *175*
Arakan (iii) (LCL) 178, 181, 183, 188, 190, 192-4
Aramco 201 127-8
Arctic II 32
Ardennes (i) 142, 147, 149
Ardennes (ii) *175-6*, 177-8, 181, 183, 187-8, 190, 192-4
Arezzo (i) 142, 144, 147, 151
Arezzo (ii) 183, 190, 193
Argentina 183-5
Argyll and Sutherland Highlanders 157
Army Catering Corps 188-9
Army Fire Service 54
Army Individual Training Organisation 191
Army Service Corps *see* Royal Army Service Corps
Arno 135
Arnold, Captain RT 11
Arromanches 98, 134, 190-1
Arromanches (i) 139, 142, 147, 149, *173*
Arromanches (ii) 183-4, 190
Arromanches (iii) (ex-*Agheila*) 191, 193
Ashburn, Second Officer 138

Atlantic Conveyor 187
Audemer (i) *119-20*, 142, 148, 167, *171*, 178-80
Audemer (ii) 183, 193
Augusta 135
Australia 49, 131, 158
Avon 153, 189

Baghdad 92, 95
Bahram 47, 67
Bahrein 127-8, 151
Balaclava 16-17
Barbados 17
Barnard, Captain Peter 144
Barr, Captain A 108
'Barrack Lines' class 72, 110
Barry 41, 129, 134
Basra 25, 91-2, 95, 97
Batavia 105
'Battle' class 54, 72, *77*, 110
Beard, Captain EL 42-3
Belgium 22-3, 163, 190
in the Second World War 70, 72, 98-9, 101
Belize 70, 162, *172*, *176*, 181-2, 183, 185, 189, 194
Benbecula 143-4, 146, 192
Benson 83, 108-9, *113*, 127-8
Benson, Major PH 178
Bermuda 17
Berry Committee 92-3
Beshik, Lake 25
Birch, Major Simon 167-8, 177
'Bird' class 32, 46, 60
Black Watch 133
Blenheim 32
Blight, AS 158
Blue Peter 47
Beach Mine Clearance vessels 82
Board of Ordnance Fleet 13-15
Boat Stores Depots 44, 49, 59, 63, 71
Boddie, RC 134
Bombay 83, 108
Borneo 49, 148-9, 161
Bosnia 187
Bourne, Captain Frank 8, 166
Boutlers 83
Boveney 83
Boy Phillip 58
Boyes, Staff Sergeant 190
Brahmaputra River 102
Bray 83
Bream 193
Britannia, HMY *176*, 179, 187, 190-2
British Honduras *see* Belize
British India Shipping Company 132
'British Rivers' class 72, 110, 157-8, 161
Brooke, General Sir Alan 61
Brunei 149, 161
Bude 153, 189
Bulwark 196
Bumble 138
Burma 49, 62, 81-2, 87, 91, 94, 96-8, 102, 104, 128
Buthidaung 96-7, 102

caiques 46, 55, 59, *73*
Cairn 162
Cairnryan 17, 111-12, 121, 134-5, 138, 143-4
Cairns, Captain JF 47

Calcutta 63, 81, 87, 91-2, 96-7, 102
Call Boy 47, 157
Cambridge 28
Cameronian 47
Campbell, Major Archie 83
Canada 24, 48, 97-8, 102, 110, 155, 182
Cape Bon 52
Captain Cuttle 47
Carrington, Major-General CEG 8
Catania 70-1
Caversham 83
Command and Control Launches 164-5, 180, 184-6
Ceylon 17, 59, 108, 128
Channel Islands 11, *79*, 85-7, 108, 111, 134, 181
Charles Macleod 110-11, 131-2
Chartney 83
Chatham 14, 16, 136
Chestnut 32
China 130, 158-9, 190-2, 194
Chindwin River 81, 87, 94, 97, 102-3
Chittagong 81, 96-8
Chubb, HE 52
Churchill, Winston 51-2, 67, 70, 98-100
Clark, Captain Tony 144
Clark, WR 46
Cleeve 83
Clifton 83, 109
Clive 32, 47, 55
Cluff, Major 146
Clyde 153
Coastal Regiment 62
Colonel Templer 166
Cook, Samuel B 15
Cookham 83, 109
Copinsay 111
Coronach 47
Corrigan, Corporal 123
Corvan, Captain 135
Courseulles 99-100
Cowes 85, 180
Cox's Bazaar 96-7
Crete 109, 122
crews 17-18, 46, 60, 64-5, 109-10, 112, 121, 124-5, 133, 135, 178, 182
Army 8, 10, 18, 21-5, 27-8, 36, *38-9*, 41-4, 46, 48-9, 51, 54-8, 60, 68-9, *73*, 81-4, 94, 96, 105, 107, 108-11, *116*, 129, 132, 135, 138, 142-3, 145, 147, 155-8, 162-3, 165, 185-6, 189, 190-1, 193, 195
civilian 8-9, 13, 18, 21, 24, 26, 28, *38*, 41, 44, 48, 55, 57-61, 68, 82, 88, 90, 94, 109-11, *117*, 122, 124, 134-6, 139, 144-6, 155-6, 158, 166-7, 181-2, 185-6, 189
locally-recruited 25, 28, 46, 48-9, 55, 59, 61, *78*, 90-2, 94, 97, 105, 110-11, 122, 149, 157-8
Merchant Navy 110, 124-6, 129, 132
RAF 26
RFA 137
Royal Navy 96, 104, 110, 124-5
training 19-20, 22, 51-5, 58, 70, *74*, 85, 93-4, 97, 126-7, 129, 165, 186, 191, 193, 195
uniforms 18-19, 26-7, 51, 53, 61-2, 72, *76*, *117*, 121, 124-5, 152, 185-6, 189

Crimean War 15
Croatia 187-8, 193-4
Crystal II 31
Cuff, Major DE 133
Culham 83
Cyprus 109, 129, 139, 142, 146, 148, 162, *174*, 182, 186, 191, 193, 195

'Dance' class 111
Dart 153
Davey, RE 45
D-Day landings 11, 53-4, 56-60, 63-71, 87, 97-100, 106, 134
fiftieth anniversary 189-91
de la Haye, John 86-7
Defence Review (1998) 10, 192, 194-5
Delacombe, Major-General R 138
Denmark 45, 181
'Derby Winner' class 47, 60, 67, *118*, 133, 157, 161, 164, 167
Devonport 14, 16
Dewar, Major AJ 48
'Dickens' class 54, 72, 110, 138, 157, 164
Dickinson, Captain Thomas 14-15
Dodecanese 59, 109
Dover 134, 163-4
Drayer, Admiral Sir Desmond 155
DUKWs 56-7, 60, 63, 66-7, *79*, 81
Dunkirk 42-3, 46, 57-8, 60, 68, 90
Durham 88

Eagle 45
Eden 153, 157
East African Army Service Corps 61-2
Egypt 25, 55, 59, 62, 90, 109, 138-42, 150
El Alamein 71
El Alamein, battle of 50-1
Elizabeth Therese 58
Elm 32
Empire Claire 121
Empire Gull 163, 182
Empire Stevedore 152-3, 164
Empress of Canada 47
Euphrates River 24-5, *79*, 91
Eureka tugs 93, 96
Evan Gibb 110, *117*, 125-6, 129

Fairmile 'B' launches 88, 107-10, 122
Falcon 17, 46
Falklands War 163, *173*, 183-4, 195
Faroe Islands 45, 59
Farrar-Hockley, Lt-General Sir Anthony 179-80
Fast Launch Companies 56-7, 63, 65, 67, 71-2, 81
Fearless, HMS 181, 196
Felixstowe 134, 167
Felstead 47
Fiddler, Major 190
fireboats 54, 56, 58, 60, 63-4, 68-9, 72, *77-8*, 108, 110, 122, 129-30, 138
First World War *see* Great War, The
Floating Workshops 71, 83
Flying Fox 47
Forth 153
Forth II 32
Foxtrot 111
France 83, 134, 138-41, 190
in the Great War 22-5, 89
in the Second World War 32, 42-4, 53, 55, 65-70, 72, 89-90, 98-

Index

101, 134
see also D-Day landings
Frederick Clover 110, 132
French 32, 48
French Guinea 50
Frost, Mr 127
Fulmar 164, 184-5
Fury, HMS 69
Fusee II 31

Gallipoli landings 25, 106
Gambia 46, 55
Gearing, Jack 106
'Geddes Axe' 29
'General' class 31-2, 42, 45, 47-8
General McHardy 29
General Skinner 21
Geoffrey Rackham GC 181
Geoffrey Stanley 29
Germany 25, 28, 31, 111, 147, 153, 163, 190
  in the Great War 22, 24
  in the Second World War 32, 42-7, 50, 54-5, 70, 85, 90, 92, 101-2, 105, 122, 167
Gibraltar 17, 22, 25, 44, 47, 56, 108, 128, 166, 182
Gill, Captain C 84
Glen 153
Gog 16, 27, 30-1, *35*, 136
Gold Coast 46, 55
Gordon 34
  class 21
Goring 83
Grand Duchess 17
Grand Parade 47
Gray Mackenzie & Co 91-3, 95
Great War, The 22-6, *37*, 38-9, 41, 52, 89, 91-2, 97, 100, 106
Greece 30, 46, 55, 58-9, 61-2, 72, 109, 121-2, 121-4, 190
Greenland 45
'Grey' class launches 50, 60
Grimsby 27, 50
Grouse 43
Guatemala 162, 183, 185, 189
Guiness, Sir Algernon 26
Gulf War 187
Gurkha Regiment 149, 160

Haig 32, 43, 45
'Ham' class minesweepers 166
Hambledon 88
Hands, Brigadier 123
harbour launches 60, 63-5, 67-9, 71-2, 81, 83, 108, 186
Hardy, Private 123
Harms, Donald 146, 158
Harris, John 26
Harwich 45-6, 70, 168
Haslar 21, 85
Heath, Major-General CE 22
Heavy Workshop Company 100
Hebrides 20, 142-5, 147, 165, 171, 178, 181
Henga (Iran) 166-7
Henry Caddell 31
Henson, Brigadier P 154
Higgins barges 93, 95-6, 103
HL 278 68-9
Holden, Mr 48
Holland 72, 101-2, 168, 177, 190
Holland, GE 23
Holy Loch 84-5
Hong Kong 17, 48-9, 108, 146, 158-61, 182, 190-2, 194
'Hong Kong' targets 29
'Honours' class 180-1, 184, 186
Hornblower II 157
hovercraft 149-50, 155, 158, 164-5, *169*
Hughes, Second Lt 123-4

Humber 153, 158
Humorist 47
Humphrey Gale 110, 129
Hurley 88
Hurst II 31
Hyperion 47, 65-7, *174*

Iceland 45, 50
Iffley 88, 109
Impulse, HMS 43
Inchcolm 111
Inchon *118*
India 25, *39*, 83, 108-9, 128, 205-8
  Indian Army 92, 128
  Royal Indian Navy 96
  in the Second World War 48-9, 62-3, 81, 90-8, 102, 102-4
Indonesia 148, 150, 161
Inland Water Tranport Service *see* Royal Engineers Fleet
Intrepid, HMS 196
Iran 91-5, 97, 163, 166
Iraq 91-7, 187
Ireland 25, 28, 30, 135, 167
Irrawaddy Flotilla 94, 96, 103-4
Irrawaddy River 102-4
Isinglass 47, *118*, 133
Isle of Wight 64, 84-5, 107-8, 180
'Isles' class 111
Israel 128-9, 139-40
Italy 43-4, 46-7, 50, 54-6, 59, 62, 71-2, 84, 90, 92, 111
Itchen 153
Ivanhoe, HMS 43

Jackdaw 31
Jamaica 17, 31, 70
James Dalton VC 180
Jameson, Captain 109
Java 108
Jersey 85-6, 108, 111, 181
John Adams 31
Joint Service Hovercraft Unit (Far East) 150, 155
Jolly, Sir Allen 155
Jones, Major Murray 167
Joseph Hughes GC 180

Kaladan River 97, 102
Kalewa 94, 102-3
Karachi 63, 108
Karmala 80
Karun River 95
Katharine 16, 27, 30
Katharine II 16, 31, 135-6, 145
Kennet 153
Keren, Lord 133
Kerr, Major-General Sir Reginald 107-8, *113*
Kestrel 43
Kingston-upon-Thames 134, 146
Kitchener 32
Korean War 11, 111, 130-2
Kut 92, 95, 97
Kuwait 95, 97, 187
Kyauktau River 97

Ladas 47
Lady of the Lea 17
Langazo, Lake 25
Langdon 30
Larak (Iran) 166-7
Landing Barges Vehicle 100
Landing Craft Logistic 163, 168, *170*, 177-8, 190, 192-4
Landing Craft Tanks 53, 82, 82-3, 104, 110-11, 132, 138-40, 142, 144, 146-50, 155-6, 157-8, 160, 163-4, 167, 178
  20 LCT Support Regiment 165-6
  Mk III 135
  Mk IV 111-12, *114*, 130, 135,

139, 142-3, 147
  Mk VIII 138-9, 142-3, 147, 153, 162, 165, 167-8, 177-9, 183
Landing Craft Vehicles 64, 82, 193
Le Havre 70, 134
Lemberg 47
Lethbridge Report 62, 71, 82
Libya 90
Light Aid Workshop Companies 100-2
Lister, Sergeant 65-6
Lodden 153
Lonsdale, Major-General EHG 155
Lord Panmure 17
Lord Plumer 29, 50, 122
Lord Wolseley 27, 29
Lowestoft *170*, 177
Landing Ships Dock 103
Landing Ships Logistic 162-3, 184, 188, 193, 195
Landing Ships Tank 11, 108, 110, *117-19*, 124, 126, 129, 131-2, 137, 156, 163, *170*
Lucien Gougby 58, 123
Luck, Captain 99

Maas River 101
Macedonia 25, *39*
Macleod Report 151
Magog (i) 16, *35*
Magog (ii) 16
Malaya 41, 62, 91, 130-1, 148-50, 161
  in the Second World War 48, 87, 94, 96, 104
Malplaquet 32, 40, 45, 59, 112, 134, 138, 145
Malta 17, 22, 25, 44, 47, 50, 72, 108, 122-3, 128-9, 137, 139, 142, 145, 157, 162, 182
Mandalay 94, 102-3
Manna 47
Maple 88
Marchwood Freighter 164
Marchwood Military Port 9-11, *120*, 134, 153, 162-7, 181-2, 184, 186-8, 191, 193, 195
Marlborough 32, 42-3
Marlow 88
Marquess of Hartington 17, 27, 30, 112, 134-7, 143
Marr, Captain *118*, 131-2
Marsh 88, 109, 122-3
Martaban 104
Masirah 128
Maungdaw 96-7, 102
Mauritius 17, 61
Maxwell Brander 14, 110-11, *118*, 124-7, 132
Mayu River 96-7, 102
McCubbin, A/B 138
Medway 153, 189
Melville, Lord 16
Menai Bridge 124
Mesopotamia *39*, 97
Mexeflotes 162-3, *174*, 195
Milford Haven 58, 179
Millreef 193
Minca barges 63, 98
Miner class 21
Minoru (i) 47
Minoru (ii) 167
ML171 84, 107
Military Oil Barges 57, 60, 63-4, 70-1, 77, 82, 84, 110
Mogadishu 61-2
Molesey (i) 88
Mombasa 61-2
Mosley, 109
Motor Boat Companies (RASC) 39, 42, 44-7, 49, 52-3, 57, 60 No. 1

42, 46-7, 74; No. 2 42, 46, 51, 74-5; No. 3 46, 50; No. 247 51-5, 58; No. 571 63; No. 624 (Fast Launch) 53, 63-4, 70; No. 625 63; No. 626 (Harbour Launch) 60, 63-5, 67, 69-70, 108; No. 697 109, 122
Moulmein 104
MT Stores Depot (RASC) 49
'Mulberry' floating harbours 61, 66-9, 98-100, 106
Mull 111, *119*, 134-5, 144-5
Myingyan 102-3
Mylchreest, A/B 138

Naaf, River 96-7
Napier of Magdala 21
Narayanganj 97
NATO 167, 163-4, 178, 181, 187-8, 194
Nelson, HMS 186
New Guinea 49
Newton Creek 64-5
Nicholas, Major David 178, 181
Nigeria 46, 55-6
Nippy 32
North Atlantic Shipping Company 132
Norway 45, 47, 157-8, 164-5, 167, 190

Oban 143
Ocean Breeze 58
Oma 11, 79, 85-7
Oman 156
Omonde 47
Omphale 48
Operation 'Corporate' 183-4
Operation 'Dynamo' *see* Dunkirk evacuation
Operation 'Gauntlet' 47
Operation 'Hardrock' 142-5
Operation 'Nest Egg' 85-6
Operation 'Overlord' *see* D-Day landings
Operation 'Regatta' 91-2
Operation 'Torch' 51
Osprey 20
Oudenarde 48
Oxna 111

Padang 105
'Paiforce' 95
Pakistan 63, 108, 128
Palembang 105
Palestine 61, 128-9
Palmer, Ralph 85-6
Pauletta 45
Powered Barges, Ramped 98-100
Perch 193
Persia *see* Iran
Petrel 164, 184
Pheby, Major Tony 153, 178
Phoenix 111
Phoenix, HMS 126
Pigeon 43
Pike 47
Pipe Line Under The Ocean 61
Plymouth 31, 50, 86, 135-6
Poole 108, 128, 146
Popperwell, Corporal K 69
Porcher 111
Port Dickson 104-5
Port Fuad 109
Port Said 59, 61, 90, 108-9, 111, 122, 128-9, 140
Port Swettenham 87, 104-5
Port-en-Bessin 99
Portsmouth 14, 16, 41, 64, 76, 125, 129, 134, 142, 146, 154, 156,

165-6, 177, 181
HM Gunwharf 8, 13, 124, 127, 143, 165-6, 186
Potts, Captain Roy 167, 179-80
Princess Victoria 135
Prome 94, 103
Prospect 111, 145
Puffin 144-5
Pulau Brani 108, 147

'Queen Bees' 129
Queen Elizabeth II 176, 187
'Queen Gannet' 138
'Queen Gull' target boats 47, *76*
Queenstown 25, 28

Royal Artillery 145-6
RAE Farnborough 26, 166
RAF Marine Craft Section 26
  transfer of ships from 167-8, 184
Raglan 32
Ramillies 32
Rampart, HMS 153
Rangoon 48, 81-3, 94, 102-4
Royal Army Ordnance Corps 49, 111, 188-9
Ras Tannurah 127-8
Royal Army Service Corps Fleet 17, 25, *39-40*, 41-5, 49, 51, 54-6, 61-3, 72-89, 105-12, 121-51, 185; 18 Amphibious Squadron 146; 37 Company 147; 46 Squadron 148; 76 Company 22, 139, 142, 146-8
  formed 26, 55-6, 61-2, 72, 107
  ensign 67-8, 88
  Fleet Repair Branch 145-6, 152
  LST Control Unit 11, 130-3
  merged into RCT Fleet 150-3
  strengths 88, 109, 132, 134-5, 137-8, 143, 145
  see also Water Transport Companies
Raven 31
Rawlinson, Captain CE 156
RB II 157
Ramped Craft Lighters 79, 99, 103, *173*, 183, 185, 190-1, 193
Royal Corps of Signals 143
Royal Corps of Transport Fleet 8-9, 151-68, 177-88;
  10 Port Squadron 161, *174*; 17 Port Regiment 155, 162, 186; 18 Maritime Squadron 165, 182; 20 Maritime Regiment 8, 165-6, 181, 186; 33 Maritime Regiment 161; 73 Squadron 184; 200 Squadron 155, 164
  formed 152, 155, 185
  ensign 154-5
  merged into Royal Logistics Corps 155, 158, 188-9
Royal Engineers Fleet 9, 11, 20-2, *36-8*, 41, 62-3, 81-2, 89-107, 134, 140, 147-8, 151,153, 161, 185
  formed 23-4
  disbanded in 1924 29, 105
  ensign *37*
  reactivated 29, 32, 41
  merged into RCT Fleet 151-4,188-9
  Port elements 11, 98, 100, 103-6, 147-8, 151, 152-3, 163, 184
  Port Training Regiment 155
  strengths 25, 89, 93-7, 103, 105
  see also Light Aid Workshop Companies, Submarine Mining Service
Reclaim, HMS 179
refrigerator barges 89
Reginald Kerr (ii) 108, 110, 132
Royal Corps of Electrical and Mechanical Engineers 49, 129, 134, 146

Fleet Repair Unit 129, 134, 138
Reynolds, GW 155
Royal Fleet Auxiliary Service 142, 162-3, 184, 188-9, 193
'Rhino' ferries 99-100
Rhodes 59
Rhu 146, 182
Richard George Masters VC 166
Richard Masters VC 180
Richborough 24
Richmond 84
'River' class launches 134
Rivett-Carnac, V/A Sir James 67-8
Royal Logistics Corps Fleet 186, 188-96
  17 Port and Maritime Regiment 9, 191
  formed 155, 188-9
  ensign 155, 189
  strengths 190-1, 193-4
Royal Maritime Auxiliary Service
  transfer of RCT Fleet to 8, 181-2, 186
Roach 193
Roberts 32
Robinson, Corporal Peter 131-3
Robinson, Major 190
Robyns, Major Peter 179
Royal Garrison Artillery 27
Royal Indian Army Service Corps 63
Royal Marines 183, 196
Royal Navy
  ship transfers from 19, 108, 110-11, 124, 142-3, 153, 168, 184
Royal Pioneer Corps 121
  merged into Royal Logistics Corps 188-9
Royalty 30
Ramped Powered Lighters 148, 152-3, 161-2, *172*, *176*, 181, 183, 185, 189, 194

Salcombe 42
Samuel Morley VC 180
Sarnia 85
Saudi Arabia 187
Scrooge 157
'Sea Mules' 99
'Seabird' class 180, 184-5
Second World War 25-6, 30, 40, 41-106, 82, 84, 123, 157, 167-8, *174*, 182
'Shakespearean Females' class 72, 110
'Shakespearean Males' class 54, 72, 110
Shearwater 164, 184
Sheerness 14, 50, 136
Shelduck 164, 184
Shepperton 88, 109
Sheppey 111
Shoeburyness 16, 22, 30
Sicily 54-7, 62, 72
Sierra Leone 17, 46, 50, 55-6
Simi 59
Simonstown Dockyard 56
Sine Boye *171*, 179-80
Singapore 17, 31, 48-9, 91, 94, 108, 131, 134-5, 138, 147-50, 158, 161-2, 182
Sir Cecil Romer 29
Sir Cecil Smith 180
Sir Desmond O'Callaghan 29
Sir Evan Gibb (i) 184
Sir Evan Gibb (ii) 181
Sir Evelyn Wood 17, 43, 68, 112, 134, 143
Sir Frederick Walker 29-30
Sir Hastings Anderson 31, 40, 49, 182
Sir Herbert Miles 27
Sir Humphrey Gale (ii) 180-1
Sir John Potter *172*, 180
Sir Noel Birch 29
Sir Paul Travers 180

Sir Redvers Buller 20, 28-9
Sir Reginald Kerr (i) 108
Sir Reginald Kerr (ii) 180
Sir Robert Wigham 31
Sir Walter Campbell 29, 49-50, 112, 134
Sir William Roe 180, 186
Sir Winston Churchill 179-80
Skua 164, 184-5
Slough 49
Smith, Sgt AE 69
Snipe 47
Snowden Smith 110
Soady, Captain Joseph 15
Solent, Army Fleet Review in 10, 107-8, *113*
Sonning 109
South Africa 56, 156
South Uist 143, 192, 194
Southampton 24, 87
Spa 137
Spabeck 137
Spabrook 137
Spaburn 137
Spalake 137
Spapool 137
Sparshott, G 58
Spion Kop 47
Spithead 66
  Army Fleet Review 8, 107-8
  Coronation Fleet Review 136-7, 179
  D-Day Commemoration Review 189-90
  Royal Review 1990 *176*, 186-7
  Silver Jubilee Fleet Review 179
Split 188, 193-4
St Edmund 173
St George 8-9, *174*, 182, 185-6
St George Barracks, Gosport 165-6, 181, 186
St Kilda 119, 143-4, *171*, 192-4
St Mary 157
St Valery 43
Star Ferry Company 159
Steward, Captain James 15
Stranraer 71
Strathewe *173*
Submarine Mining Service 9, 11, 19, 20-1, *36-7*
Sudan 48, 90
Suez 61-2, 90-1, 108, 128
  Suez Canal crisis 138-42, 143
Sunbury 109, 122-4
Sunstar 47
Swale 26
Swallow 43, 46, 60, 64-8

Tahog 59
Taigo 157
Task Force 135 85-6
Teal 43
Tern 164, 184
Territorial Army 134
Train Ferry vessels 24
'Thames Lock' class 83
Thrush 47
TID (Towing in Dock) tugs 63, *80*, 99, 107
Tigris River 24-5, 91-2, 95
Titlark 32
Tobruk 50, 109, 137, 140, 142
Toft, Staff Sergeant Jack 11, 51, 53, 60, 64-6, 68, 70, 84, 87-8, 108-9, 128
tongkangs 23, 31
Torre del Greco 62
Travers, General Sir Paul 182
Travis, Henry 29
Trevose 150
Trewhearne, Sergeant 123
Trinidad 71
Tripoli 145
Tripolitania 61

Tromso 157, 167-8
Trout 47
Tunis 54
Tunisia 52, 55
Turks and Caicos Islands 71
Turner, Captain CG 48
Tye, Staff Sergeant 'Pop' 158-9

Unicraft barges 102-3
Uniflotes 161
United Friends 135-6
United Nations 130, 141, 187-8, 194
Unst 147-8

Valse 111
Vawdrey 31
Venice 84
Venning, Sir Walter 43
Vernon, HMS 8, 184
Victoria 48
Vincent, Major Norman 11, 131-3
Vistafjord (GB) 187
Vulture 43

Wadi Halfa 90
'Waggon Trail' exercise 155
Waja 50
Wales, FJ 43
Walter Cleall GC 181, 184
Waltham Abbey 17
Warsash Sea School 84
Water Transport Companies (RASC) 41, 44, 49-54, 56-7, 59-63, 71, 78, 124-5, 155-6; No. 37 149; No. 247 62, 72; No. 510 61-2; No. 615 127; No. 616 82; No. 624 54, 60, 72; No. 626 87; No. 630 82; No. 632 133; No. 647 84; No. 697 61; No. 698 61, 109; No. 782 59, 61; No. 793 55-6; No. 797 72; No. 798 61, 72; No. 801 61, 72; No. 841 85-7; No. 856 81-2; No. 884 81, 87; No. 899 70
  inspectorate 52, 57
  strengths 61, 71
Waterborne Training Centre 84
Watson, Lance-Corporal 66
Watts, Captain OM 84
Wavell, Earl *118*, 133
War Department Fleet 15-20, 41-72
Wellington 32
West Africa Army Service Corps 55-6
West Indies 17, 70-1
West Mersea Training Unit 51-4, 70
Winchelsea, HMS 43
Windsor Lad 47
Winter, Mr 127
Wolf 32
Wolfe 43
Wolseley 32
Wood, Captain Tom 108
Woodlark 164
Woolwich 14-16, 23, 27, 30, 41, 49, 135
Worcester, HMS 156
Wright, Lt-Col DM 134
Wuzzer 31
Wyndham 28, *34*
Wynn-Werninck, Major BV 84, 107, 109, 179-80, 187

Yarmouth Navigator 8, 129-30, 145, 186
Yarmouth Seaman 130, 145
Yeabsley, Sgt RJ 69
Yeoman, Lt-Col GJ 8, 181
Yugoslavia 46, 55, 62, 72, 187-8, 193-5

'Z' craft 90-1, 97, 104, 140, 152, 161